Phonics Teacher's Book

Teaching *Jolly Phonics* with

Phonics Student Books 1, 2, and 3

Written by

Sara Wernham and Sue Lloyd

Edited by Louise Van-Pottelsberghe

Contents

PART 1

Introduction

For ease of use, this *Teacher's Book* has been divided into two distinct parts. The first part (with yellow page borders) gives a comprehensive introduction to *Jolly Phonics*, and explains the *Jolly Phonics* teaching method in detail. It is a good idea to read this part of the *Teacher's Book* before using the *Phonics Student and Teacher's Books* in the classroom. The second part of the *Teacher's Book* provides a thorough and structured lesson plan for each day of phonics teaching. The lesson plans in this part of the book are designed specifically for use with the corresponding pages in *Phonics Student Books 1, 2,* and *3.*

The *Phonics Teacher's Book* and *Student Books* provide a program for teaching the skills of reading and writing in English. The focus of the program is on the teaching of the English alphabetic code; this includes teaching the ways in which the code knowledge is put into practice. The phonics teaching, covered in Part 2 of this book, is not intended to take up all the time allocated for English lessons. This means that teachers are free to teach the other aspects of literacy, such as comprehension and poetry, in the remaining time.

The *Jolly Phonics* program is multi-sensory, active, and specifically designed for young children. There are activities in the *Phonics Student Books* and corresponding lesson plans in the *Teacher's Book* for each day. Useful supplementary materials are also mentioned in this book, although all the teaching can be carried out without the support of these extra materials. For instance, whiteboard software called *Phonics for the Whiteboard*, is available for those teachers who have interactive whiteboards in their classrooms. This product includes reproducible worksheets, which support the phonics teaching. *Phonics Student Books* 1, 2, and 3, and the *Phonics for the Whiteboard* software cover the same teaching and can be used together in the classroom. The *Phonics Student Books* are designed so that each book follows the same teaching as the corresponding step in the whiteboard software.

With the *Phonics Student Books*, the students are not just taught the alphabet sounds, but all the 42 main letter sounds, and how they are written. With this knowledge, they are taken through stages of blending sounds together to form words, and then on to reading. At the same time, the students are taught to write by listening for the sounds in spoken words and identifying the letters corresponding to those sounds. This skill is also referred to as "segmenting."

The main 42 letter sounds are introduced at a rate of one a day. Most students are very capable of coping with this fast and stimulating pace. However, the rate of introduction can be adjusted according to the number and duration of lessons available, and the age of the students.

The *Teacher's Book* offers step-by-step lesson plans, which bring a better understanding of the *Jolly Phonics* program and the activities in the *Phonics Student Books*. Teachers using the *Phonics Teacher's Book* and *Student Books* can be assured that their students will read and write independently at an earlier-than-average age.

In this introduction, the teaching program has been divided into the following five basic skills, each of which has its own section:

1. Learning the Letter Sounds
2. Learning Letter Formation
3. Reading (Blending)
4. Identifying the Sounds in Words
5. Tricky Words

In this introduction, the teaching has been separated into these five basic skills, but in the *Phonics Student Books* the first four skills are taught simultaneously from the beginning and the fifth skill, learning the tricky words, is taught after the first few weeks.

Learning to read and write fluently is vital for children. All parents know this and want their children to master these skills. The majority of parents are keen to help, but are not sure how to go about it. It is a good idea to invite new parents to a meeting, where it is explained to them how reading and writing is taught in the school. These meetings provide an opportunity to introduce the *Phonics Student Books*, and to explain how the parents can support their children.

The *Jolly Phonics* method of teaching was developed and tested over a period of time at Woods Loke Primary School in Lowestoft, England. Before 1975, reading was taught at this school using an essentially visual, whole-word approach. Most students read well. However, there was always a group of students who had problems remembering words and who could not cope satisfactorily with reading or writing. These students did not pick up letter sounds easily, or relate them to words. It was, therefore, decided to teach the letter sounds first, to see if early letter knowledge would help them. This approach proved to be much more successful for the students as a group, and those students who had problems were much fewer in number.

This outcome reflects the findings of several research studies, which found that knowing the letters was the best predictor of success in learning to read.

Later, in the early 1980s, Woods Loke Primary School introduced some structured blending, in addition to the letter-sound work. The school then took part in an external research experiment. The students were first taught to listen carefully for the sounds in words, to identify them, and to relate them to the letters (phonemic awareness). This teaching method made it much easier for the students to learn to read and write. They became fluent readers much earlier than before, and best of all, the group of students with reading problems was almost non-existent. It was rare to have a student in the school scoring below 90 on the Young's Reading Test, and the average was between 110 and 116. (The Young's Reading Test is designed so that a score of 100 is the average. It is also designed so that half of all students will fall in the range 90-110). The students learned to read much faster when they knew the letter sounds and could work out words for themselves. Independent writing started much earlier than usual and accurate spelling developed more quickly.

These results also reflect the findings of independent research studies, which show that both blending skills and phonemic awareness are strong predictors of reading success.

The key advantages of *Jolly Phonics* are that it teaches the students to recognize all the main letter sounds early on, and that it shows them how to relate the sounds to the symbols, and so, to understand the alphabetic code used for reading and writing. At an early stage, the students have a way of writing every letter sound and this means that they are soon able to write whatever they wish. With *Jolly Phonics*, the students can be taught to read at a young age, even at a pre-school age.

The effectiveness of *Jolly Phonics* has been highlighted by numerous research studies, in which the achievements of students taught with *Jolly Phonics* have been much greater than those of students taught with other methods. A number of research studies can be viewed on the Jolly Learning Website:

www.jollylearning.com

The letter sounds of the English language

a	ant, sand, catch	
ai	aim, aid, drain	(long /a/)
b	bat, bend, crab	
c	cat, cot, duck	
d	dog, dip, sudden	
e	egg, end, shed	
ee	eel, creep, tree	(long /e/)
f	fog, lift, fluff	
g	goat, gap, digger	
h	hop, hit, hill	
i	ink, instant, drink	
ie	pie, tie, die	(long i)
j	jelly, jet, jump	
k	king, kind, kettle	
l	leg, lost, shell	
m	man, mill, shrimp	
n	nut, nip, spin	
o	ostrich, on, spot	
oa	oak, oats, boat	(long /o/)
p	plug, pet, step	
qu	queen, quick, quack	
r	run, rabbit, barrel	
s	sand, sun, twist	
t	top, tug, mat	
u	up, under, lung	
ue	value, argue, cue	(long /u/)
v	van, vet, give	
w	wind, went, swim	
x	x-ray, ox, flex	
y	yell, yes, yellow	
z	zoo, zebra, buzz	
sh	ship, shop, wish	
ch	chop, chick, much	
th	this, then, with	(voiced /th/)
th	thin, thick, thimble	(unvoiced /th/)
ng	song, bang, string	
oo	look, book, foot,	(little /oo/)
oo	moon, spoon, shoot	(long /oo/)
ar	art, arm, start	
er	herb, stern, sister	
or	order, corn, storm	
oi	oil, ointment, spoil	
ou	out, cloud, found	

These letter sounds can be heard at: www.jollylearning.com/research.htm

1. Learning the Letter Sounds

All words are made up of sounds. There are at least 42 sounds in English, but only 26 letters are used to represent these sounds. For reading and writing, the students need to be fluent at saying the sounds that go with the letters.

Initially, only one way of representing each sound is taught. Afterwards, the main alternatives are covered. For example, at first, the /ai/ sound is taught with the ‹ai› spelling, as in *rain*. Later on, the alternatives ‹ay› as in *day*, and ‹a_e› as in *came* are taught.

All the main 42 letter sounds are introduced in *Phonics Student Book 1* (43 letter sounds are listed, but ‹c› and ‹k› make the same sound). One page is devoted to each letter sound, with a number of activities designed to teach the basic skills. Each letter sound is introduced through a story, which is provided in the *Teacher's Book*. Pictures, linked to the story and the action, are provided in the *Phonics Student Books* for the students to color.

Young children learn particularly quickly when there is a physical activity involved. By doing an action for each letter sound, the students use movement, sight, hearing, and speech to help them remember. This multi-sensory approach is a very effective way of teaching, as well as being fun for the students. The action box is provided in the *Phonics Student Books* as a guide for the parents and as a reminder for the students. Merely introducing the letter sounds will not ensure that the students have learned them; the letter sounds must be reviewed regularly. The letter sound practice is usually carried out with flash cards showing the letter sounds. Teachers can either make these flash cards, or purchase the *Jolly Phonics Cards*.

Every day, flash cards showing the letter sounds that have been taught should be held up for the students to say the sound and do the action. Alternatively, letter sounds can be written on the board for this purpose. The aim of this frequent practice is to develop fluency and an automatic response to the letters.

Occasionally, the students should be encouraged to say the letter sounds without doing the action. On these occasions, you could tell the students to sit on their hands; this amuses them, and helps them to avoid doing the actions.

Rate of introduction

The first letter sound can be introduced on the students' first day. Their enthusiasm for learning is high and this provides a meaningful start for the students.

Where possible, it is recommended that the letter sounds be introduced at the rate of one letter sound a day. Although this may seem a great deal at first, most students are able to cope with it and look forward to their new letter sound every day. All the 42 letter sounds are introduced at this rate, so that they can be covered in about nine weeks. The result is that the students become competent readers much sooner, and can use all these letter sounds to produce more expressive independent writing at a much earlier stage than is usual.

If the students are younger than four or five, if they do not have a lesson every day, or if there are other special factors, then the rate of introduction of the letter sounds is likely to be slower. The teacher will need to decide on the appropriate pace for his or her own class. If a slower pace is adopted, then it is important to avoid asking the students to read books that contain letter sounds that they have not yet been taught. The students will not be able to decode (work out) words, if the relevant letter sounds have not yet been taught.

Introducing each letter sound

In the first lesson, the /s/ sound is introduced. Start the lesson by telling a story about the /s/ sound, or by reading the story from the *Teacher's Book*. The sound and the action are incorporated into each story. In this case, the snake makes the /ssss/ sound, and the movement of the snake provides the action; the students weave their arm like a snake saying /ssss/. The students are told that /s/ is one of the letter sounds.

If the *Finger Phonics Books* are available, they can be used at this stage to help illustrate the stories. These books also have grooved letters, which allow the students to see and feel the shape of the letters. A *Jolly Phonics Wall Frieze* is also useful in the classroom. This can be used to make a cheerful wall display, which acts as a visual reminder of each letter sound. Young students may also enjoy singing the songs linked to each letter sound, which are available as *Jolly Songs* and *Jolly Jingles*.

Once the /s/ sound has been introduced with the story, the students should look at the letter ‹s› in *Phonics Student Book 1*. The students can then be shown the letter ‹s› on a flash card, on the *Wall Frieze*, or in the *Finger Phonics Books* before being shown how to form the letter correctly. The teaching of correct letter formation is covered in Section 2: Learning Letter Formation. The students then look at the picture of the snake, and the action box in their *Phonics Student Books*. The pictures on the *Phonics Student Book* page can then be colored in. In the first few lessons, the students can play "hunt the letter sound" by searching for it in books, or around the classroom. This helps the students to understand the link between the letter sounds and the words in books.

In *Phonics Student Book 1*, the emphasis should be on the lower-case letters. The capital letters, although shown in the book, need only be referred to incidentally. Capital letters are dealt with in more depth in *Phonics Student Books 2* and *3*. In the very early stages, it is important that all letters are introduced by their sounds and not by their names. In this case, say /sssss/ and not /ess/ when introducing the /s/ letter sound.

The other letters are introduced in a similar fashion. When /a/, /e/, /i/, /o/ and /u/ are taught, the students need to know that they are "special letters," and are called *vowels*. Later, they will be told useful rules that relate to the vowels, which will help them with reading and spelling. The students can then be taught that the other letters are called *consonants*.

Reinforcement of the letter sounds is very important. Flash cards showing the letters that have been taught should be held up during every lesson for the students to call out the sounds. It is important that the cards are shown in a random order so that the students truly recognize the letters and do not simply recite the sounds in order. The faster students are at recognizing the letters and saying the sounds, the easier it is for them to read and write.

Learning to read and write in English is complicated because there are more than 42 sounds, but only 26 letters with which to write them. This means that sometimes two letters are put together to make a new sound, as with /sh/, /ee/, /ou/, and /ng/. These are called *digraphs*, and they are different from blends. A digraph has just one sound, for example, the /sh/ in *ship*, whereas a blend has two or more sounds, for example, the /s-t/ in *stop*. This is an important difference, as will be seen in Section 4: Identifying the Sounds in Words.

The ‹oo› and ‹th› digraphs are initially introduced in two sizes. This helps the students to understand that they each make two sounds, as in *book* and *moon*, and *this* and *thin*.

oo	(little /oo/ in *book*)
oo	(long /oo/ in *moon*)
th	(voiced /th/ in *this*)
th	(unvoiced /th/ in *thin*)

Order of the letter-sound groups

The letter sounds are arranged in groups of six. They have been ordered carefully, so as to aid learning. For instance, the first six letters can be used to make many simple words, such as *pin, tip, pan, sat*. This means that it is possible for the students to make words at an early stage in their learning. Furthermore, the letters that are often confused, such as ‹b› and ‹d›, are in separate groups. The ‹c› is introduced early on, because it forms a template for writing the letters ‹a›, ‹d›, ‹o›, ‹g›, ‹q›. The letter-sound groups, listed below, are used throughout the *Jolly Phonics* materials.

The letter-sound groups

1. s, a, t, i, p, n
2. c k, e, h, r, m, d
3. g, o, u, l, f, b
4. ai, j, oa, ie, ee, or
5. z, w, ng, v, little oo, long oo
6. y, x, ch, sh, voiced th, unvoiced th
7. qu, ou, oi, ue, er, ar.

Reinforcing the letter sounds

As well as holding up flash cards, there are lots of activities that will help the students to learn the letter sounds. Large letters could be placed in the corners of the room and the students told to run to the correct corner when they see or hear one of the letter sounds. By taking part in a number of activities, all of which aim to achieve the same goal (learning the letter sounds), the students are stimulated and become more enthusiastic.

Letter names

Initially, it is helpful to use only the letter sounds when teaching students to read and write. When letter names are introduced at the same time as the letter sounds, many students become confused. For this reason, it is recommended that the teaching of letter names is left until *Phonics Student Books 2* and *3*. A good way of introducing the letter names is through the alphabet.

The alphabet is introduced in four color-coded sets in *Phonics Student Book 2*. This helps to prepare the students for using a dictionary, as each set of letters corresponds to roughly a quarter of the words in a dictionary. Once the letter names have been taught, you could ask the students to say letter names when flash cards are held up.

Alternative spellings of vowels

Once students have learned the 42 letter sounds taught in *Phonics Student Book 1*, they need to be aware of the alternative ways in which some of the vowel sounds can be written. The table opposite details the alternative vowel spellings, most of which are taught in *Phonics Student Books 2,* and *3*.

Alternative vowel spellings

Long /a/:	**ai** a_e ay	rain, waist, drain date, plate, flame day, stay, play
Long /e/:	**ee** e_e ea	seed, bleed, street these, theme, seat, cream, read
Long /i/:	**ie** i_e y igh	pie, tie, lie pipe, line, shine my, fly, cry night, fight, bright
Long /o/:	**oa** o_e ow	boat, float, goat bone, close, smoke snow, slow, pillow
Long /u/:	**ue** u_e ew	value, argue, cue cube, fuse, mule few, pew
Little /oo/:	**oo** u	book, foot, shook put, push, pudding
Long /oo/:	**oo** ue ew u_e	moon, fool, shoot glue, blue, true blew, flew, brew rude, flute, rule
/er/:	**er** ir ur	supper, sister, blister bird, shirt, third turn, burn, purse
Short /o/:	**o** au aw al	dog, pond, lost fault, pause, taunt claw, saw, shawl talk, walk, chalk
/oi/:	**oi** oy	oil, coin, spoil boy, toy, enjoy
/ou/:	**ou** ow	loud, mouse, cloud cow, clown, brown

Supplementary work

In most classes, there will be a few students who are not learning the sounds fast enough to keep up with the others. This could be for a number of reasons:

1. The student may have a poor memory for letter sounds and words.
2. The student's attendance is, for some reason, limited.
3. The student's concentration is poor.
4. There is little individual help given at home.

Whatever the reason, the problem must be overcome. Extra individual or group teaching in class may be necessary. Sometimes, a student who knows the letter sounds well is able to listen to a struggling student go through the letter sounds and help the struggling student to learn them.

The cooperation of parents is also invaluable. At the parents' meeting, it helps to inform parents that approximately 20% of students have some problems with learning to read and write, not because they are unintelligent, but because they have a poor memory for symbols and words. If their child is not managing to learn a letter sound a day, it is likely that they are amongst this 20%, and will benefit from some extra help.

Parents need to know when their child is struggling, so they can understand their child's problem, and give their time to helping him or her. Young children are keen to learn and enjoy the attention of their parents. One idea would be to write out the 42 letter sounds on small pieces of card or paper. The known letter sounds could be put in a box or envelope for the struggling student to take home and practice. The remaining letter sounds should be added to the box gradually, at a pace with which the student can cope. The aim of this exercise is to reinforce knowledge and develop fluency.

Once the main aspects of the alphabetic code are mastered, and reading and writing are relatively fluent, students will generally manage well in school and keep up with the others.

Conclusions

It is vital that the students know the letter sounds; they need to be able to say the sound as soon as they see the letter(s).

However, learning the letter sounds is not enough. The students need to know how to apply their letter knowledge. From the beginning the students should be taught to blend the sounds and hear the words for reading. This is a technique that can be taught, and is explained in Section 3: Reading. For writing, the students need to be taught to hear the sounds in words and know which letter(s) are needed for those sounds; this is explained in Section 4: Identifying the Sounds in Words.

2. Learning Letter Formation

For young students to learn fluent, neat handwriting they need to be taught how to hold their pencil and form their letters correctly. Early mastery is well worth the extra effort involved. Anyone who has tried to correct an older student's bad pencil hold, or incorrect formation, knows how difficult, if not impossible, it can be. It is far better to teach it correctly from the start.

Pencil hold

The pencil rests between the thumb and the first finger. The next finger prevents the pencil falling down; the last two fingers are tucked away. The hand rests on the table and the movement of the pencil is through the thumb and first finger. It is important that the knuckles point outwards. Young students are amused if their fingers are likened to "froggy legs." They move the pencil forwards and backwards with their "froggy legs"!

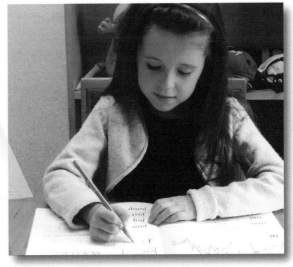

Letter formation

A multi-sensory approach to teaching helps the students to learn more easily. For this reason, the students are introduced to the formation of each letter in the following ways:

1. The teacher shows the formation on the board.

2. The teacher shows the formation in the air, taking care when facing the students that the letter is formed the correct way round for the students (in mirror writing, from the teacher's own point of view). The students hold up their fingers and follow the movement, saying the

sound at the same time. They do this several times.

3. In the *Phonics Student Books*, a line of dotted letters is provided for the students to write on. Arrows guide the students in the correct direction. The teacher, if possible, watches them write and tries to check that they are forming the letters correctly. The dotted line helps the students to understand that all the letters are the same size, except for the tall sticks and the tails.

4. The students feel the formation in the cutout letter grooves in the *Finger Phonics Books*.

5. The students can watch the formation of the letters on the *Phonics for the Whiteboard* software, *Jolly Phonics DVD*, or the *Phonics Games CD*. The *Phonics Games CD* also gives the students a chance to form the letters themselves.

The following list covers the basic letter knowledge needed for good handwriting:

1. All the letters are the same size except the seven letters that have sticks above the body of the letter: ‹b›, ‹d›, ‹f›, ‹h›, ‹k›, ‹l› and ‹t›, (note that the ‹t› is not quite as tall as the other tall letters), and the five letters that have tails that go below the line: ‹g›, ‹j›, ‹p›, ‹q› and ‹y›.

2. Most letters go down towards the line first: ‹b›, ‹h›, ‹i›, ‹j›, ‹k›, ‹l›, ‹m›, ‹n›, ‹p›, ‹r›, ‹t›, ‹u›, ‹v›, ‹w›, ‹x›, ‹y› and ‹f›. (Note that ‹f› has a little arch backwards before it goes down.)

3. The following letters start like a ‹c›: ‹a›, ‹d›, ‹o›, ‹g›, ‹q›. In *Jolly Phonics*, these are referred to as the "caterpillar c" letters.

4. ‹z› and ‹e› start by going towards the end of the page. Note that ‹e› starts lower than the other letters and comes back over like a "caterpillar c."

Parents can be invaluable here. They are in a good position to encourage correct formation and a good pencil hold. This can be explained at the parents' meeting.

The students are told that the letters in a word are written close together, but without bumping. They are also told to leave a space between words. It is important to practice the formation of each letter regularly. When the students are writing, especially during dictation, it is a good idea to check the pencil hold and make sure the letter formation is correct.

Capital letters

Phonics Student Book 1 concentrates on the formation of lower-case letters. Later, in *Phonics Student Book 2*, the formation of the capital letters is taught. Capital letters are the same size as tall letters. They all go down to the line first, apart from ‹C›, ‹G›, ‹O›, ‹Q›, and ‹S›, which go around anticlockwise first. Capital letters are never joined.

Joined-up writing

There is evidence to suggest that joined handwriting helps the students to develop greater fluency in their writing and encourages better spelling. The students feel how the letters go together by writing the word in one continuous movement and this reminds them to put the letters in the correct order. If joined handwriting is preferred, a good time to introduce it is when the digraphs are being taught. The students can be shown how the letters join together and reminded that sometimes two letters are needed to make one sound.

That said, joined handwriting is not necessarily better than print handwriting. Indeed, it has been argued that students should learn to use print letters first, because these more closely resemble the letters they will come across in books. The reality is that the style of handwriting taught makes little difference to the students' phonic understanding. Ultimately, the teacher should be guided by their school's handwriting policy when deciding whether he or she should teach joined handwriting.

Supplementary work

Some students have poor motor control. They need more practice if they are to form letters correctly and neatly. Coloring the pictures, and tracing the letters and patterns in their *Phonics Student Books* can help the students to develop this skill. In addition, using lined paper encourages the students to limit the size of their letters, and allows for greater accuracy when it comes to their letter formation.

Conclusions

By concentrating on correct letter formation and pencil hold from the beginning, bad habits can be prevented. It also makes it easier for the students to develop neat, fluent handwriting, and to take pride in their work.

3. Reading (Blending)

When reading, students need to understand the meaning of the words. Before they can do this, they have to be able to work out what the words say. The phonic skill for this is to look at the letters, say the sounds, and hear the word. This is called "blending." Blending is sometimes referred to as "synthesizing," which is why *Jolly Phonics* is known as a "synthetic phonics" program.

In the beginning, most students are not able to blend and need to be taught how. With the ability to blend, the students are able to read unknown regular words. They are also in a far better position to attempt the so-called irregular words, as no words are completely irregular. The pages of *Phonics Student Book 1* are a good starting place for teaching blending. Take the /s/ page; the teacher should ask the students if they can see a picture of a /s-u-n/. Only a few students in the class will hear the word *sun*, after it has been split into its individual sounds. After a few more examples, such as /s-p-ie-d-er/, /s-n-ai-l/ and /f-l-ow-er/ one or two more students might be tuned in to hear the words. The following day, after teaching the next letter sound, a few examples from the /a/ page could be called out, such as /a-n-t/ and /a-rr-ow/. Any object on the page could be used, although short words are preferable. Each day, a few more students will be able to hear the words. Some students have a natural ability for blending, but success comes to all in the end.

Once the students can hear the word when an adult says the letter sounds, they are ready to try saying the sounds for themselves and try listening for the word. Blending needs practice, and should be started as soon as possible. On most days, teachers should try to write short regular words, using the letters that have been taught, on the board or on flash cards. Examples of such words are: *tap*, *pan*, *pit*, *sit* and *pin*. The students say the sounds and listen for the word. The daily Word banks in Part 2 of the *Teacher's Book* is useful for this activity. In addition to the Word banks, there are words to blend each day on the letter sound pages in *Phonics Student Book 1* (although the pages for /s/ and /a/ show only the sounds). The students should not use any actions when blending words. Those students who can hear the words understand how the alphabetic code works for reading. They realize that it is something they can work out for themselves. This knowledge fascinates them and their confidence grows.

For most students, blending is relatively easy. However, some students find it difficult and need to be taught exactly what to do. There are two main reasons for students not being able to hear the word when they have said the sounds:

1. **They do not know the letter sounds well enough.**
   As soon as the student sees a letter, the sound should come automatically to them. If they have to pause to think, they lose track of the word. To correct this, it is necessary to practice the sounds regularly with flash cards, actions and other letter-sound activities.

2. The letter sounds are emphasized wrongly.

The emphasis should be on the first letter sound, for example, on the /d/ of /d-o-g/. If the students put the emphasis on the last letter sound, they may try to start the word with that sound and fail to hear the word.

There are two types of sound in English. One sort makes a pure, continuous sound; examples are the sounds, /sssssss/, /fffffffffff/, /rrrrrrrrr/, /mmmmmm/, /nnnnnnn/, /vvvvvvv/. The other sort has a "schwa" on the end. The schwa is like an /uh/ sound on the end of the letter sounds. For example, /b/ cannot be said without a schwa: /buh/. The continuous sounds can be said with, or without the schwa. Sounds should be said with as little schwa as possible.

With blending, the first sound needs to be louder than the others. This helps the students to remember the sound the word starts with. The sounds that follow in the word need to be spoken softly and quickly, and the schwa should be avoided where possible. This technique has been found to be effective, and about three quarters of the students master it quite quickly. Although blending is more difficult for the other quarter of the group, all they need is more practice. Frequently, in a whole-class situation, the students who are good at blending call out the answer too quickly and the less able copy them, as they do with letter sounds on flash cards. To remedy this situation, teachers can provide an extra blending session for the weaker students.

Blending skills can be improved if the students practice saying initial consonant blends in isolation. Examples of common consonant blends are: /cr/, /fl/, and /str/. It is important to make sure that the students have been taught the individual letter sounds and are just learning to blend separate sounds together. For example, if the /w/ letter sound has not yet been introduced, then avoid using the /sw/ blend. Saying the blend makes it easier to read the words that have initial consonant blends. The students are encouraged to work the word out by saying the blend, followed by the individual sounds, for example, /pl-a-n/, and not /p-l-a-n/. In *Phonics Student Book 1*, words with initial consonant blends are introduced from page 17 onwards.

When blending words with digraphs, the students have to remember to look at the two letters and say one sound. This more complicated skill is mastered when regular words, using the digraphs, are blended. For example, flash cards can be made showing regular /ai/ words, like *pain, rain, train, Spain, hail,* and *snail* so that, when the /ai/ sound has been taught, they can be held up for the students to sound out aloud and blend. Alternatively, the words could be written on the board for the class or for a group to blend.

Another way to develop speedy blending is to snap together the initial consonant(s) and the short vowel. Teachers can, on a regular basis, write a few of these consonant-vowel combinations on the board, and encourage those students who are weaker at blending to read them.

pa	pe	pi	po	pu
na	ne	ni	no	nu
ra	re	ri	ro	ru
fra	fre	fri	fro	fru
sta	ste	sti	sto	stu
gra	gre	gri	gro	gru

Initially, the students blend words by calling out the sounds aloud, but gradually, they should be encouraged to blend silently in their head. This promotes fluency for reading.

One activity for developing this skill involves the teacher doing the actions for a word without saying the sounds. For example, with the word *pin*, the teacher does the actions for the letter sounds, in this case puffing on the finger for the /p/, wiggling fingers on the nose for the /i/, and the arms out for the /n/ sound. The students try to work out the word and either write it down or call it out. Alternatively, a student could mime the actions for the sounds in a word, or three students could do one letter-sound action each. Another simple way to help students learn to blend sounds in their heads is as follows; the teacher writes letters randomly on the board and then points to one letter after another, spelling out a word. The students watch this and try to put the sounds together in their head to identify the word.

Once the students have started to blend simple words, it is important to provide many words for them to read, using their newly acquired blending skills. This will develop the essential fluency that is needed. Eventually blending should become an automatic response from the students every time they are confronted with a word that they have not seen or read before. Many words are provided in the *Teacher's Book*. More words are available in the *Jolly Phonics Cards*, the *Jolly Phonics Word Book* and in the Word Bank, which can be printed from the *Jolly Phonics Resources CD*. Other blending activities are available on the *Phonics Games CD* and in the *Jolly Phonics Workbooks*.

Introducing storybooks

During the first nine weeks, the aim is to prepare the students for reading books. Stories and poems can be read to the students, but they should not be expected to try to read books for themselves until they have learned the 42 letter sounds and the twelve tricky words that are introduced in *Phonics Student Book 1*.

Teachers and parents may find it difficult not to give the students books to read for themselves in the first few weeks. However, spending this extra time devoted to letter work at the beginning means that the benefits of following this program can be greater, with higher reading abilities gained and much lower levels of remedial help needed. The students gain confidence and can enjoy storybooks independently at an earlier stage.

Storybooks intended for students to read themselves are best introduced once the student can work out simple regular words independently, and after *Phonics Student Book 1* has been completed. Ideally, decodable readers, such as the *Jolly Phonics Readers*, should be used initially. There are a number of progressively difficult levels in the *Jolly Phonics Readers*. In addition, there are two sets of *Read and See* books for any students who have not yet mastered the necessary skills and who need extra blending practice and letter-sound knowledge.

Jolly Phonics Readers: Red Level (first level)
The words in these books are spelled regularly and can be read using knowledge of the 42 letter sounds and the tricky words taught in *Phonics Student Book 1*. The students will also need to recognize the tricky word *of*.

Jolly Phonics Readers: Yellow Level (second level)
These books follow on from the Red Level and can be read when the new sound for ‹y›, which occurs in the words *funny, happy,* and *floppy,* has been introduced, and the next ten tricky words have been learned. This teaching is covered at the beginning of *Phonics Student Book 2*.

Jolly Phonics Readers: Green Level (third level)
These books follow on from the Yellow Level and can be read when the "magic ‹e›" words, such as *late, these, fine, hope* and *cube,* have been introduced and the next twenty tricky words have been learned. This teaching is covered in *Phonics Student Book 2*.

Jolly Phonics Readers: Blue Level (fourth level)
These books follow on from the Green Level and can be read when the remaining tricky words have been learned, and when the following alternative vowel spellings have been taught: ‹ay›, ‹ea›, ‹igh›, ‹ow›, ‹ew›, ‹ir› and ‹oy›. These are common spellings found in words such as: *day, seat, light, snow, brown, stew, bird* and *boy*. This teaching is covered in *Student Books 2,* and *3*.

Note that the amount of text increases with each level, and light type is used for those few letters that should not be sounded out, such as the silent ‹b› in *lamb*.

When students can read the Blue Level Readers fluently and have completed *Phonics Student Books 1, 2,* and *3,* they are able to read any material that is appropriate for their intellectual age and knowledge of vocabulary.

Reading schemes

If it is not possible to use decodable readers, then the next most effective books are those linked to a reading scheme. Reading scheme books should use a controlled vocabulary, which is initially limited as much as is possible to regular words, and gradually increases to include words that have alternative or irregular spellings. Most students, who have been taught with *Jolly Phonics*, are able to cope well with this limited structure. However, the weaker students can struggle.

Great care should be taken to match the structure of the books to the reading ability of the students. When students are given books that use words that they cannot work out, they lose confidence in blending and start trying to remember the words by their shape, or simply to guess. This frequently leads to serious reading problems. Good readers are good at blending and they use this technique every time they meet an unknown word. Conversely, poor readers are poor at blending and rarely use this technique. It is important that teachers do not cause their students problems by failing to develop their blending skills sufficiently well, or by giving them the wrong type of books too early.

Once there is fluency in the reading and in the working out of unknown words, the students have the ability to read anything that is appropriate for their intellectual age. If they understand text when it is spoken to them, they will understand it when they read it themselves. It is at this stage that the students start reading to learn instead of learning to read. They also begin to read for pleasure, which encourages them to read more books. This, in turn, further improves their literacy skills and increases their vocabulary.

Helpful hints for blending

The following hints enable the students to blend more words. The extra knowledge helps to develop their understanding and confidence.

1. **When two vowels go walking, the first does the talking**
   When two vowel letters appear together in a word, the sound made is often the long vowel sound of the first letter. The second vowel says nothing. The following type of words can be worked out with this understanding: *dream* and *people*. The saying, "When two vowels go walking, the first does the talking," amuses the students and helps to remind them that usually the first vowel is spoken and the second vowel is silent. Occasionally, it is the second vowel that gives the sound, as in the words *young* and *field*, and the students delight in finding the "naughty" second vowel!

2. **If the short vowel doesn't work, try the long one**
   This saying is a good hint to know for blending. It helps with words like *he*, *be*, *blind*, *mind*, *acorn*, *union*, *able*, *emu* and *item*. The saying

also helps the students cope with words containing split digraphs, introduced in *Phonics Student Book 2*, which are often called "magic ‹e›" words. The following words have a "magic ‹e›" in them: *late, theme, pipe, home, cube.* The ‹e› on the end of the word does not say a sound itself, but the so-called "magic" hops back over the consonant and changes the first vowel from a short vowel to a long one.

3. Shy ‹i› and toughy ‹y›

The letter ‹i› is very "shy" and "toughy ‹y›" takes its place. The words *day* and *boy* are not written *dai* or *boi*, because ‹i› is too "shy" to go on the end, so "toughy ‹y›" takes its place. The letter ‹i› is replaced by ‹y› in words like *funny, system,* and *toy.* For young students, it is enough for them to know that when a ‹y› is not the first letter, it often takes the place of the ‹i›, and it is then a vowel. When blending a ‹y›, which is not the first letter, the students should first try the short ‹i› and, if that doesn't work, try the long ‹i›. With some accents, ‹y› can make an /ee/ sound when it comes at the end of words such as *happy, merry,* and *holly.*

4. Soft ‹c› and soft ‹g›

If the letter ‹c› is followed by the vowels ‹e›, ‹i›, or ‹y›, the sound is usually softened to a /s/, as in the words *ice, race, city, circle,* and *cycle.* Similarly, when a letter ‹g› is followed by an ‹e›, ‹i›, or ‹y›, the /g/ sound usually changes to /j/, as in *gently, giant,* and *gymnastics.* This teaching is covered in *Phonics Student Book 3.* Flash cards showing these types of words help to reinforce the pattern.

5. Alternative vowel spellings

Lastly, the seven alternative ways of writing the vowels, listed in the table below, cannot be worked out using the above helpful hints, and will need to be learned as alternative spellings.

/igh/	/ew/	/ir/	/ur/	/au/	/aw/	/al/
night	few	bird	turn	pause	saw	ball
light	skew	girl	nurse	haunt	draw	talk
high	pew	shirt	curl	taunt	straw	small

Supplementary work

Students need to have plenty of blending practice. In Part 2 of this book, lists of words and sentences are provided for blending practice in an exercise entitled: Further Blending Practice. For this exercise, the teacher writes the words and sentences on the board for the students to read as a class. The students should be encouraged to spot any tricky words, and to blend any unknown words. Once the students have read the sentences with their teacher, they can discuss them and the teacher can explain the meanings of any words that the students do not understand.

A few students seem to have great difficulty learning to blend. It is easy to think that they may never achieve this skill. However, with extra support and practice, they will succeed. These students tend to be those who have a poor visual memory. The ability to blend will be even more essential for these students, as they will always have difficulty memorizing words.

The Word Banks and Further Blending Practice in the Daily Lesson Plans section of this book provide words for this extra practice. When the students have developed the necessary skills and are ready to read books for themselves, it is important that they are given decodable books. The decodable books used should contain only the letter sounds and tricky words that have been taught and learned. Once the students use their blending skills automatically, know the letter sounds and read fluently, they are able to read any books that are suitable for their age and intellect.

Conclusions

Students who can blend words fluently have few problems with reading. Once the fluency is there, reading extension and comprehension become the more important aspects. Early phonic teaching with *Jolly Phonics* makes reading and writing easier for all students. For those students with a poor memory for words, it is absolutely essential.

4. Identifying the Sounds in Words

Hearing the sounds in words is one of the main skills needed for writing. For example, when students can hear each sound in a simple word, and know how to write the letters for those sounds, they can write hundreds of words by themselves, such as *mat, pen, hop, lid, fun, run,* and *sunset.*

From the beginning, the students are taught how to write the letter sounds as they are introduced to them. This was covered in Section 2: Letter Formation. At the same time, the students are taught to identify the sounds in words. The first step is to encourage them to listen for the sound that is being taught. There is an example of this kind of activity for every lesson in *Phonics Student Book 1*. For example, the first letter sound is /s/ and the students have to look at the pictures of a *sun, snail, spider,* and *flower* and decide which word does not have a /s/ sound in it. Initially, only a few students will have the ability to hear this. Gradually, all the students listen more carefully and start to answer correctly. They may even be able to say whether the sound comes at the beginning, in the middle, or at the end of the word.

The second step, which starts after the first few pages of *Phonics Student Book 1*, is to ask the students to listen and identify all the sounds in a word, and to hold up a finger for each sound. For example, *pan, sit,* and *rain* each have three sounds: /p-a-n/, /s-i-t/, and /r-ai-n/. Identifying sounds is a skill known as *phonemic awareness*. A few examples should be done every day. At the beginning, you should use the letter sounds that have been taught. For example, the word *pat* could be used when the /p/ letter sound has been taught. Ask the students what sound comes at the beginning of *pat*. When a student identifies the /p/, hold up a finger (usually the thumb), and ask the students to do the same. Then ask for the next sound in *pat*, placing a strong emphasis on the /a/. When the /a/ is identified, hold up the second finger (usually the index finger), and ask for the last sound. Hold up the next finger when the /t/ sound is called out. Then do the same with other words, such as *sit, at,* and *sat*. Call the word out and encourage the students to say the sounds with you, holding up a finger for each sound. In the beginning, the students are guided by their teacher, but after a short while the students will hold up their fingers and call out all the sounds by themselves.

Teachers could also demonstrate the skill of writing by asking for the sounds in the words and writing the letters on the board as the students call them out. The word can then be blended and read. This allows the students to see the significance of encoding to write and decoding to read. It is this understanding that makes the students confident and the program so successful. Later on, the students learn that the English language is not quite so simple. There are several alternative ways of writing the letter sounds, and sometimes there are quite bizarre spelling patterns. However, by going from simple skills and gradually introducing the more complex ones, virtually all the students become successful readers and writers.

When most of the students can call out the sounds in three-letter words, longer words can be tackled. This often involves hearing the single sounds in consonant blends. Frequently, the students fail to hear one of the consonants, and might write "fog'" instead of *frog*, or "wet" instead of *went*.

Initial consonant blends:

bl-, cl-, fl-, pl-, sl-, br-, cr-, dr-, fr-, gr-, pr-, tr-, st-, sc-, sm-, sn-, tw-, shr-, thr-, scr-, spr-, str-.

Final consonant blends:

-lb, -ld, -lf, -lk, -lm, -ln, -lp, -lt, -ct, -ft, -nt, -pt, -xt, -mp, -nd.

In order to help the students hear all the sounds in initial and final consonant blends, call out the blends and ask the students to say the sounds, holding up a finger for each sound. For example, say /cr/ and ask the students to respond with the sounds /c/ (holding up the thumb) and /r/ (holding up the index finger). Repeat with a few other consonant blends. Take care that these letter sounds have already been taught. Then, on a regular basis, call out a few words with consonant blends, so that the students can count the sounds. Any of the following examples could be used for this exercise:

Examples of words with initial consonant blends:

bran	clap	clip	club	flag	flat	flap	flip	glad
plan	plug	plum	plot	slap	slim	slug	crab	crop
drag	drip	drop	drug	drum	frog	from	grab	grim
grip	print	prop	trim	trap	trip	smog	snap	snip
snug	swam	swim	swum	twig	twin	spin	span	stop

Examples of words with final consonant blends:

bulb	held	golf	milk	silk	film	help	gulp	belt
melt	quilt	gift	lift	soft	ant	pant	bent	went
tent	mint	hunt	kept	next	camp	damp	lamp	bend
mend	wind	pond	felt	desk	risk	best	nest	lost
must	sank	west	ramp	plump	slept	frost	grand	crisp

When the digraphs are being taught, the students need to understand that sometimes they have to write two letters for one sound. The first digraph taught is the /ai/ sound. The students listen for the sounds in a word, such as *nail*, and call out /n-ai-l/, holding up a finger for each of the three sounds. Then other /ai/ words can be called out for the students to identify the sounds in them, such as *rain*, *paint*, *sail*, *fail*, *pain*, *drain*. Once the students can hear the sounds in these words, it is relatively easy for them to write similar words during dictation, in their *Phonics Student Books*. There are also games on the *Phonics Games CD*, which encourage students to identify the sounds in words, providing them with the practice they need.

Letter board

This can be made from a large piece of card. Three smaller strips of card are stapled across the first sheet, so that letters can be slotted into the strips. The vowels are placed on the top row and some consonants, needed for making words, are placed on the bottom row.

The teacher asks a student to make a word by putting the letters in the middle strip. For example, with the word *peg*, the students listen for the sounds and one student is chosen to pick out the letters and place them in the correct left to right order. Then the rest of the class can indicate if they think the word is correct or not (thumbs up for "yes", and thumbs down for "no"). Then, all the students blend the word to check if it is correct. If it is wrong, the student might like to have another go. After that, the teacher could ask, "Who can change it from *peg* to *pen*?" and then, "Who can change *pen* to *spend*?"

Regular word building with the letter board shows the students, in a practical way, how regular words are built up. Alternatively, a similar activity could be carried out with magnetic letters.

Dictation

Dictating letters, words and sentences is important for developing writing skills. Dictation begins almost immediately in *Phonics Student Book 1*, with the teacher calling out letter sounds that have been taught. All the students attempt to write the letter sounds. Then the teacher can write the letter sounds on the board and the students look to see if they have written them correctly. The number of letters dictated increases as confidence grows. In the beginning the standard of achievement will probably range from very good to hardly legible.

Word dictation starts at the time the letter sound /c k/ is taught. First of all, a few letter sounds are dictated and then the words *it* and *at*. Each student has to try and identify the sounds and write the letters for the sounds. Encourage the students to write the letters in a word close together, but with no bumping. When the first word has been attempted, ask the students to call out the sounds and watch you write the letters on the board. Then the students can see if they have written their word correctly. Some teachers encourage the students to put a little tick next to the word if they are correct. At this stage, not all students will be able to write the words; they may only get the first letter sound. However, it is not long before they start to tune in to the sounds and realize what is expected of them. Some students may need extra support at home or at school.

Dictation of regular words with consonant blends and digraphs should follow on from the dictation of simple CVC words (consonant-vowel-consonant words).

Once the students are familiar with some tricky words, and know how to spell a few of them, sentences can be dictated. The sentences should be made up of regular words, which can be written by listening for the sounds, and can include those tricky words that have been taught. Sentence writing begins in *Phonics Student Book 2* and is the start of independent writing. The exercises in *Phonics Student Book 2* not only provide the opportunity for practicing writing words, but also give the students a feeling for what a sentence is and that a capital letter and period are needed. Additional sentences suitable for this exercise are available on the *Jolly Phonics Resources CD*.

The dictation of capital letters, once they have been taught, is needed to make sure that the students know how to write them. This is also covered in *Phonics Student Book 2*. Frequently, young students have the ability to recognize the capital letters, but this does not necessarily mean they know how to write them. In the beginning, only one way of writing a digraph is used; for example the long /a/ sound is taught as ‹ai›. So words used for dictation should be restricted to those with the ‹ai› spelling, such as *rain, drain, tail, Spain, pain*.

Independent writing

Independent writing is the desired outcome. When the students have learned the letter sounds, can identify the sounds in words and have done some dictation, they are well on their way to being able to write independently.

As soon as students can hear the sounds in words and know one way of writing each sound, they can write anything they want to write. In the early stages, students might not use conventional spelling, but their work will still be readable; for example, "mie momee poot mie book in mie scool bag." Accurate spelling comes through reading many books, knowing the alternative letter sounds and following a systematic spelling program.

This is an example of a student's writing after just over half a year (reduced to half of its original size):

Notice how this student has joined up some of the digraphs: ‹ar›, ‹ch›, ‹ee›. However, she needs to listen more carefully to some words, so that she can hear the /t/ in *lots*, and that *had* does not have a /n/ in it.

Developing independent writing

Independent writing starts in *Phonics Student Book 2*. At this stage, the students are used to word building, listening for the sounds and writing the appropriate letters. In *Phonics Student Book 2*, a themed picture is provided and the students are asked to say sentences about the picture and make up a little story about it. The students are then given a model sentence to copy into their books. In *Phonics Student Book 3*, the students are provided with a theme only; they have to draw their own picture and write about it. Some of the words, those that are difficult to spell accurately through listening for the sounds, can be written on the board. Guidance for each independent writing exercise is provided in the *Teacher's Book*.

Initially, the teacher reads out the model sentence that is provided in the notes, and the students, with help from the teacher, work out how to write it. The sentence has a controlled vocabulary so that it uses only those tricky words that have been taught, and regular words using the 42 letter sounds. This enables the students to work out the sentence for themselves by calling out the letters for the tricky words, and identifying the sounds in the regular words, which the teacher writes on the board. The students are then encouraged to copy this sentence under their picture.

When those students who are good at writing words from dictation finish copying their sentence, they can be encouraged to write some more sentences by themselves. Naturally, at a young age, it is impossible to spell all the words correctly and close attempts are acceptable.

Marking policy

The students' earliest efforts at independent writing do not need rigorous marking. Missing sounds can be pointed out and any tricky words already taught can be corrected.

It is impossible for young students to have the freedom to write exactly what they want to say and spell all the words correctly. If everything is corrected it is demoralizing, and discourages the students from writing freely. Generally speaking, it is best to restrict the errors marked to about four words. These words can be learned with the "Look, Copy, Cover, Write and Check" method, referred to in Section 5, once the work has been marked.

By the end of the second year at school the majority of words are written correctly. If the error is one that the student should have known not to make, it should be marked. However, if the error is not due to carelessness, and the word is out of the ordinary, a dot can be placed underneath it. This tells the student that the word is spelled wrongly, but that their attempt was a good one and the correct spelling will be taught later. Teachers should select four words, which the student has spelled wrongly, for them to practice underneath.

Those students who have a good visual memory and a certain amount of maturity, but have been careless, need more rigorous marking than those students who are less able. In the end, it comes down to judgment. It is not encouraging to have too many red pen marks over a piece of work, but as they get a bit older the students need to know when they are wrong, and to learn from their mistakes. The use of dictionaries is encouraged once the skill of looking up words has been mastered. This skill is taught in *The Grammar Handbooks 1* and *2*.

Supplementary work

Most students will learn to hear the sounds in words during class lessons. The few who are finding it difficult may need to be taught in the same manner, but in a smaller group, or if necessary individually.

The Further Blending Practice words, provided in the Daily Lesson Plans, are ideal for improving the students' blending skills, but they can also be used to encourage the students to hear the sounds in words. The teacher copies the list of words onto the board and blends them with the students. Then the teacher reads each word again, more slowly this time, and asks the students to identify the individual sounds, holding up a finger for each sound. In the Daily Lesson

Plans sections for *Phonics Student Books 2* and *3*, the Further Blending Practice words often contain some of the alternative letter-sound spellings that the students have learned. For example, after the students have been introduced to the soft ‹c› and soft ‹g› in *Phonics Student Book 3*, words like *space* and *fragile* are included in the Further Blending Practice section. Teachers can ask the students to spot the alternative letter-sound spellings when the list of words is written on the board.

Conclusions

The aim of this teaching is to enable the students to hear the sounds in regular words and to write the letters that relate to those sounds. A different technique is needed for coping with words that are spelt irregularly. This is covered next, in Section 5: Tricky Words.

In every class, there will be a few students who find it difficult to memorize the letter sounds and who struggle to blend and segment words. These students tend to have a weak visual memory and poor auditory skills. However, this does not mean that they need different teaching from the more able students; they simply need the same teaching, but more of it.

It is necessary to identify any struggling students at an early stage. It is a good idea to provide some extra teaching for these students if possible. Not all of the students who are struggling will be at the same stage; there will be a range of abilities. Some students will only need extra support for a few weeks before they begin to make steady progress. Other students may have more significant difficulties. Despite their differences, all the students should receive the same type of teaching. With regular blending and writing practice and by reviewing the letter sounds, teachers can ensure that the students master these skills.

5. Tricky Words

Tricky words are either irregular, such as *to*, *your*, *one*, and *said*, or are frequently used words that can only be read with phonic knowledge that has not yet been taught, for example the words *made*, *like*, *my*, *right*. The students think of the awkward bits as being out to trick them! Despite this, some part of a tricky word will be regular. For example, in the word *come*, the ‹c› and ‹m› are regular. The students might find it helpful to underline the tricky part(s) of each tricky word in their *Phonics Student Books*.

Students are more able to read tricky words when they have knowledge of letter sounds and can relate those sounds to symbols. They should, initially, blend the letter sounds and then learn the correct pronunciation. The students find it interesting to look carefully for the "tricky" part in the words; by doing this they start to analyze words. The students' extra attention to the details helps to store the word in their memories. For example, if the students recognize that the letter ‹a› in the word *was* has an /o/ sound, they are more likely to remember the correct spelling. The first set of tricky words is introduced towards the end of *Phonics Student Book 1*. It is important that tricky words are taught in a systematic way and with plenty of practice.

Learning to spell tricky words

The students should learn how to spell the tricky words after they have been taught to read them. Some fortunate students have a sufficiently good visual memory to master the spelling of the tricky words just by reading them, but most students have to be taught. The following six techniques for teaching spelling, listed below, are all useful.

1. Look, copy, cover, write, check

This is the principal method for teaching the spelling of tricky words in the *Phonics Student Books*. First, the students look at the word and identify the tricky part(s). For instance, the word *said* has an /e/ sound in the middle, but it is spelled with an ‹ai›. The ‹s› and ‹d› are regular. Then the students say the letter names (not the letter sounds) several times. The reason for saying the names and not the sounds is that the letter names trot off the tongue more easily and these particular words do not sound out reliably. After that, the students trace the word in the air or on the table, saying the letter names as they do so. Following that, they copy the word by going over the dots in their *Phonics Student Books*, saying the letter names again. Then they cover up the dotted word, and write it on their own in the next column, looking back to see if it is correct. This is repeated in the last column. Encourage the students to continue saying the letter names as they write the word. Regular practice and dictation ensure that the spelling of these words is mastered.

2. Word wall

In *Jolly Phonics*, the tricky words are divided into six color-coded groups, of twelve tricky words each. The blue group comes first, then yellow, and so on. The colored groups correspond to the colors suggested for the tricky word flowers in the *Phonics Student Books* and on the *Phonics for the Whiteboard* software. These colors are also used on the *Jolly Phonics Tricky Word Wall Flowers*, which are designed to be used as a wall display. Each flower can be pinned to the wall once the tricky word it contains has been taught; in this way, the wall display builds up week by week. Alternatively, you could make your own display by writing the tricky words onto card shapes and pinning them to the wall as you teach the words.

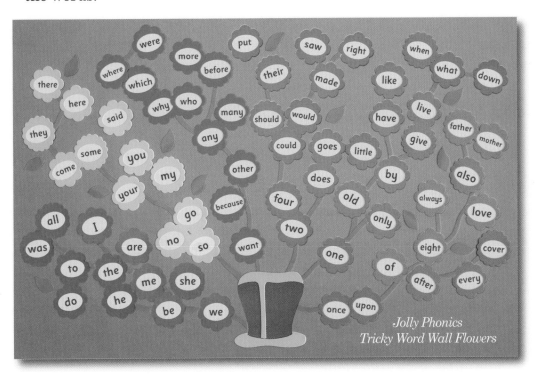

*Jolly Phonics
Tricky Word Wall Flowers*

3. Say it as it sounds

This spelling method is useful for words, though not necessarily high-frequency ones, which have one element that makes the word difficult to spell. Take, for example, the word *Monday*. The difficult part is the ‹o›, because instead of having an /o/ sound, it has an /u/ sound. It helps the students to remember this awkward spelling if they say the word as it should be spoken, so that *Monday* starts like the word *monster*. Frequently, these odd spellings have other words that follow the same pattern, in this case words like *monk*, *monkey*, *month,* and *money.* Sometimes it helps to introduce the other words at the same time, depending on how useful you think it will be for the students at this stage, and how capable they are.

Another awkward aspect of spelling is the fact that we often swallow the pronunciation of the vowels, particularly in words with more than one syllable. For example, the ‹e› in *children* has an /uh/ sound, which is known as a *schwa*. It often helps the children to spell these words if they "say it as it sounds," in this case by emphasizing the /e/.

Silent letters can also be taught in this way. By pronouncing the ‹w› at the beginning of words like *write, wrong, wrap,* and *wring*, the students find it much easier to spell the words correctly. Teachers can make a list of these words as they occur and then, in odd moments, call out the words so that the students can say them as they are written, pronouncing the silent letters and the swallowed vowels.

Teacher says:	Students respond:
"mother"	"m**o**ther" (to rhyme with *bother*)
"doctor"	"doct**or**" (emphasising the /or/)
"Wednesday"	"**Wed-nes**-day"
"front"	"fr**o**nt" (with an /o/ sound and not an /u/)
"knock"	"***k***-nock"
"island"	"***is***-land"

4. Word families or patterns

When one word is taught, it is helpful to show others with the same spelling pattern. For example, the word *like* could be linked to *bike, like, hike, pike,* and other words ending in ‹ike›. Each word family can then be linked to a wider group, in this case, ‹i_e› words, such as *hive, pine, pipe, shine, line, mine, time, rice.*

Later, more awkward patterns can be taught, including the worst letter combination of all, the ‹ough›, found in words like *rough, ought, bough, doughnut,* and *through*. Note that in each of these words the ‹ough› has a different sound. Fortunately, there are not too many of this type of word.

5. Does it look right?

When students are uncertain about how to spell a word, they can write it down on some scrap paper, trying different ways of writing it. This is particularly useful for working out the vowels, which often have more than one way of being written. For instance, *brown* could be written *broun* or *brown* and *bird* could be *berd, burd,* or *bird*. The students choose the one that looks right. At a later stage, the students should be encouraged to look up the correct spelling in a dictionary, especially when their dictionary skills are good enough.

By dictating the tricky words regularly, teachers can check how well the students are learning to spell them. Similarly, frequent use of tricky word flash cards will help the students to read these words. On the *Phonics Games CD* the students can practice reading and spelling the tricky words by playing the relevant games.

Vowels and helpful hints for spelling

The way vowels work is probably the least understood aspect of phonic teaching. Many of the vowels have more than one way of being written. In addition, vowels often have irregular spellings. Some knowledge about vowels is useful, but it is important that you do not get too bogged down in rules.

Generally, the early rules relate to the short vowels /a/, /e/, /i/, /o/, and /u/. When the students have been taught to listen for the short vowel and can easily identify it in words, they can understand the following rules:

1. A short word with a short vowel, followed by a /ck/ sound, is written with a ‹ck›, as in *black, neck, tick, tock, duck*. If the word does not have a short vowel, then only the ‹k› is required, as in *look, dark, jerk,* and *leek.*

2. In a short word with a short vowel, ending in ‹f›, ‹l›, ‹s›, or ‹z›, the final consonant needs to be doubled, as in *cliff, spill, miss, buzz*. The few exceptions include the very short words *if, is,* and *of.*

3. If the suffixes ‹ing›, ‹ed›, ‹er›, or ‹y› are added to a short word with a short vowel, there must be at least two consonants before the suffix. If the short word has only one consonant at the end, then this consonant is usually doubled before the suffix is added. This means that in *running, stopped, thinner,* and *funny,* the final consonants of the original words, *run, stop, thin,* and *fun* have been doubled. If there are already two consonants at the end of the word, no such doubling is needed. Furthermore, if the word does not have a short vowel, it is not necessary to have two consonants before the suffix, so *looking, heated, lighter,* and *dreamy* have only one consonant.

Conclusions

The tricky words in English always cause problems. Learning to read these words is easier than learning to spell them. By teaching the students to observe the irregularities, and by giving them techniques and simple rules, you are enabling them to be more accurate in their spelling. A certain amount of rigor is needed when teaching the awkward spellings, particularly when teaching students who do not have a good visual memory.

PART 2

Teaching with Phonics Student Book 1

The *Phonics Student Books* are designed so that each page is a complete lesson. The majority of *Phonics Student Book 1* is devoted to the letter sound pages, which introduce the students to the main 42 sounds of the English language. With the letter sound pages, the students are not only taught how to recognize each letter sound, but are also introduced to one way of writing each sound. Towards the end of *Phonics Student Book 1*, the students are taught how to read and spell the first twelve tricky words and there are a number of activity pages, which help the students to begin to use their letter-sound knowledge for reading and writing.

The letter sound pages
There is one page for each of the letter sounds, but the teaching on each page follows the same pattern and the following four activities are covered daily.

1. Learning the letter sound

- Each letter sound is introduced with a story, which is provided for the teacher in the Daily Guidance section.
- Throughout each story, the letter sound of the day is repeatedly emphasized, and a letter-sound action emerges from the story, which helps to make the letter sound more memorable for the students.
- A picture, linked to the story, and an illustration of the action are provided on the *Phonics Student Book* pages as a further reminder for the students.

2. Letter Formation
- The letter of the day is printed at the top of each page. Both the capital letter and the lower-case letter are shown, but the students need only learn the formation of the lower-case letter at this early stage. The capital letters are taught thoroughly in *Phonics Student Book 2*, and should only be referred to incidentally at this point.
- The Daily Guidance section gives instructions for teaching the students how to form the letters correctly. A corresponding activity on each *Phonics Student Book* page shows precisely how each letter is written and provides dotted letters for the students to write over.

3. Blending
- There are words for the students to blend in the colored panels on each page and a number of extra words for blending practice provided in a daily Word Bank. All the blending words use only the letter sounds that have been covered at that point.
- For more information about blending, see pages 16 to 22 of the introduction.

4. Identifying the sounds
- A number of pictures are provided on each letter sound page.
- The students say the words corresponding to each picture. When they come across a word that does not contain the sound of the day, they cross out its picture.
- A number of further activities are explained in the Daily Guidance section, along with the letters and the words for dictation.

The tricky word pages
- Once the main 42 letter sounds have been introduced, the students are taught to read and spell some of the most common tricky words. For more information, see pages 30 to 33 of this book for the section on tricky words.
- The tricky words introduced in *Student Book 1* are as follows:

  the, he she, me, we, be,
  I, was, to, do, are, all.

- The tricky words are introduced in color-coded sets in the *Phonics Student Books*. This first set of twelve words is referred to as the blue set and the words are displayed in blue flowers in the *Phonics Student Books*.

The reading and writing pages
- The reading activities on these pages help the students to consolidate their letter-sound and tricky word knowledge and provide them with the opportunity to practice their blending skills.
- Whenever the students are expected to write a word, a line is provided for each sound in that word, with a longer line indicating that a digraph is required. This reminds the students that they have to listen for all the sounds in a word in order to write it.
- At this point, the students are only expected to write single words.

Letter Sound /s/

Story
· Introduce the sound /s/ using a story, such as the one below, and the action.

It is a sunny morning, and Sam is taking his dog, Sampson, for a walk. They like to walk down to the pond. Sam looks around as they walk along. He sees a toadstool, a red and yellow caterpillar, and a blackbird on her nest. When they get to the pond, Sam and Sampson spend some time watching the fish swim around. After a while, Sampson goes off and snuffles around in the grass. He finds a stick, which he brings back to Sam. Then he barks at Sam, and Sam throws the stick for Sampson to fetch. Sampson runs around, looking for the stick in the grass. Suddenly, Sampson starts barking, "woof, woof, woof!" Sam skips over to see what Sampson has found. He hears a "ssssss" sound, "ssssss!" In front of Sampson is a spotty snake. It is rearing up and hissing loudly. Sam grabs hold of Sampson, and the snake slithers quickly away.

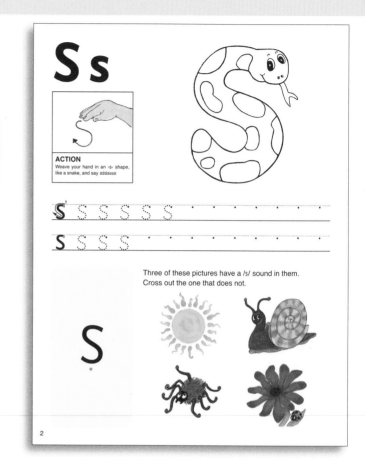

Three of these pictures have a /s/ sound in them. Cross out the one that does not.

Action
· The students weave their arms like a snake while making a continuous /ssssss/ sound.

Formation
· Explain how the letter ‹s› is written.
· The students write over the dotted letters in their books.

Blending
· Encourage the students to try making the /s/ sound.
· No words can be read at this stage, as the students have only been taught one letter sound. However, even at this early stage, teachers can begin auditory blending by encouraging the students to listen for the word when they have said the sounds.
· For example, the teacher says, /s-u-n/ and the students call out *sun*.

Sounding
· Say the words corresponding to the pictures on the page: *sun, snail, spider, flower*.
· The students listen for the word without the /s/ sound (*flower*), and cross out its picture.

Further Ideas
· Sing the song from the *Jolly Jingles* or the *Jolly Songs*.
· Put up on the wall, or hold up, the /s/ section of the *Wall Frieze*.
· Paint or collage a snake shape.
· Make snake shapes from dough or modeling clay.

Letter Sound /a/

Flashcards
• Practice the sound /s/.

Story
• Introduce the sound /a/ using a story, such as the one below, and the action.

The Smith family is going on a picnic. The children help their mother pack the food. Adam packs the apples and Annie helps to make the sandwiches. At last, they are ready and set off for their picnic. When they arrive, they spread out a big picnic blanket and lay all the food on it. Annie rubs her arm. "Something is tickling me," she says. "Something is tickling me, too," says Adam, eating his apple. Then Annie shouts, "a, a, a ants!" They all look at Annie and see some ants crawling up her arm. They all jump up. There are ants all over the picnic cloth! "Oh dear," says Dad. "We must have put our cloth over an ants' nest." They pack up their things and move to a nicer spot.

Action
• The students pretend that ants are crawling up their arms and say "a, a, a."

Formation
• Explain how the letter ‹a› is written.
• The students write over the dotted letters in their books.

Blending
• Point to the letters and say the sounds /s/ and /a/.
• No words can be read at this stage, as the students have only been taught two letter sounds. However, teachers can begin auditory blending by encouraging the students to listen for the word when they have said the sounds.
• For example, the teacher says, /a-n-t/ and the students call out *ant*.

Sounding
• Say the words corresponding to the pictures on the page: *cobweb, arrow, ant, apple.*
• The students listen for the word without the /a/ sound (*cobweb*), and cross out its picture.

Dictation
• Call out the sounds /a/ and /s/ for the students to write.

Further ideas
• Sing the /a/ song from the *Jolly Jingles* or the *Jolly Songs.*
• Put up on the wall, or hold up, the /a/ section of the *Wall Frieze.*
• Cut out a large letter ‹a› shape from paper or card for each student. The students collage or paint their letter ‹a›.
• Cut some apples in half and use them to print shapes.

Letter Sound /t/

Flash cards
• Practice the sounds /s/, and /a/.

Story
• Introduce the sound /t/ using a story, such as the one below, and the action.

This morning, Tom and Tamiko watched an important tennis match on television. There was a big crowd waiting for the match to begin. When the players came on to the court, the crowd clapped. Then the match began, and the two tennis players hit the ball to each other, "t, t, t." The people in the crowd turned their heads from side to side, watching the tennis ball. Now, Tom and Tamiko are outside, pretending to be the tennis players they saw on television. They hit the tennis ball to each other, "t, t, t." Among the tulips, some animals are watching Tom and Tamiko play. The animals turn their heads from side to side, watching the ball, just like the crowd at the tennis match.

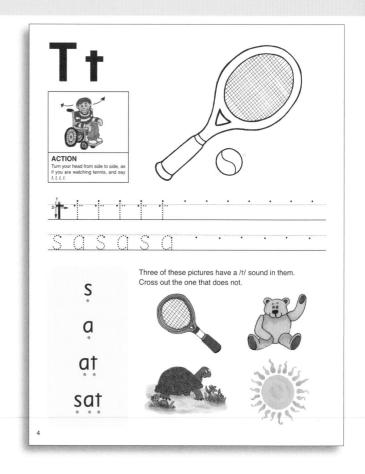

Action
• The students imitate watching tennis, turning their heads from side to side and saying "t, t, t."

Formation
• Explain how the letter ‹t› is written. It is a tall letter and starts slightly higher up than the letters ‹s› and ‹a›.
• The students write over the dotted letters in their books.

Blending
• Point to the letters and say the sounds /s/ and /a/.
• Blend the words *at* and *sat*.
• Say the sounds with the students, then blend the sounds together and read the words.
• Encourage the students to point to the dot underneath each sound as they say it.

Sounding
• Say the words corresponding to the pictures on the page: *tennis racket, teddy bear, turtle, sun.*
• The students listen for the word without the /t/ sound (*sun*), and cross out its picture.

Dictation
• Call out the sounds /t/, /a/, and /s/ for the students to write.

Further ideas
• Sing the song from the *Jolly Jingles* or the *Jolly Songs*.
• Put up on the wall, or hold up, the /t/ section of the *Wall Frieze*.
• Play tennis.
• Have a teddy bear day.
• Make model turtles from modeling clay.

Letter Sound /i/

Flash cards
- Practice the sounds /s/, /a/, and /t/.

Story
- Introduce the sound /i/ using a story, such as the one below, and the action.

Zack has a white pet mouse. She lives in a cage on the desk in his bedroom. One evening, Zack forgets to close the cage door properly. The little mouse climbs out of the cage and starts looking around the desk. Suddenly, she sees the cat watching her. She squeaks, "i, i, i," and quickly runs across the top of the desk. Crash! She bumps into a bottle of ink and knocks it over. As the bottle falls, the lid comes off, and the ink spills out everywhere, even over the little mouse. The mouse keeps on running as fast as she can, scampering off the desk and across the room to a mouse hole she had seen from her cage. Safe in the mouse hole, she scrubs and scrubs at her fur, but she cannot get all the ink off. She decides that from now on she will make the mouse hole her new home and call herself "Inky Mouse." In the morning, Zack finds the mouse missing and sees a little set of inky footprints across the carpet, leading from the desk to the little mouse hole.

Action
- The students wiggle their fingers on the end of their nose, like whiskers, saying, "i, i, i."

Formation
- Explain how the letter ‹i› is written. The students write over the dotted letters in their books.

Blending
- Point to the letters and say the sounds /a/ and /i/.
- Blend the words *it* and *sit*.
- Say the sounds with the students, then blend the sounds together and read the words.
- Encourage the students to point to the dot underneath each sound as they say it.

Sounding
- Say the words corresponding to the pictures on the page: *igloo, arrow, insects, ink.*
- The students listen for the word without the /i/ sound (*arrow*), and cross out its picture.

Dictation
- Call out the sound /i/ and the other sounds already covered for the students to write.

Further ideas
- Sing the song from the *Jolly Jingles* or the *Jolly Songs*.
- Put up on the wall, or hold up, the /i/ section of the *Wall Frieze*.
- Make inky fingerprints.
- Hunt for the letter ‹i› around the classroom, for example, in books, or on posters on the walls.

Letter Sound /p/

Flash cards
- Practice the sounds /s/, /a/, /t/, and /i/.

Story
- Introduce the sound /p/ using a story such as the one below, and the action.

Paul likes to visit the city zoo near his home. His favorite animal there is the polar bear. "The polar bear has big paws for paddling in the pool," says the zookeeper. It is Paul's birthday soon and his mom asks if he would like a teddy bear as his present. Paul thinks about this, and says that he would prefer a polar bear! When his birthday arrives, Paul's friends Peng, Pavlo, and Pat come to his party. They all play games and eat the party food: pineapple, pizza, and popcorn. Then Paul's mom gives Paul his present. He unwraps the paper to find a perfect toy polar bear. After that, Paul's mom produces a big birthday cake, with purple icing. She has put trick candles on the cake. Every time Paul blows out a candle, it lights up again! He tries to puff out the candles, "p, p, p, p, p," but they keep re-lighting. Everyone laughs and claps and tries to puff out the candles, "p, p, p."

Action
- The students pretend their finger is a candle and try to puff out the trick candle, saying "p, p, p."

Formation
- Explain how the letter ‹p› is written. It has a stick that goes down under the line.
- The students write over the dotted letters in their books.

Blending
- Blend the words *pit, pat, tap, tip*.
- Say the sounds with the students, then blend the sounds together and read the words.
- Encourage the students to point to the dot underneath each sound as they say it.

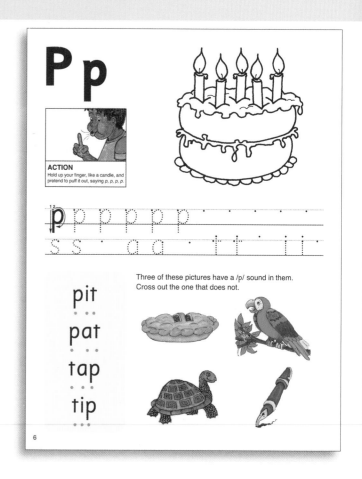

Sounding
- Say the words corresponding to the pictures on the page: *pie, parrot, turtle, pen*.
- The students listen for the word without the /p/ sound (*turtle*), and cross out its picture.

Word bank
pit, pat, tip, tap, sap, sip.

Dictation
- Call out the sound /p/ and the other sounds already covered for the students to write.
- Call out some words from the Word Bank.
- The students listen to the words and hold up a finger for each sound.

Further ideas
- Sing the song from the *Jolly Songs* and pin up the /p/ section of the *Wall Frieze*.
- Collage parrot pictures with feathers.
- Paint pictures of pink poodles or spiny porcupines.

Letter Sound /n/

Flash cards
• Practice the sounds /s/, /a/, /t/, /i/, /p/.

Story
• Introduce the sound /n/ using a story, such as the one below, and the action.

Nicola has always wanted to go fishing with her Grandfather. Until now, he has always said, "No, you will make too much noise and scare the fish away. You can come when you get bigger." But now Nicola is five, her Grandfather has agreed to take her fishing for an afternoon. Grandfather sets up the fishing rod and puts his net in the pond. Then he places a bucket on the ground and they both settle down to fish. Nicola sits very still and waits very quietly. She watches the birds and insects flying around the pond. It is very peaceful. Suddenly, Nicola and her Grandfather hear a very loud and nasty noise, "nnnn!" An airplane is flying overhead! The airplane does a noisy loop-the-loop in the sky above them. Grandfather doesn't like the nasty noise and puts his hands over his ears. Nicola looks at her Grandfather and laughs. "You were worried I would make too much noise! Even I am never that noisy." Then she runs along the bank, pretending that she is an airplane, "nnnnn!"

Action
• The students put their arms out and pretend to be a "nasty noisy airplane," making a continuous /nnnnnnnnnnnnnn/ sound.

Formation
• Explain how the letter ‹n› is written.
• The students write over the dotted letters in their books.

Blending
• Blend the words *nap, ant, pan, tin*.
• Say the sounds with the students, then blend the sounds together and read the words.
• Encourage the students to point to the dot underneath each sound as they say it.

Three of these pictures have a /n/ sound in them. Cross out the one that does not.

nap
ant
pan
tin

Sounding
• Say the words corresponding to the pictures on the page: *nest, pie, net, neck*.
• The students listen for the word without the /n/ sound (*pie*), and cross out its picture.

Word bank
nap, nip, pan, pin, tin, tan, ant, pant, snip, snap, span, spin.

Dictation
• Call out the sound /n/ and the other sounds already covered for the students to write.
• Call out some words from the Word Bank.
• The students listen to the words and hold up a finger for each sound.

Further ideas
• Sing the song from the *Jolly Songs* and pin up the /n/ section of the *Wall Frieze*.
• Think of some "nasty, noisy things," and draw pictures of them.

Letter Sound /c k/

Flash cards
- Practice some of the sounds already learned: /s/, /a/, /t/, /i/, /p/, /n/.

Story
- Introduce the sound /c k/ using a story, such as the one below, and the action.

The Khan family is on vacation in Spain. Mr. Khan has hired a car and the family decides to drive to a nearby village to visit the castle there. On the way, they pass a donkey carrying a big bundle of sticks. After they have looked around the castle, the family stops off at a café for a snack. Outside the café is the same donkey they saw before, enjoying a bucket of water. Beside the donkey, a cat and her kittens are playing. As the clock strikes four, some Spanish dancers skip into the courtyard in front of the café. The ladies carry castanets and wear dresses in bright crimson, yellow, and black. They clap and dance and click their castanets, "ck, ck, ck!"

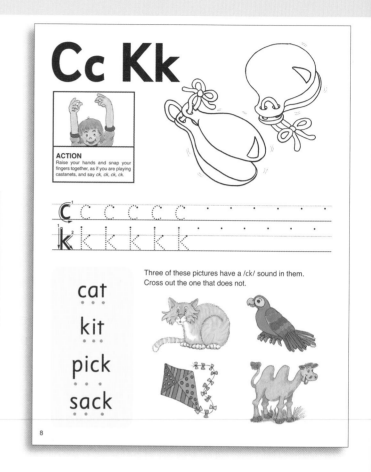

Action
- The students click their fingers above their heads saying "ck, ck, ck."

Formation
- Explain how the letters ‹c› (caterpillar /c/) and ‹k› (kicking /k/) are written. The letter ‹k› is a tall letter and the students need to be careful to come up only a little way before doing the "little kick."
- The students write over the dotted letters.

Blending
- Blend the words *cat, kit, pick, sack*.
- Say the sounds with the students, then blend the sounds together and read the words.
- Encourage the students to point to the dot underneath each sound as they say it.

Sounding
- Say the words corresponding to the pictures on the page: *cat, parrot, kite, camel*.

- The students listen for the word without the /c k/ sound (*parrot*), and cross out its picture.

Word bank
cat, cap, can, kit, kin, sack, sick, pack, pick, tick, tack, tank, sank, stack, snack, stick.

Dictation
- Call out the sounds /i/, /t/, /p/, and /n/ for the students to write down. Then ask the students to write a "caterpillar /c/" and a "kicking /k/".
- Now tell the students that you are going to dictate a word: *it*.
- The students should say the word to themselves, listening for the sounds in *it*, and then write the word.
- Repeat this exercise with the word *at*.

Further ideas
- Sing the song from the *Jolly Songs* and pin up the /c k/ section of the *Wall Frieze*.
- Collage pictures of cats and kittens.

Letter Sound /e/

Flash cards
- Practice some of the sounds already learned: /s/, /a/, /t/, /i/, /p/, /n/, /c/, /k/.

Story
- Introduce the sound /e/ using a story, such as the one below, and the action.

It is almost the end of the summer. Eric and his family have gone to stay on Ten Acre Farm for seven days' holiday. Every morning, they get up early to watch the cows being milked. After that, Eric likes to help out with the farm chores. He helps fetch buckets of water from the well. Then he pours the water into troughs for the cows to drink. Then Eric helps to feed the hens and collect the eggs. He takes the eggs into the kitchen for breakfast. Ellie, the farmer's wife, cracks open the eggs by tapping their shells on the side of the pan, "e, e, e." Then everyone eats fried eggs for breakfast.

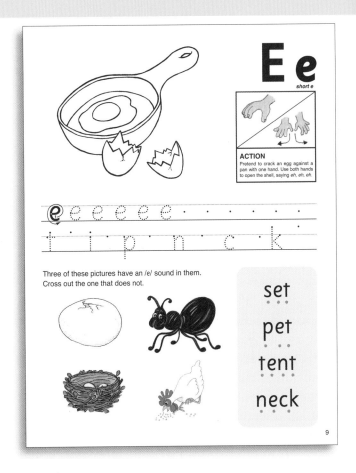

Action
- The students pretend to hold an egg in one hand and tap it against a pan saying "e, e, e." Then, they use both hands to open the imaginary eggshell, and say "e."

Formation
- Explain how the letter ‹e› is written. It is an unusual letter, as it starts in the middle.
- The students write over the dotted letters in their books.

Blending
- Blend the words *set, pet, tent, neck*.
- Say the sounds with the students, then blend the sounds together and read the words.
- Encourage the students to point to the dot underneath each sound as they say it.

Sounding
- Say the words corresponding to the pictures on the page: *egg, ant, nest, hen*.

- The students listen for the word without the /e/ sound (*ant*), and cross out its picture.

Word bank
set, ten, pen, peck, neck, kept, net, pet, sent, tent, step, nest, pest, test, spent.

Dictation
- Call out the sound /e/ and some of the other sounds already covered for the students to write.
- Dictate the words *net* and *pen*.
- Call out some words from the Word Bank.
- The students listen to the words and hold up a finger for each sound.

Further ideas
- Sing the song from the *Jolly Songs* and pin up the /e/ section of the *Wall Frieze*.
- Paint egg shapes.
- Plant mustard or cress seeds in empty eggshells.

Letter Sound /h/

Flash cards
- Practice some of the sounds already learned:
/s/, /a/, /t/, /i/, /p/, /n/, /c/, /k/, /e/.

Story
- Introduce the sound /h/ using a story, such as the one below, and the action.

It is the school's summer fun day. In the morning, the students do fun things in the classroom, and in the afternoon there are races. Helen, Harry, Hanif, and Harriet are in the hopping race. Mr. Heath starts the race. "One, two, three, GO!" he shouts and waves his hat in the air. Helen, Harry, Hanif, and Harriet hop as fast as they can. It is a hot day and hopping is hard work. Harriet is huffing and puffing by the time she finishes, "h, h, h, h!" Miss Hopkins gives everyone huge drinks.

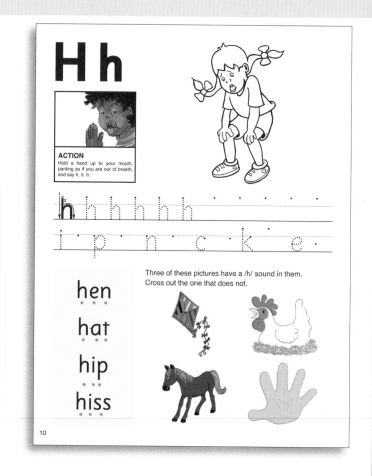

Three of these pictures have a /h/ sound in them. Cross out the one that does not.

hen
hat
hip
hiss

10

Action
- The students pretend to pant, and say "h, h, h."

Formation
- Explain how the letter ‹h› is written.
- It is a tall letter.
- The students write over the dotted letters in their books.

Blending
- Blend the words *hen, hat, hip, hiss*.
- Say the sounds with the students, then blend the sounds together and read the words.
- Encourage the students to point to the dot underneath each sound as they say it.
- Say /h-i-s/ and not /h-i-s-s/, when blending the word *hiss* with the students.
- Explain to the students that, when two letters making the same sound are next to each other, the sound is only said once.

Sounding
- Say the words corresponding to the pictures on the page: *kite, hen, horse, hand*.

- The students listen for the word without the /h/ sound (*kite*), and cross out its picture.

Word bank
hat, hit, hip, hen, hiss, hint.

Dictation
- Call out the sound /h/ and some of the other sounds already covered for the students to write.
- Dictate the words *hen* and *hat*.
- Call out some words from the Word Bank.
- The students listen to the words and hold up a finger for each sound.

Further ideas
- Sing the song from the *Jolly Songs* and pin up the /h/ section of the *Wall Frieze*.
- Have a hopping race.
- Make hedgehogs with handprint prickles.

Letter Sound /r/

Flash cards
- Practice some of the sounds already learned: /s/, /a/, /t/, /i/, /p/, /n/, /c/, /k/, /e/, /h/.

Story
- Introduce the sound /r/ using a story, such as the one below, and the action.

Robert's family has a new puppy. They have to choose a name for him. Robert's parents like "Rover," but Robert likes "Ben." Robert can't decide. He goes up to his bedroom with the puppy to fetch his roller skates. While Robert looks for the roller skates, the puppy explores the bedroom. Suddenly, Robert hears a loud "ruff, rrrrrrrrrr!" The puppy has found a blanket and is shaking it from side to side. Robert gets hold of the blanket and tries to pull it away, but the puppy hangs on tightly, going "rrrrrrrr!" The blanket rips. "Oh dear," says Robert, holding up the ripped blanket. "This looks like a rag now. I know, we'll call you Rags!"

Three of these pictures have a /r/ sound in them. Cross out the one that does not.

rat

rip

ran

rest

Action
- The students pretend to be a puppy holding the blanket, shaking their heads and making a continuous /rrrrrrrrrrr/ sound.

Formation
- Explain how the letter ‹r› is written.
- The students write over the dotted letters in their books.

Blending
- Blend the words rat, rip, ran, rest.
- Say the sounds with the students, then blend the sounds together and read the words.
- Encourage the students to point to the dot underneath each sound as they say it.

Sounding
- Say the words corresponding to the pictures on the page: rabbit, dress, egg, rocket.
- The students listen for the word without the /r/ sound (egg), and cross out its picture.

Word bank
rat, ran, rack, rip, rest, rap, trap, trip, track, crack, crest, crisp, strap, scrap.

Dictation
- Call out the sound /r/ and some other sounds already covered for the students to write.
- Dictate the words *rat* and *rip*.
- Call out some words from the Word Bank.
- The students listen to the words and hold up a finger for each sound.

Further ideas
- Sing the song from the *Jolly Jingles* or the *Jolly Songs*.
- Put up on the wall, or hold up, the /r/ section of the *Wall Frieze*.
- Make model rabbits from modeling clay.
- Paint a rocket picture.

Letter Sound /m/

Flash cards
- Practice some of the sounds already learned: /s/, /a/, /t/, /i/, /p/, /n/, /c/, /k/, /e/, /h/, /r/.

Story
- Introduce the sound /m/ using a story, such as the one below, and the action.

Mrs. Morris and her son Marvin have invited his friends, Milly and Molly for supper. The children are playing outside when they hear the call for supper. They all come inside, wash their hands and sit down at the table. "I'm hungry!" says Marvin, rubbing his tummy, "mmmmm, I hope it's spaghetti and meat balls." "I hope it's hot dogs, mmmmm," says Molly. "I hope it's hamburgers," says Milly, rubbing her tummy. Then Mrs. Morris comes in, carrying a steaming dish. "Lamb and peas," say the children, "mmmmm." "I like that meal most of all!" says Marvin, "mmmmmm!"

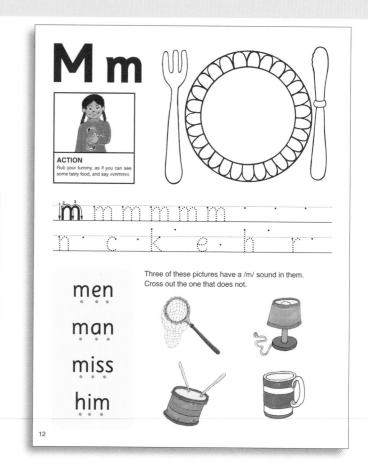

Action
- The students rub their tummies, as though eating their favorite foods, and make a continuous /mmmmmm/ sound.

Formation
- Explain how the letter ‹m› is written.
- The students write over the dotted letters in their books.

Blending
- Blend the words *men, man, miss, him*.
- Say the sounds with the students, then blend the sounds together and read the words.
- Encourage the students to point to the dot underneath each sound as they say it.

Sounding
- Say the words corresponding to the pictures on the page: *net, lamp, drum, mug*.
- The students listen for the word without the /m/ sound (*net*), and cross out its picture.

Word bank
am, mat, met, map, man, men, ram, him, mist, ham, camp, ramp, mint, rim, imp, hem, stem, stamp, smack, mess, miss.

Dictation
- Call out the sound /m/ and some other sounds already covered for the students to write.
- Dictate the words *rim* and *map*.
- Call out some words from the Word Bank.
- The students listen to the words and hold up a finger for each sound.

Further ideas
- Sing the song from the *Jolly Jingles* or the *Jolly Songs*.
- Put up on the wall, or hold up, the /m/ section of the *Wall Frieze*.
- Make a collage of different foods.

Letter Sound /d/

Flash cards
- Practice some of the sounds already learned: /s/, /a/, /t/, /i/, /p/, /n/, /c/, /k/, /e/, /h/, /r/, /m/.

Story
- Introduce the sound /d/ using a story, such as the one below and the action.

Dan is tidying his toy cupboard. He pulls out his teddy, his old donkey and a duck. Then, he finds a box of dominoes. He plays with them for a while. Next, he sees his yellow digger and takes it out for a drive. Suddenly, from downstairs, Dad asks, "Dan, have you finished yet?" "Not yet," says Dan, and he goes back to the cupboard. He finds a bag of marbles and some dice. He plays with these for a little while, and then hears his Dad again. "Dan, have you finished yet?" "No, not yet," says Dan, and he goes back to the cupboard. At the very back of the cupboard, he sees his old red and blue drum. He picks it up and marches up and down, banging the drum, "d, d, d!" Dad comes in to see what all the noise is. "Do you know you have spent all day tidying your cupboard?" he says. Dan smiles. "I've found lots of things I had forgotten all about," he replies.

Action
- The students pretend to be playing a drum, moving their hands up and down, and saying "d, d, d."

Formation
- Explain how the letter ‹d› is written. It starts with a "caterpillar c," and is a tall letter.
- The students write over the dotted letters in their books.

Blending
- Blend the words *dip, dad, pad, hid*.
- Say the sounds with the students, then blend the sounds together and read the words.
- Encourage the students to point to the dot underneath each sound as they say it.

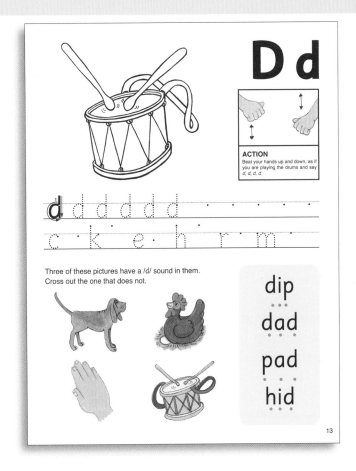

Three of these pictures have a /d/ sound in them. Cross out the one that does not.

Sounding
- Say the words corresponding to the pictures on the page: *dog, hen, hand, drum*.
- The students listen for the word without the /d/ sound (*hen*), and cross out its picture.

Word bank
dad, did, den, din, dip, hid, had, red, deck, pad, sad, mad, end, hand, and, sand, desk, drip, dent, send, skid, spend, add.

Dictation
- Call out the sound /d/ and some other sounds already covered for the students to write.
- Dictate the words *dad* and *hid*.
- Call out some words from the Word Bank.
- The students listen to the words and hold up a finger for each sound.

Further ideas
- Sing the song from the *Jolly Songs* and pin up the /d/ section of the *Wall Frieze*.

Letter Sound /g/

Flash cards
- Practice some of the sounds already learned: /s/, /a/, /t/, /i/, /p/, /n/, /c/, /k/, /e/, /h/, /r/, /m/, /d/.

Story
- Introduce the sound /g/ using a story, such as the one below, and the action.

Gail is staying with her grandmother, who has a big garden and keeps some animals. This morning, Gail and Gran went outside to check on the goat and the geese. While they were outside, Gail found a frog next to the water bucket. She watched it hop off under the gate. When they came in, Gran sent Gail to the bathroom to have a wash. Gail put the plug in the sink, filled the basin and washed her hands and face, but when she pulled the plug out, the water didn't go away. Her grandmother came to have a look. "Oh dear, the sink must be blocked," she said. Gran phoned the plumber. When he arrived, the plumber unblocked the sink and the water ran gurgling out of the basin, "g, g, g, g, g."

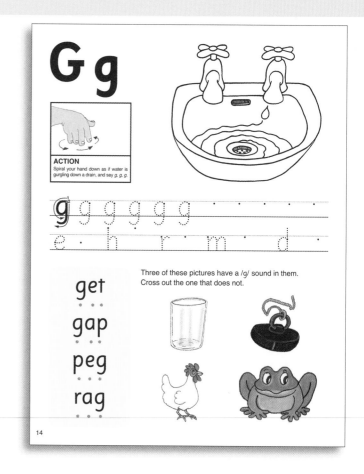

Action
- The students pretend their hand is the water spiraling down the drain saying, "g, g, g, g."

Formation
- Explain how the letter ‹g› is written. It starts with a "caterpillar c," and has a tail that goes down under the line.
- The students write over the dotted letters.

Blending
- Blend the words get, gap, peg, rag.
- Say the sounds with the students, then blend the sounds together and read the words.
- Encourage the students to point to the dot underneath each sound as they say it.

Sounding
- Say the words corresponding to the pictures on the page: glass, plug, hen, frog.

- The students listen for the word without the /g/ sound (hen), and cross out its picture.

Word bank
get, gap, peg, dig, tag, gas, rag, sag, gram, grim, grip, grid, grin, snag, stag, grand.

Dictation
- Call out the sound /g/ and some other sounds already covered for the children to write.
- Dictate the words sag, peg, dig, get.
- Call out some words from the Word Bank.
- The students listen to the words and hold up a finger for each sound.

Further ideas
- Sing the song from the Jolly Jingles or the Jolly Songs.
- Put up on the wall, or hold up, the /g/ section of the Wall Frieze.
- Read the story, The Three Billy Goats Gruff.
- Paint some green frogs.

Letter Sound /o/

Flash cards
- Practice some of the sounds already learned: /s/, /a/, /t/, /i/, /p/, /n/, /c/, /k/, /e/, /h/, /r/, /m/, /d/, /g/.

Story
- Introduce the sound /o/ using a story, such as the one below, and the action.

Oliver and Holly have moved to a new house. They have a new bedroom with bunk beds in it. Near the bed is a light switch, so they can turn the light on and off by themselves when they are in bed. That night, Holly curls up with Oscar, her toy rabbit, and Oliver reads his comic. "You can turn the light out when you've finished," says Dad. Oliver leans over to the light switch and turns it off. "Off it goes," he says. Then he turns the light back on, saying "o, on it goes." He turns the light on and off, saying, "o, on it goes. Off it goes; o, on it goes." Then he hears Dad's voice. "Stop turning the light on and off, Oliver! You will break it. Turn it off, and go to sleep." Oliver turns the light off and goes to sleep.

Action
- The students point their finger, as if pushing a switch on and off, saying "o o o."

Formation
- Explain how the letter ‹o› is written. It starts with a "caterpillar c."
- The students write over the dotted letters in their books.

Blending
- Blend the words *hot, mop, pots, dog*.
- Say the sounds with the students, then blend the sounds together and read the words.
- Encourage the students to point to the dot underneath each sound as they say it.

Sounding
- Say the words corresponding to the pictures on the page: *bat, octopus, sock, pond*.

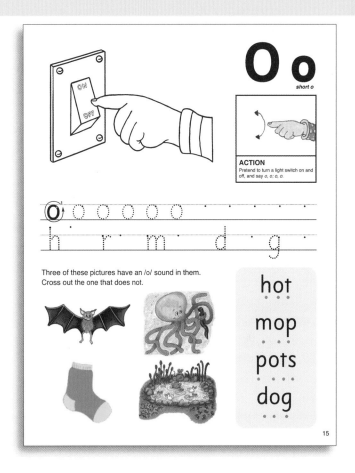

- The students listen for the word without the /o/ sound (*bat*), and cross out its picture.

Word bank
top, pot, dot, pod, dog, sock, tock, rock, mock, dock, hop, mop, hog, pond, spot, cod, cog, cot, got, hot, nod, not, pop, rod, drop, trod, stop, cost, odd, moss, cross.

Dictation
- Call out the sound /o/ and some other sounds already covered for the students to write.
- Dictate the words *hog, hop, dot*, and *mop*.
- Call out some words from the Word Bank.
- The students listen to the words and hold up a finger for each sound.

Further ideas
- Sing the song from the *Jolly Songs* and pin up the /o/ section of the *Wall Frieze*.
- Print ‹o› shapes using the end of cardboard tubes and add legs to make octopus pictures.

Letter Sound /u/

Flash cards
• Practice some of the sounds already learned: /s/, /a/, /t/, /i/, /p/, /n/, /c/, /k/, /e/, /h/, /r/, /m/, /d/, /g/, /o/.

Story
• Introduce the sound /u/ using a story, such as the one below, and the action.

Uncle Bud often comes to visit his niece and nephew, Anna and Ulric. Today, he has brought them each an umbrella. Anna's umbrella is spotty, and Ulric's umbrella has stripes. In the afternoon, the whole family goes out for a walk. Although it is sunny, Anna and Ulric bring their umbrellas. Everyone laughs, except Uncle Bud. "I'll take my umbrella, too," he says. The family sets off for their walk in the sunshine. After a while, they notice some black clouds on the horizon. A little while later, they feel the first raindrops starting to fall. Soon it is pouring with rain! Uncle Bud, Anna, and Ulric put up their umbrellas, shouting, "u, u, up umbrellas!" They are the ones laughing now! They have a lovely time splashing in the puddles.

Three of these pictures have an /u/ sound in them. Cross out the one that does not.

Action
• The students mime opening an umbrella, with one hand holding the handle and the other moving up, saying "u, u, u."

Formation
• Explain how the letter ‹u› is written.
• The students write over the dotted letters.

Blending
• Blend the words *sun, mud, cup, dug*.
• Say the sounds with the students, then blend the sounds together and read the words.
• Encourage the students to point to the dot underneath each sound as they say it.

Sounding
• Say the words corresponding to the pictures on the page: *umbrella, dog, mug, drum*.

• The students listen for the word without the /u/ sound (*dog*), and cross out its picture.

Word bank
up, us, sun, run, mug, tug, dug, rug, hug, cup, cut, hum, hut, mud, nut, pup, sum, snug, suck, duck, muck, gull, hunt, dump, hump, pump, dusk, tusk, dust, must, crust, trust, skunk, stump, truck, stuck.

Dictation
• Call out the sound /u/ and some other sounds already covered for the students to write.
• Dictate the words *run, sum, cut*, and *mug*.
• Call out some words from the Word Bank.
• The students listen to the words and hold up a finger for each sound.

Further ideas
• Sing the song from the *Jolly Songs* and pin up the /u/ section of the *Wall Frieze*.

Letter Sound /l/

Flash cards
- Practice some of the sounds already learned: /s/, /a/, /t/, /i/, /p/, /n/, /c/, /k/, /e/, /h/, /r/, /m/, /d/, /g/, /o/, /u/.

Story
- Introduce the sound /l/ using a story, such as the one below, and the action.

It is Luca's birthday and he is having a party. Luca's friends have brought lots of presents for him. Luca and his friends play some party games while the food is set out. There are lettuce sandwiches, little cakes, licorice laces and lemonade to drink. Most importantly, there is a big birthday cake in the shape of a lion. Luca and his friends play "blind man's buff" and "pin the tail on the donkey." Lucy wins "pin the tail on the donkey" and gets a lime lollipop as a prize. She licks her lollipop, going "lllllllll."

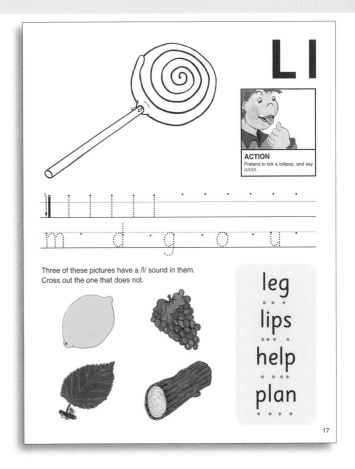

Three of these pictures have a /l/ sound in them. Cross out the one that does not.

leg
lips
help
plan

Action
- The students stick out their tongues, pretending to be licking a lollipop, and say "llllllll."

Formation
- Explain how the letter ◊ is written. It is a tall letter.
- The students write over the dotted letters in their books.

Blending
- Blend the words *leg, lips, help, plan*.
- Say the sounds with the students, then blend the sounds together and read the words.
- Encourage the students to point to the dot underneath each sound as they say it.

Sounding
- Say the words corresponding to the pictures on the page: *lemon, grapes, leaf, log*.
- The students listen for the word without the /l/ sound (*grapes*), and cross out its picture.

Word bank
lap, lad, leg, log, lip, led, let, lid, lit, lot, clap, clip, clog, glad, glum, plan, plot, plug, plum, plus, slam, slip, slug, held, milk, help, lent, lump, list, slept, ill, hill, kill, mill, pill, till, doll, loss, spell, smell, lick, lock, luck, click, trick, stick, clock.

Dictation
- Call out the sound /l/ and some other sounds already covered for the students to write.
- Dictate the words *lap, log, lad,* and *lit*.
- Call out some words from the Word Bank.
- The students listen to the words and hold up a finger for each sound.

Further ideas
- Sing the song from the *Jolly Jingles* or the *Jolly Songs*.
- Put up on the wall, or hold up, the /l/ section of the *Wall Frieze*.
- Make lemonade.

Letter Sound /f/

Flash cards
· Practice some of the sounds already learned.

Story
· Introduce the sound /f/ using a story, such as the one below, and the action.

Freda, Fred, and their friend Felix are at the beach. Freda has a new sun hat and a bucket and spade. Fred has a large, floating, inflatable fish. At first, all the children play in the water with the inflatable fish. Then, Freda and Felix decide to build sand castles and Fred leaves his inflatable fish on the sand to dry. Freda's castle has four towers and she puts a flag on each one. Felix finds some shells and seaweed for his castle. Fred puts on his flippers and goes off for a swim. Suddenly, Fred calls out. When the others look around, they see his inflatable fish getting smaller and smaller. The plug has come out and all the air is escaping, "fffffffff!"

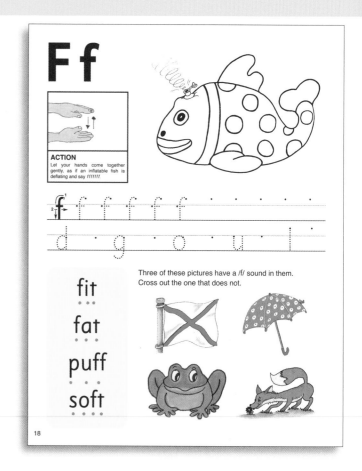

Action
· The students bring their hands together, as if the inflatable fish is deflating, and make a continuous /fffffffff/ sound.

Formation
· Explain how the letter ⟨f⟩ is written. It is a tall letter.
· The students write over the dotted letters.

Blending
· Blend the words *fit, fat, puff, soft*.
· Say the sounds with the students, then blend the sounds together and read the words.
· Encourage the students to point to the dot underneath each sound as they say it.

Sounding
· Say the words corresponding to the pictures on the page: *flag, umbrella, frog, fox*.
· The students listen for the word without the /f/ sound (*umbrella*), and cross out its picture.

Word bank
fit, fat, fun, fan, fed, fig, fin, fog, flag, flap, flat, flop, frog, from, elf, self, golf, film, felt, left, gift, lift, loft, soft, tuft, fund, fist, frost, fill, fuss, flock.

Dictation
· Call out the sound /f/ and some other sounds already covered for the students to write.
· Dictate the words *fan, fin, fog,* and *fun*.
· Call out some words from the Word Bank.
· The students listen to the words and hold up a finger for each sound.

Further ideas
· Sing the song from the *Jolly Jingles* or the *Jolly Songs*.
· Put up on the wall, or hold up, the /f/ section of the *Wall Frieze*.
· Paint a fish picture.
· Find out about different sorts of fish.

Letter Sound /b/

Flash cards
- Practice some of the sounds already learned.

Story
- Introduce the sound /b/ using a story, such as the one below and the action.

Granny is looking after Bill and his baby brother, Ben. Granny takes Bill and baby Ben to the park. Granny stops to watch the boats on the lake, and to listen to the band playing. She finds a bench and sits down. Soon she and baby Ben are dozing in the sun. Bill sees his friend, Rob, who has a bat and ball. They find some more of their friends and have a game of baseball. Bill throws the ball for Rob. As the bat hits the ball, it goes "b!" Then, it is Betty's turn. She bashes the ball as hard as she can. It just misses Granny, but bounces and hits the bench. Granny and baby Ben wake up. "I think I had better keep a safe distance from the baseball," says Granny and she pushes baby Ben along the path at the side of the boating lake.

Action
- The students pretend to hold a bat and hit a ball saying "b b b."

Formation
- Explain how the letter ‹b› is written. It is a tall letter. Tell the students to go down for the bat and bounce up and around for the ball.
- The students write over the dotted letters in their books.

Blending
- Blend the words *bag, big, cub,* and *crab.*
- Say the sounds with the students, then blend the sounds together and read the words.
- Encourage the students to point to the dot underneath each sound as they say it.

Sounding
- Say the words corresponding to the pictures on the page: *bib, rabbit, frog, crab.*

- The students listen for the word without the /b/ sound (*frog*), and cross out its picture.

Word bank
bat, bad, bag, ban, cab, bed, beg, bet, bib, big, bin, bit, rob, bud, bug, bus, but, cub, rub, club, crab, crib, grab, scab, bulb, belt, bent, bend, bump, best, bill, bell, boss, back, beck, buck, black, block, brick, blend.

Dictation
- Call out the sound /b/ and some other sounds already covered for the students to write.
- Dictate the words *bed, but, bat,* and *bib.*
- Call out some words from the Word Bank.
- The students listen to the words and hold up a finger for each sound.

Further ideas
- Sing the song from the *Jolly Songs* and pin up the /b/ section of the *Wall Frieze.*
- Play bat and ball.

Letter Sound /ai/

Flash cards
- Practice some of the sounds already learned. /s/, /a/, /t/, /i/, /p/, /n/, /c/, /k/, /e/, /h/, /r/, /m/, /d/, /g/, /o/, /u/, /l/, /f/, /b/.
- The sound /ai/ is written using two letters.
- When these two letters come together they make a different sound.
- When two letters make one sound it is called a *digraph*.

Story
- Introduce the sound /ai/ using a story, such as the one below, and the action.

Ainsley has been having trouble with his hearing. Whenever his mother speaks to him, he puts his hand to his ear and says, "ai?" His mother tells him that he should say "pardon," not "ai." After a while, his mother takes him to the doctor to have his hearing checked. In the waiting room there is a box of toys. Ainsley plays with a whale and a train. As he is pushing the train around the room, Dr. Ail comes out and calls his name. Dr. Ail looks in Ainsley's ears. "You have a lot of wax in your ears, Ainsley. That's why you're having trouble with your hearing." Dr. Ail gives him some eardrops. "Not another "ai" now, Ainsley," says his mother.

Action
- The students cup a hand over one ear and say "ai."

Formation
- Explain how the digraph ‹ai› is written.
- Tell the students that they need to write both an ‹a› and an ‹i› for the /ai/ sound.
- The students write over the dotted letters.

Blending
- Blend the words *rain, tail, paid, snail*.
- Say the sounds with the students, then blend the sounds together and read the words.
- Encourage the students to point to the dot underneath each sound as they say it.

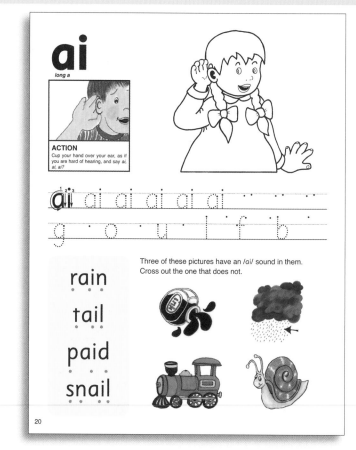

Three of these pictures have an /ai/ sound in them. Cross out the one that does not.

rain
tail
paid
snail

Sounding
- Say the words corresponding to the pictures on the page: *ink, rain, train, snail*.
- The students listen for the word without the /ai/ sound (*ink*), and cross out its picture.

Word bank
aid, aim, bait, fail, hail, laid, maid, mail, main, nail, paid, pail, pain, raid, rail, rain, sail, tail, claim, plain, brain, drain, trail, train, snail, strain, faint, paint, saint.

Dictation
- Call out the sound /ai/ and some other sounds already covered for the students to write.
- Dictate the words *aid, rail, pain,* and *bait*.
- Call out some words from the Word Bank.
- The students listen to the words and hold up a finger for each sound.

Further ideas
- Sing the song from the *Jolly Songs* and pin up the /ai/ section of the *Wall Frieze*.

Letter Sound /j/

Flash cards
• Practice some of the sounds already learned.
/s/, /a/, /t/, /i/, /p/, /n/, /c/, /k/, /e/, /h/, /r/, /m/, /d/,
/g/, /o/, /u/, /l/, /f/, /b/, /ai/.

Story
• Introduce the sound /j/ using a story, such as the one below, and the action.

Jane loves Jello. Jane's mother has promised to make her some Jello this afternoon. When Jane gets home from school, she eats a peanut butter and jelly sandwich and has a glass of orange juice. She tells her mother that she and her friend Javinda made a giant jigsaw of a juggler at school. Jane's mother shows Jane the Jello she has made. "Wow," says Jane. The Jello is tall and red and has four layers. As Jane carries it to the table, it wobbles and wobbles. Jane pretends to wobble just like the Jello, saying, "Jello on a plate, jello on a plate, j, j, j, j, Jello on a plate."

Action
• The students pretend to be the Jello and wobble, saying "j j j."

Formation
• Explain how the letter ‹j› is written. It has a tail that goes down and under the line.
• The students write over the dotted letters in their books.

Blending
• Blend the words *jam, jog, just, jump.*
• Say the sounds with the students, then blend the sounds together and read the words.
• Encourage the students to point to the dot underneath each sound as they say it.

Sounding
• Say the words corresponding to the pictures on the page: *Jello, jellyfish, jam, cow.*
• The students listen for the word without the /j/ sound (*cow*), and cross out its picture.

Word bank
jet, job, jab, jug, jog, jig, jot, jut, just, jacket, jail, jam, jump, junk.

Dictation
• Call out the sound /j/ and some other sounds already covered for the students to write.
• Dictate the words *jet, job, jab,* and *jug.*
• Call out some words from the Word Bank.
• The students listen to the words and hold up a finger for each sound.

Further ideas
• Sing the song from the *Jolly Jingles* or the *Jolly Songs.*
• Put up on the wall, or hold up, the /j/ section of the *Wall Frieze.*
• Make a multi-colored Jello.
• Make a jellyfish with a paper cup body and crêpe paper tentacles.

Letter Sound /oa/

Flash cards
- Practice some of the sounds already learned.

Story
- Introduce the sound /oa/ using a story, such as the one below, and the action.

A bad-tempered goat lives in a field at the side of a road. The goat gets very cross if any other animal comes into his field. Mona and her brother, Jonah, often walk past the field and talk to the goat. One windy day, Mona and Jonah are going to the park to have a picnic and to sail Jonah's model boat. As they pass by, they can see the goat is very cross. He is stamping his hooves and snorting beside an oak tree, which is blowing in the wind. Up in the tree are two cheeky robins and a squirrel. The robins have been flying down and stealing oats from the goat. The goat charges at the tree and butts the trunk as hard as he can. CRASH! The tree falls on top of the goat. "Oh!" say Mona and Jonah. They run to get the farmer, who rescues the goat.

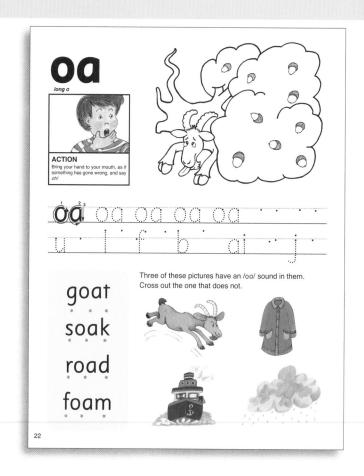

Action
- The students bring one hand up to their mouth, as if they see something go wrong, and say "oh!"

Formation
- Explain how the digraph ‹oa› is written.
- Tell the students that they need to write both an ‹o› and an ‹a› for the /oa/ sound.
- The students write over the dotted letters.

Blending
- Blend the words *goat*, *soak*, *road*, *foam*.
- Say the sounds with the students, then blend the sounds together and read the words.
- Encourage the students to point to the dot underneath each sound as they say it.

Sounding
- Say the words corresponding to the pictures on the page: *goat, coat, boat, rain cloud*.

- The students listen for the word without the /oa/ sound (*rain cloud*), and cross out its picture.

Word bank
oak, oats, boat, coal, coat, foal, foam, goal, goat, load, loaf, moan, moat, road, soak, soap, toad, cloak, float, croak, groan, boast, coast, roast, toast.

Dictation
- Call out the sound /oa/ and some other sounds already covered for the students to write.
- Dictate the words *oak, moan, soap,* and *coat*.
- Call out some words from the Word Bank.
- The students listen to the words and hold up a finger for each sound.

Further ideas
- Sing the song from the *Jolly Songs* and pin up the /oa/ section of the *Wall Frieze*.
- Make paper boats and see if they float.

Letter Sound /ie/

Flash cards
- Practice some of the sounds already learned. /s/, /a/, /t/, /i/, /p/, /n/, /c/, /k/, /e/, /h/, /r/, /m/, /d/, /g/, /o/, /u/, /l/, /f/, /b/, /ai/, /j/, /oa/.

Story
- Introduce the sound /ie/ using a story, such as the one below, and the action.

Clive has been invited to a party. Clive's dad is a sailor in the navy and he has given Clive a hat from his ship. Clive wants to dress up as a sailor like his dad and wear the hat to the party. His mother makes him a sailor's outfit. Just before the party, Clive's dad comes home on leave. Clive insists on wearing his new outfit to meet him off the ship. He waves and waves when he sees his dad and runs up and gives him a big hug. Dad admires his outfit and says, "If you are a sailor, you will have to learn how to salute and say, 'ie, ie!'" When they get home, he shows Clive how to salute. Clive has a go in front of the mirror, saluting and saying, "ie, ie!"

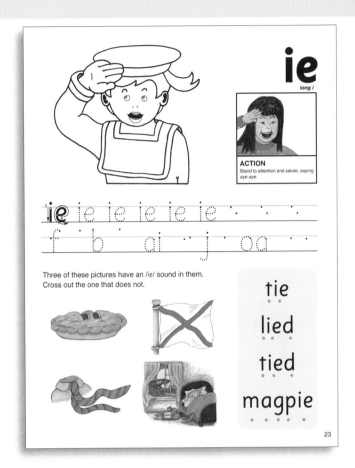

Action
- The students pretend to be a sailor and salute, saying "ie, ie."

Formation
- Explain how the digraph ‹ie› is written.
- Tell the students that they need to write both an ‹i› and an ‹e› for the /ie/ sound.
- The students write over the dotted letters.

Blending
- Blend the words *tie, lied, tied,* and *magpie.*
- Say the sounds with the students, then blend the sounds together and read the words.
- Encourage the students to point to the dot underneath each sound as they say it.

Sounding
- Say the words corresponding to the pictures on the page: *pie, flag, tie, night.*

- The students listen for the word without the /ie/ sound (*flag*), and cross out its picture.

Word bank
pie, tie, lie, die, died, lied, magpie, tried, spied, fried, cried, dried.

Dictation
- Call out the sound /ie/ and some other sounds already covered for the students to write.
- Dictate the words *pie, tie, lie,* and *die.*
- Call out some words from the Word Bank.
- The students listen to the words and hold up a finger for each sound.

Further ideas
- Sing the song from the *Jolly Jingles* or the *Jolly Songs.*
- Put up on the wall, or hold up, the /ie/ section of the *Wall Frieze.*
- Cut out paper tie shapes for the students to decorate.

Letter Sounds /ee/ and /or/

Flash cards
• Practice some of the sounds already learned.

Story
• Introduce the sounds /ee/ and /or/ using a story, such as the one below, and the action.

An old donkey and some sheep live next to a small cornfield. Nora and Jakeem like to go and talk to the donkey. He is always very pleased to see them. He brays, "ee or!" and waggles his ears up and down in greeting. One August morning, the children go for a walk to see the donkey. He brays happily, "ee or!" Jakeem gives the donkey a carrot. "The carrot comes from my garden," says Nora. "I have carrots and sweetcorn growing there." As the children talk to the donkey, big raindrops begin to fall. Behind the children is an enormous rain cloud. "I think we had better get home quickly," says Jakeem. "There is a storm coming. We will have to run home as fast as we can." The children run off, waving to the donkey.

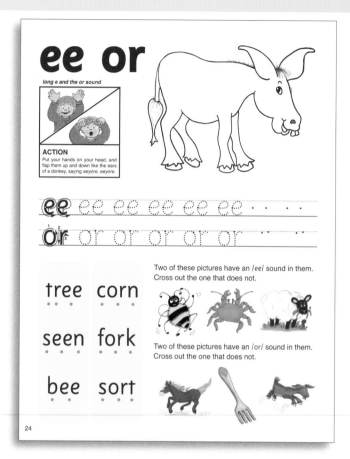

Action
• The students pretend their hands are the donkey's ears. Their hands point straight up for the /ee/ sound and point down for /or/.

Formation
• Explain how the digraphs ‹ee› and ‹or› are written.
• The students write over the dotted letters.

Blending
• Blend the following words with the students: *tree, seen, bee; corn, fork, sort.*
• Encourage the students to point to the dot underneath each sound as they say it.

Sounding
• Say the words corresponding to the pictures on the page: *bee, crab, sheep; horse, fork, goat.* The students listen for the words without the /ee/ and /or/ sounds (*crab; goat*), and cross out these pictures.

Word bank
• /ee/ words:
eel, bee, beef, been, deep, feed, feel, feet, heel, jeep, keen, keep, leek, meet, need, peel, peep, reef, see, seed, seek, seem, seen, bleed, sleep, creep, free, greed, green, tree, speed.
• /or/ words:
lord, cork, fork, form, born, corn, horn, morn, fort, port, sort, sport, stork, storm.

Dictation
• Call out the sounds /ee/ and /or/ and some other sounds already covered for the students to write.
• Dictate the words *feet, seed, born, form.*
• Call out some words from the Word Banks.
• The students listen to the words and hold up a finger for each sound.

Further ideas
• Sing the song from the *Jolly Songs* and pin up the /ee/-/or/ section of the *Wall Frieze.*
• Collage a storm picture with scrap-paper trees.

Letter Sound /z/

Flash cards
- Practice some of the sounds already learned: /s/, /a/, /t/, /i/, /p/, /n/, /c/, /k/, /e/, /h/, /r/, /m/, /d/, /g/, /o/, /u/, /l/, /f/, /b/, /ai/, /j/, /oa/, /ie/, /ee/, /or/.

Story
- Introduce the sound /z/ using a story, such as the one below, and the action.

Zara is sitting outside on the grass one sunny morning. She is playing with Zebadee, her toy zebra. Suddenly, Zara hears a loud buzzing sound, "zzzZZZzzz". She looks around and sees a big honeybee, buzzing around the flowers. The bee is collecting pollen to be made into honey, back at the hive. Zara watches the bee as it buzzes from flower to flower, landing on each one and collecting the pollen. Then Zara stands up and runs around, flapping her arms like the wings of the bee and saying, "zzzZZZzzz!" She stops by a gazania and bends down to pretend to collect the pollen from the flower. Then, "zzzZZZzzz," she buzzes and off she goes to collect more pollen from the daisies.

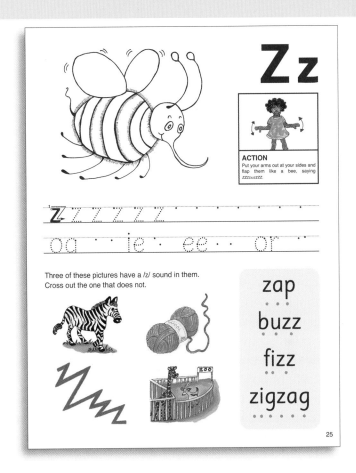

Action
- The students pretend to be a bee, flapping their arms up and down like wings, and saying "zzzZZZzzz."

Formation
- Explain how the letter ‹z› is written.
- The students write over the dotted letters.

Blending
- Blend the words *zap, buzz, fizz, zigzag*.
- Say the sounds with the students, then blend the sounds together and read the words.
- Encourage the students to point to the dot underneath each sound as they say it.

Sounding
- Say the words corresponding to the pictures on the page: *zebra, wool, zigzag, zoo*.

- The students listen for the word without the /z/ sound (*wool*), and cross out its picture.

Word bank
zip, zit, zap, buzz, fizz, jazz, zigzag, zest.

Dictation
- Call out the sound /z/ and some other sounds already covered for the students to write.
- Dictate the words *zip, zest, zit,* and *zap*.
- Call out some words from the Word Bank.
- The students listen to the words and hold up a finger for each sound.

Further ideas
- Sing the song from the *Jolly Jingles* or the *Jolly Songs*.
- Put up on the wall, or hold up, the /z/ section of the *Wall Frieze*.
- Make a zoo with toy animals.
- Make bees by painting paper plates with black and yellow stripes and adding paper wings.

Letter Sound /w/

Flash cards

• Practice some of the sounds already learned: /s/, /a/, /t/, /i/, /p/, /n/, /c/, /k/, /e/, /h/, /r/, /m/, /d/, /g/, /o/, /u/, /l/, /f/, /b/, /ai/, /j/, /oa/, /ie/, /ee/, /or/, /z/.

Story

• Introduce the sound /w/ using a story, such as the one below, and the action.

Aesop told a fable about the wind and the sun. The west wind and the sun are having an argument about which of them is the strongest. The west wind says to the sun, "You see that man down there? I bet I can blow so hard that his coat comes off." The west wind blows and blows, "wwwwwww," but the man hangs on to his warm coat. The harder the wind blows, the more tightly the man holds on to his coat. "My turn! Let me try," says the sun. The sun shines and shines and the man gets warmer and warmer, then hotter and hotter. Then the man gets too hot and takes off his coat. "I win," smiles the sun, and the west wind storms off, "wwwwww!"

Action

• The students cup their hands and blow on them, saying "w, w, w, w."

Formation

• Explain how the letter ‹w› is written.
• The students write over the dotted letters in their books.

Blending

• Blend the words *web, wig, swam, wind.*
• Say the sounds with the students, then blend the sounds together and read the words.
• Encourage the students to point to the dot underneath each sound as they say it.

Sounding

• Say the words corresponding to the pictures on the page: *window, swan, apple, well.*

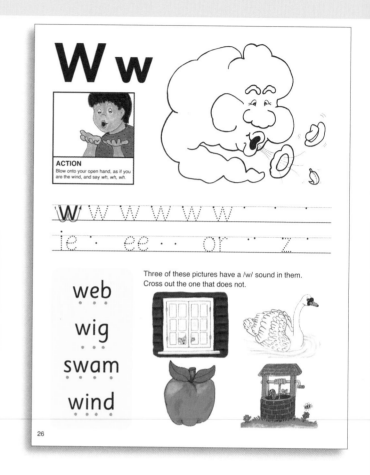

• The students listen for the word without the /w/ sound (*apple*), and cross out its picture.

Word bank

web, wag, wig, win, wet, swim, swam, wind, went, well, wait, will, twist, sweet, sweep, waist, twig, weep, weekend.

Dictation

• Call out the sound /w/ and some other sounds already covered for the students to write.
• Dictate the words *wag, win, wet,* and *swim.*
• Call out some words from the Word Bank.
• The students listen to the words and hold up a finger for each sound.

Further ideas

• Sing the song from the *Jolly Songs* and pin up the /w/ section of the *Wall Frieze.*
• Paint the view from the classroom window.
• Make a spider's web with wool.

Letter Sound /ng/

Flash cards
• Practice some of the sounds already learned.

Story
• Introduce the sound /ng/ using a story, such as the one below, and the action.

It is Saturday afternoon, and Bing has come to play at Mark's house. They start by having a game of ping-pong. Then they play with a racing car. "Let's see what's on television," says Mark, "There might be some motor racing." They put on the television. "Look at that man!" says Bing. "He's a weightlifter," says Mark. Bing and Mark watch the man as he lifts some huge weights. The man grunts as he lifts, "ngngngng!" "He must be strong," says Bing. "Let's be weightlifters," says Mark. They use a broom and a mop as weights. As they pretend to lift the heavy weights, they go "ngngngngng," just like the weightlifter.

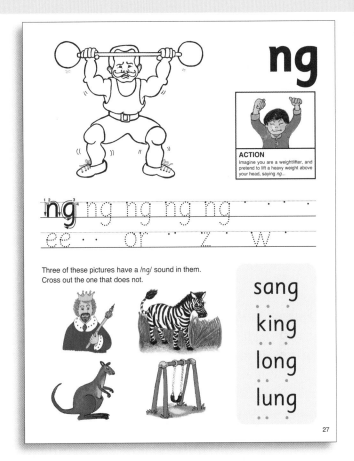

Action
• The students pretend to lift a heavy weight and say, "ng, ng, ng."

Formation
• Explain how the digraph ‹ng› is written.
• Tell the students that they need to write both an ‹n› and a ‹g› for the /ng/ sound.
• The students write over the dotted letters in their books.

Blending
• Blend the words *sang, king, long, lung.*
• Say the sounds with the students, then blend the sounds together and read the words.
• Encourage the students to point to the dot underneath each sound as they say it.

Sounding
• Say the words corresponding to the pictures on the page: *king, zebra, kangaroo, swing.*

• The students listen for the word without the /ng/ sound (*zebra*), and cross out its picture.

Word bank
sang, king, long, lung, ping-pong, song, sing, bang, gang, hang, rang, ring, wing, zing, hung, rung, cling, sling, bring, sting, swing, string, strong, clung, stung, swung.

Dictation
• Call out the sound /ng/ and some other sounds already covered for the students to write.
• Dictate the words *song, bang, lung,* and *wing.*
• Call out some words from the Word Bank. The students listen to the words and hold up a finger for each sound.

Further ideas
• Sing the song from the *Jolly Songs* and pin up the /ng/ section of the *Wall Frieze.*
• Play ping-pong.

Letter Sound /v/

Flash cards
- Practice some of the sounds already learned: /s/, /a/, /t/, /i/, /p/, /n/, /c/, /k/, /e/, /h/, /r/, /m/, /d/, /g/, /o/, /u/, /l/, /f/, /b/, /ai/, /j/, /oa/, /ie/, /ee/, /or/, /z/, /w/, /ng/.

Story
- Introduce the sound /v/ using a story, such as the one below, and the action.

One day during the summer, Uncle Vic arrives at Zack and Jess's house. "Would you like to come and help me, today?" he asks. "Yes, please," they reply. "Come on, then, we have a lot to do," says Uncle Vic. They all drive off to the station in his van, "vvvvv!" "I need to collect an order from Val's Fruit and Veg," says Uncle Vic. "Vvvvvv!" They stop outside the door and Uncle Vic collects the order. Then, "vroom," they are off again. Next, Uncle Vic delivers the vegetables to old Mrs. Vernon. They are busy all day, driving around, "vvvvvv!" Eventually, it is time for Zack and Jess to go home. "Good-bye," call Zack and Jess, as they wave to Uncle Vic.

Action
- The students pretend to be driving, holding the steering wheel and saying "vvvvvvv."

Formation
- Explain how the letter ‹v› is written.
- The students write over the dotted letters.

Blending
- Blends the words *van, vim, vat, vest*.
- Say the sounds with the students, then blend the sounds together and read the words.
- Encourage the students to point to the dot underneath each sound as they say it.

Sounding
- Say the words corresponding to the pictures on the page: *violin, van, fish, volcano*.
- The students listen for the word without the /v/ sound (*fish*), and cross out its picture.

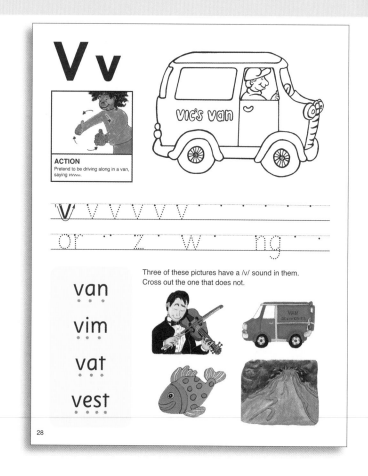

Word bank
van, vat, vet, vent, vain, velvet, vest, vivid, visit, seven, seventeen, invent.

Dictation
- Call out the sound /v/ and some other sounds already covered for the students to write.
- Dictate the words *vat, van, vent*, and *vet*.
- Call out some words from the Word Bank.
- The students listen to the words and hold up a finger for each sound.

Further ideas
- Sing the song from the *Jolly Jingles* or the *Jolly Songs*.
- Put up on the wall, or hold up, the /v/ section of the *Wall Frieze*.
- Wrap up some things for Uncle Vic to deliver.
- Set up a veterinarian's surgery for toy animals.

Letter Sounds /oo/ and /oo/

Flash cards
- Practice some of the sounds already learned.
- The digraph ‹oo› has two sounds, the /oo/ in *book* and the /oo/ in *moon*.
- Initially the two sounds are represented by two sizes of letter.

Story
- Introduce the /oo/ and /oo/ sounds using a story, such as the one below, and the action.

Oona is going to visit Great Aunt Ivy. Oona likes visiting Great Aunt Ivy because she has lots of interesting things and a large friendly cat called Noodle. The thing Oona likes best is Great Aunt Ivy's cuckoo clock. On the hour, a little wooden cuckoo pops out from the little wooden door at the top, calling, "oo oo, oo oo." Noodle and Oona like to wait underneath the clock, knowing that the cuckoo will come out soon. As the cuckoo goes in and out, Oona pretends to be the cuckoo, and says, "oo oo, oo oo!"

Action
- The students pretend to be the cuckoo in the clock, moving their heads forward for the /oo/ sound and back for the /oo/ sound.

Formation
- Explain how the digraph ‹oo› is written. One size of writing is used for the two /oo/ sounds.
- The students write over the dotted letters.

Blending
- Blend the following words with the students: *foot, look, book; zoo, soon,* and *moon.*
- Encourage the students to point to the dot underneath each sound as they say it.

Sounding
- Say the words corresponding to the pictures on the page: *book, hook, bed; moon, ring, spoon.* The students listen for the words without the /oo/ and /oo/ sounds (*bed; ring*), and cross out the pictures.

Word bank
- /oo/ words:
  look, foot, woof, wool, hook, book, cook, good, rook, took, wood, stood.
- /oo/ words:
  zoo, hoop, zoom, moon, boot, boo, moo, too, boom, cool, food, hoot, mood, noon, pool, roof, root, soon, tool, bloom, scoop, spook, spoon, stool.

Dictation
- Call out the /oo/ sounds and some other sounds already covered for the students to write.
- Dictate the words *wood, good, boot* and *zoom.*
- Call out some words from the Word Banks.
- The students listen to the words and hold up a finger for each sound.

Further ideas
- Sing the song from the *Jolly Songs* and pin up the /oo/ section of the *Wall Frieze.*
- Make a model cuckoo clock.

Letter Sound /y/

Flash cards
- Practice some of the sounds already learned: /s/, /a/, /t/, /i/, /p/, /n/, /c/, /k/, /e/, /h/, /r/, /m/, /d/, /g/, /o/, /u/, /l/, /f/, /b/, /ai/, /j/, /oa/, /ie/, /ee/, /or/, /z/, /w/, /ng/, /v/, /oo/, /oo/.

Story
- Introduce the sound /y/ using a story, such as the one below, and the action.

It is lunchtime and Yasmin, Ron, and Yamal are having something to eat. Yamal eats his sandwiches quickly, so that he can play with his yo-yo. Yasmin's mom has given her some yogurt. "That looks nice," says Ron. "Yes, it is," says Yasmin. "I chose it when we went shopping yesterday. It's a yellow banana yogurt. I love yellow." "Please may I try some?" asks Ron. "Yes," says Yasmin. "It's nice," says Ron, "a yummy, yellow yogurt!"

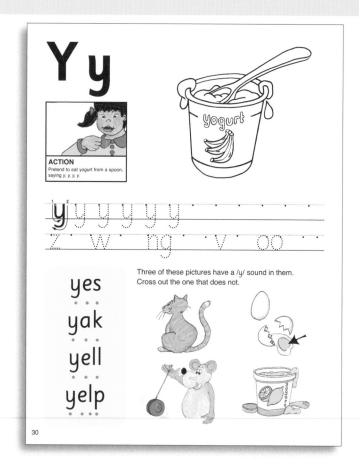

Action
- The students pretend to be eating yogurt from a spoon and say, "y, y, y, y, y."

Formation
- Explain how the letter ‹y› is written. It has a tail that goes under the line.
- The students write over the dotted letters.

Blending
- Blend the words *yes, yak, yell, yelp.*
- Say the sounds with the students, then blend the sounds together and read the words.
- Encourage the students to point to the dot underneath each sound as they say it.

Sounding
- Say the words corresponding to the pictures on the page: *cat, yolk, yo-yo, yogurt.*
- The students listen for the word without the /y/ sound (*cat*), and cross out its picture.

Word bank
yes, yen, yak, yell, yelp, yet, yuck, yam, yap.

Dictation
- Call out the sound /y/ and some other sounds already covered for the students to write.
- Dictate the words *yam, yet, yap,* and *yen.*
- Call out some words from the Word Bank.
- The students listen to the words and hold up a finger for each sound.

Further ideas
- Sing the song from the *Jolly Jingles* or the *Jolly Songs.*
- Put up on the wall, or hold up, the /y/ section of the *Wall Frieze.*
- Paint a yellow picture.
- Collage a yak using wool.

Letter Sound /x/

Flash cards
- Practice some of the sounds already learned.
- The sound /x/ is really two sounds: a /k/ and a /s/. However, when the students see the letter ‹x›, they need to be able to say /ks/ together in order to hear the word.

Story
- Introduce the sound /x/ using a story such as the one below, and the action.

Max and Ti are playing. They are pretending to be spacemen. Max, the alien, chases Ti, the astronaut, up a tree. Ti falls out of the tree and hurts his arm. Dad takes Ti and Max to hospital, where Ti has to have an x-ray. Ti has to keep his arm very still while the nurse takes the x-ray, "ks, ks, ks, ks, ks, ks." "Ti's arm is broken," explains the doctor. The nurse puts a plaster cast on Ti's arm, so that he cannot move it and the bones will mend properly.

Action
- The students pretend to take an x-ray picture of someone and say "x, x, x, x, x, x, x."

Formation
- Explain how the letter ‹x› is written.
- The students write over the dotted letters in their books.

Blending
- Blend the words *box, six, exit, next*.
- Say the sounds with the students, then blend the sounds together and read the words.
- Encourage the students to point to the dot underneath each sound as they say it.

Sounding
- Say the words corresponding to the pictures on the page: *box, sheep, six, fox*.
- The students listen for the word without the /x/ sound (*sheep*), and cross out its picture.

Word bank
fox, fax, box, six, mix, tax, wax, sax, exit, fix, sixteen, next, boxing, toolbox, expect, exam, flex, fixing, Mexican.

Dictation
- Call out the sound /x/ and some other sounds already covered for the students to write.
- Dictate the words *fox, sax, mix,* and *fax*.
- Call out some words from the Word Bank.
- The students listen to the words and hold up a finger for each sound.

Further ideas
- Sing the song from the *Jolly Jingles* or the *Jolly Songs*.
- Put up on the wall, or hold up, the /x/ section of the *Wall Frieze*.
- Look at pictures of skeletons and x-rays.
- Make x-ray pictures with white straws and black paper.

Letter Sound /ch/

Flash cards
- Practice some of the sounds already learned. /s/, /a/, /t/, /i/, /p/, /n/, /c/, /k/, /e/, /h/, /r/, /m/, /d/, /g/, /o/, /u/, /l/, /f/, /b/, /ai/, /j/, /oa/, /ie/, /ee/, /or/, /z/, /w/, /ng/, /v/, /oo/, /oo/, /y/, /x/.

Story
- Introduce the sound /ch/ using a story, such as the one below, and the action.

The students in Charlie's class are studying transport. Their teacher has arranged an outing to a transport museum. In the afternoon, the students get to ride on a steam train. They are very excited. They all climb into the carriage. The train starts chugging, "ch, ch, ch, ch." The train goes faster, "ch, ch, ch, ch!" Then, steam comes out of the funnel, and the whistle blows. "Choo! Choo!" The next day at school, all the students pretend to be trains, going, "ch, ch, ch, ch!" They chuff around, pretending to stop at lots of different places so the passengers can get on and off.

Action
- The students move their arms at their sides, like a steam train and say, "ch, ch, ch, ch."

Formation
- Explain how the digraph ‹ch› is written.
- The students write over the dotted letters in their books.

Blending
- Blend the words *chops, chips, bunch, chain*.
- Say the sounds with the students, then blend the sounds together and read the words.
- Encourage the students to point to the dot underneath each sound as they say it.

Sounding
- Say the words corresponding to the pictures on the page: *cheese, chimney, butterfly, chick*.

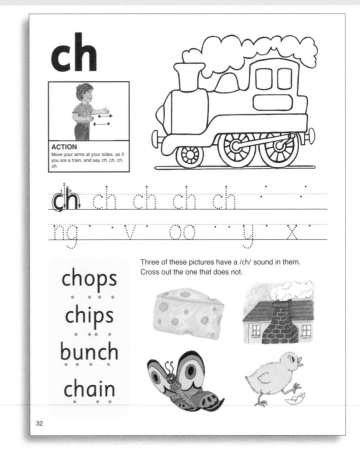

- The students listen for the word without the /ch/ sound (*butterfly*), and cross out its picture.

Word bank
chat, chest, chess, check, chin, chip, chill, chick, chimp, chop, rich, much, such, bench, drench, pinch, bunch, lunch, munch, chain, cheek, speech, coach, torch.

Dictation
- Call out the sound /ch/ and some other sounds already covered for the students to write.
- Dictate the words *much, such, chat,* and *chin*.
- Call out some words from the Word Bank.
- The students listen to the words and hold up a finger for each sound.

Further ideas
- Sing the song from the *Jolly Songs* and pin up the /ch/ section of the *Wall Frieze*.
- Pretend to be a train and chuff around saying "ch, ch, ch!"

Letter Sound /sh/

Flash cards
- Practice some of the sounds already learned: /s/, /a/, /t/, /i/, /p/, /n/, /c/, /k/, /e/, /h/, /r/, /m/, /d/, /g/, /o/, /u/, /l/, /f/, /b/, /ai/, /j/, /oa/, /ie/, /ee/, /or/, /z/, /w/, /ng/, /v/, /oo/, /oo/, /y/, /x/, /ch/.

Story
- Introduce the sound /sh/ using a story such as the one below, and the action.

Mrs. Shaw has just had a baby. The baby is called Shannon. Sam is the baby's elder brother. Sam thinks Shannon is okay, but she cries a lot. While his mother tries to get Shannon to sleep, Sam goes and plays with his toys. He plays in his store, with his cash register. It makes a very loud "ting" when the cash drawer opens. "Shshshshsh," whispers Mrs. Shaw, putting her finger to her lips. "Shannon is nearly asleep. Let's go downstairs for a while." "Okay," says Sam, adding, "shshshsh," as they tiptoe quietly from the room.

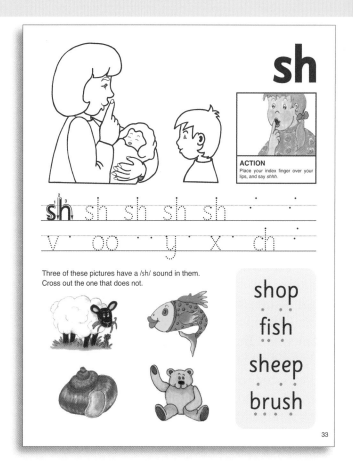

Action
- The students place their finger over their lips, saying, "shhh!"

Formation
- Explain how the digraph ‹sh› is written.
- The students write over the dotted letters in their books.

Blending
- Blend the words *shop, fish, sheep, brush.*
- Say the sounds with the students, then blend the sounds together and read the words.
- Encourage the students to point to the dot underneath each sound as they say it.

Sounding
- Say the words corresponding to the pictures on the page: *sheep, fish, shell, teddy bear.*
- The students listen for the word without the /sh/ sound (*teddy bear*), and cross out its picture.

Word bank
shed, shelf, shell, shin, ship, shift, shop, shot, shock, shut, shrimp, ash, bash, cash, mash, rash, dish, fish, wish, hush, rush, crash, splash, fresh, brush, sheep, sheet, shoot, shook, short, shampoo, mushroom, shopping, paintbrush.

Dictation
- Call out the sound /sh/ and some other sounds already covered for the students to write.
- Dictate the words *ash, wish, sheet,* and *shed.*
- Call out some words from the Word Bank.
- The students listen to the words and hold up a finger for each sound.

Further ideas
- Sing the song from the *Jolly Songs* and pin up the /sh/ section of the *Wall Frieze.*
- Make sheep with cotton wool fleeces.
- Set up a class store.

Letter Sounds /th/ and /th/

Flash cards
- Practice some of the sounds already learned.
- The digraph ‹th› has two sounds, the voiced sound /th/, in *this, that, then,* and the unvoiced /th/, in *thin, thick, three.*

Story
- Introduce the /th/ and /th/ sounds using a story, such as the one below, and the action.

Matthew and Nathan have gone to the circus. The ringmaster opens the circus and introduces the acts. First, there is a juggler, throwing three rings high into the air. Then, two naughty clowns throw water at the ringmaster, who tells them off. One clown, a thin fellow, is rather rude. He sticks his tongue out at the ringmaster, but only a little way; "th," he goes. The other clown, who is much bigger, is very rude. He sticks his tongue right out; "ththth!" he goes. Then the clowns chase one another and tickle each other with feathers. Everyone laughs at them.

Action
- The students pretend to be naughty clowns and stick out their tongues: a little way for the /th/ sound and further for the /th/ sound.

Formation
- Explain how the digraph ‹th› is written.
- The students write over the dotted letters in their books. One size of writing is used for the two /th/ sounds.

Blending
- Blend the following words with the students: *this, that, them; moth, three, thin.*
- Encourage the students to point to the dot underneath each sound as they say it.

Sounding
- Say the words corresponding to the pictures on the page: *three, feather, frog, moth.*

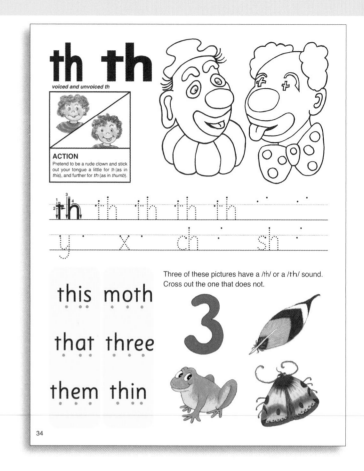

- The students listen for the words without a /th/ or /th/ sound (*frog*), and cross out its picture.

Word bank
- /th/ words:
  than, them, this, that, then, with, smooth.
- /th/ words:
  thank, theft, thin, thing, think, thick, throb, thump, sixth, moth, cloth, froth, teeth, three, throat, tooth, north, thud, thorn, toothbrush.

Dictation
- Call out the /th/ sounds and some other sounds already covered for the students to write.
- Dictate the words *than, with, tooth,* and *thud.*
- Call out some words from the Word Banks.
- The students listen to the words and hold up a finger for each sound.

Further ideas
- Sing the song from the *Jolly Songs* and pin up the /th/ section of the *Wall Frieze.*

Letter Sound /qu/

Flash cards
- Practice some of the sounds already learned.
- The sound /qu/ is really two sounds: a /k/ and a /w/. However, when the students see the letters ‹qu› they need to be able to say /kw/ together in order to hear the word.

Story
- Introduce the sound /qu/ using a story, such as the one below, and the action.

Quentin quite enjoys going to the park with his family. They always take some stale bread so that they can feed the ducks and Quentin likes to give some to the squirrels too. When they see Quentin with a bag of bread, the squirrels scamper over quickly. Two squirrels grab the same slice. They begin to quarrel, squeaking at each other and tugging at the bread. The ducks also see the bread and rush to the side of the pond, quacking loudly, "qu, qu, qu!" Quentin throws pieces of bread into the pond for the ducks. Then Quentin pretends that he is a duck. He goes, "qu, qu, qu," and opens and shuts his hands like a beak.

Action
- The students make their hands into a duck's beak and say, "qu, qu, qu."

Formation
- Explain how the digraph ‹qu› is written.
- The students write over the dotted letters.

Blending
- Blend the words *quick, quilt, liquid, squid*.
- Say the sounds with the students, then blend the sounds together and read the words.
- Encourage the students to point to the dot underneath each sound as they say it.

Sounding
- Say the words corresponding to the pictures on the page: *queen, squirrel, map, question mark*.

- The students listen for the word without the /qu/ sound (*map*), and cross out its picture.

Word bank
quit, quiz, quick, quilt, quins, squid, liquid, queen, quill, quack, quest, quench, quail.

Dictation
- Call out the sound /qu/ and some other sounds already covered for the students to write.
- Dictate the words *quit, quiz, queen*, and *quail*.
- Call out some words from the Word Bank.
- The students listen to the words and hold up a finger for each sound.

Further ideas
- Sing the song from the *Jolly Jingles* or the *Jolly Songs*.
- Put up on the wall, or hold up, the /qu/ section of the *Wall Frieze*.
- Draw a picture of ducks on a pond.
- Collage a squirrel with a wool tail.

Letter Sound /ou/

Flash cards
•Practice some of the sounds already learned.

Story
•Introduce the sound /ou/ using a story, such as the one below, and the action.

Emily has gone to stay at her grandmother's house. Emily's grandmother does a lot of sewing. Emily asks if she can do some sewing, too. Granny gets out a piece of cloth from her sewing basket. Emily has found a reel of brown cotton and Granny helps her to thread the needle. Emily sits down on the couch and does a few stitches. Then, as she pushes the needle through the cloth, she pricks her thumb. She frowns and shouts, "ou, ou! That hurt!" "You must be careful, Emily," says Granny. By the end of her visit, Emily has done a lot of sewing. She is much better at it now, and she has made a little mat as a present for her parents. She has embroidered a brown owl on it.

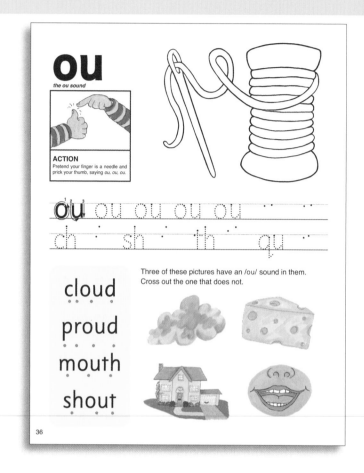

Action
•The students pretend that their finger is a needle and use it to prick their thumb, saying "ou, ou, ou."

Formation
•Explain how the digraph ‹ou› is written.
•The students write over the dotted letters in their books.

Blending
•Blend the words *cloud, proud, mouth, shout*.
•Say the sounds with the students, then blend the sounds together and read the words.
•Encourage the students to point to the dot underneath each sound as they say it.

Sounding
•Say the words corresponding to the pictures on the page: *cloud, cheese, house, mouth*.
•The students listen for the word without the /ou/ sound (*cheese*), and cross out its picture.

Word bank
out, loud, noun, cloud, trout, scout, snout, spout, sprout, joust, found, round, sound, ground, count, shout, couch, mouth, south, crouch, about, around, aloud.

Dictation
•Call out the sound /ou/ and some other sounds already covered for the students to write.
•Dictate the words *out, loud, shout,* and *noun*.
•Call out some words from the Word Bank.
•The students listen to the words and hold up a finger for each sound.

Further ideas
•Sing the song from the *Jolly Songs* and pin up the /ou/ section of the *Wall Frieze*.
•Do some sewing or lacing.
•Draw houses and describe them.

Letter Sound /oi/

Flash cards

- Practice some of the sounds already learned: /s/, /a/, /t/, /i/, /p/, /n/, /c/, /k/, /e/, /h/, /r/, /m/, /d/, /g/, /o/, /u/, /l/, /f/, /b/, /ai/, /j/, /oa/, /ie/, /ee/, /or/, /z/, /w/, /ng/, /v/, /oo/, /oo/, /y/, /x/, /ch/, /sh/, /th/, /th/, /qu/, /ou/.

Story

- Introduce the sound /oi/ using a story, such as the one below, and the action.

Roy's dad has a little boat, called Sailor Boy. Sometimes, in the summer, Roy is allowed to join his dad on the boat. One morning, Roy, Dad, and Uncle Martin are taking the boat out. They pack all their things, climb aboard and set off. They are really enjoying themselves, when, BANG! There is a loud noise as they hit something in the water. It is an oil drum. "Oh dear," says Dad. "It's made a hole." Just then, they see a ship, steaming along. "Quick," says Dad, pointing at the ship. "We'll shout for help." "Oi, oi, ship ahoy!" The sailors from the ship hear their voices and yell back, "oi, ship ahoy, are you in trouble?" "Yes, we're sinking. Help!" they cry. The sailors help Roy and his dad get the boat back to port.

Action

- The students cup their hands around their mouth and shout, "oi, oi, ship ahoy!"

Formation

- Explain how the digraph ‹oi› is written.
- The students write over the dotted letters in their books.

Blending

- Blend the words *soil, joint, point,* and *void*.
- Say the sounds with the students, then blend the sounds together and read the words.
- Encourage the students to point to the dot underneath each sound as they say it.

Sounding

- Say the words corresponding to the pictures on the page: *train, boil, point, oil*.
- The students listen for the word without the /oi/ sound (*train*), and cross out its picture.

Word bank

oil, boil, coil, coin, foil, join, soil, toil, spoil, joint, point, moist, boiling, toilet, tinfoil, oilcan, avoid.

Dictation

- Call out the sound /oi/ and some other sounds already covered for the students to write.
- Dictate the words *oil, boil, join,* and *coin*.
- Call out some words from the Word Bank.
- The students listen to the words and hold up a finger for each sound.

Further ideas

- Sing the song from the *Jolly Songs* and pin up the /oi/ section of the *Wall Frieze*.

Letter Sound /ue/

Flash cards
- Practice some of the sounds already learned.
- The digraph ‹ue› is sometimes pronounced as a long /oo/ sound, for example in the words: *glue, blue, clue.*

Story
- Introduce the sound /ue/ using a story, such as the one below, and the action.

It is Samuel's birthday and he is having a party. First, Samuel and his friends play musical chairs. After that, a magician performs a magic show. He uses a magic wand and he has a big magic box with a unicorn on the side. The magician does a few card tricks, and then he asks for someone to come and help him. "You," he says, pointing at Samuel, "You are the birthday boy," he continues, "will you come and help me?" "Me?" asks Samuel. "You!" shout the children. Samuel helps the magician do a trick. He has to wave the magic wand and say, "ue, ue, ue." Right on cue, a rabbit pops out from under the magician's table! After the magic show, they all go outside and have a barbecue.

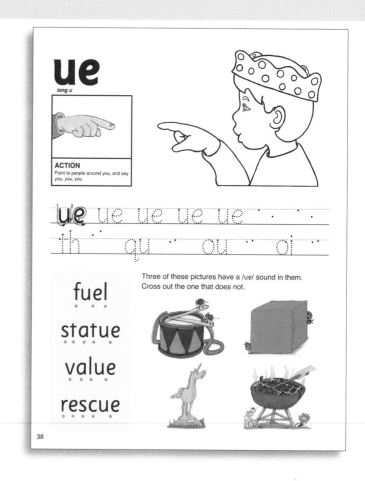

Three of these pictures have a /ue/ sound in them. Cross out the one that does not.

fuel
statue
value
rescue

Action
- The students point to each other and say, "ue, ue, ue."

Formation
- Explain how the digraph ‹ue› is written.
- The students write over the dotted letters in their books.

Blending
- Blend the words *fuel, statue, value, rescue.*
- Say the sounds with the students, then blend the sounds together and read the words.
- Encourage the students to point to the dot underneath each sound as they say it.

Sounding
- Say the words corresponding to the pictures on the page: *drum, cube, statue, barbecue.*

- The students listen for the word without the /ue/ sound (*drum*), and cross out its picture.

Word bank
cue, due, fuel, value, rescue, statue.

Dictation
- Call out the sound /ue/ and some other sounds already covered for the students to write.
- Dictate the words *value, cue* and *due.*
- Call out some words from the Word Bank.
- The students listen to the words and hold up a finger for each sound.

Further ideas
- Sing the song from the *Jolly Songs* pin up the /ue/ section of the *Wall Frieze*.
- Paint a unicorn.
- Build a model with cubes and tubes.

Letter Sound /er/

Flash cards
• Practice some of the sounds already learned.

Story
• Introduce the sound /er/ using a story, such as the one below, and the action.

Bert's teacher, Mr. Bird, has been reading *The Gingerbread Man* to his class. When Bert gets home, he asks if he can make some gingerbread for supper. First, he and his sister, Jennifer, help to weigh the butter, sugar, flour, eggs, and the ground ginger. Then they put all the ingredients in a bowl and stir. "Erererer," goes the mixer. Bert and Jennifer roll their hands over and over, pretending to be the mixer; "er, er, er, er, er," they go. Next, Bert and Jennifer roll out their mixture, cut out the gingerbread shapes, and bake them in the oven. When the gingerbread has cooked and cooled, Bert decorates it with frosting and currants. He makes a special gingerbread man to take into school for his teacher.

Action
• The students roll their hands over each other, like a mixer, and say "er-er-er-er-er".

Formation
• Explain how the digraph ‹er› is written.
• The students write over the dotted letters in their books.

Blending
• Blend the words *verb, letter, winter, runner*.
• Say the sounds with the students, then blend the sounds together and read the words.
• Encourage the students to point to the dot underneath each sound as they say it.

Sounding
• Say the words corresponding to the pictures on the page: *spider, tiger, letter, kite*.
• The students listen for the word without the /er/ sound (*kite*), and cross out its picture.

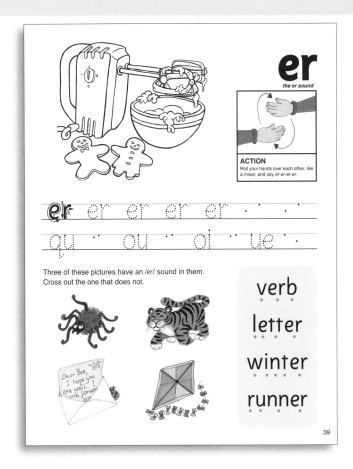

Word bank
her, fern, silver, deeper, summer, winter, dinner, ladder, longer, stronger, sister, chatter, helper, sender, jester, blender, litter, printer, singer, trucker, jumper, zipper, duster, waiter, thunderstorm, cooker, helicopter, corner, understand.

Dictation
• Call out the sound /er/ and some other sounds already covered for the students to write.
• Dictate the words *her, silver, winter*, and *fern*.
• Call out some words from the Word Bank.
• The students listen to the words and hold up a finger for each sound.

Further ideas
• Sing the song from the *Jolly Songs* and pin up the /er/ section of the *Wall Frieze*.
• Make gingerbread people and decorate them.
• Make summer and winter pictures.

Letter Sound /ar/

Flash cards
• Practice some of the sounds already learned.

Story
• Introduce the sound /ar/ using a story, such as the one below, and the action.

The Smart family is on vacation by the ocean. Charlie, Carla, and Barbara are having a great time. So far, they have visited the farm and looked for starfish on the beach. They have even been to see the sharks at the aquarium. Today Mrs. Smart and the girls are going to the market to buy souvenirs, and Dad and Charlie go to the harbor. At the harbor, Dad and Charlie see a sign with a seal painted on it. "They do boat trips over to the island to see the seals," says Dad. "We could go tomorrow." Just then, Dad and Charlie hear a loud "ar, ar, ar!" Over by the rocks is a big brown seal. It is flapping its flippers and barking "ar!" Charlie pretends to be a seal, flapping his hands together and saying "ar, ar, ar!"

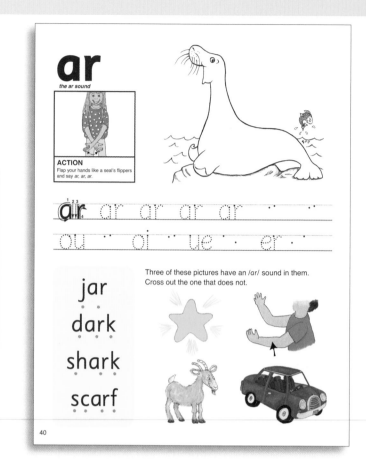

Action
• The students flap their hands like a seal's flippers and say "ar ar ar."

Formation
• Explain how the digraph ‹ar› is written.
• The students write over the dotted letters in their books.

Blending
• Blend the words *jar, dark, shark, scarf.*
• Say the sounds with the students, then blend the sounds together and read the words.
• Encourage the students to point to the dot underneath each sound as they say it.

Sounding
• Say the words corresponding to the pictures on the page: *star, arm, goat, car.*
• The students listen for the word without the /ar/ sound (*goat*), and cross out its picture.

Word bank
art, ark, bar, car, arm, jar, bark, barn, card, cart, dark, dart, farm, hard, harm, harp, park, part, tart, yard, star, scar, spark, start, scarf, smart, shark, sharp, charm, chart, marsh, arch, march, farmer, barnyard, cartoon.

Dictation
• Call out the sound /ar/ and some other sounds already covered for the students to write.
• Dictate the words *art, card, star,* and *march.*
• Call out some words from the Word Banks.
• The students listen to the words and hold up a finger for each sound.

Further ideas
• Sing the song from the *Jolly Jingles* or the *Jolly Songs.*
• Put up on the wall, or hold up, the /ar/ section of the *Wall Frieze.*
• Make stars from shiny paper.
• Design a park using a construction set.

Tricky Words

Flash cards
- Practice some of the basic 42 sounds: /s/, /a/, /t/, /i/, /p/, /n/, /c/, /k/, /e/, /h/, /r/, /m/, /d/, /g/, /o/, /u/, /l/, /f/, /b/, /ai/, /j/, /oa/, /ie/, /ee/, /or/, /z/, /w/, /ng/, /v/, /oo/, /**oo**/, /y/, /x/, /ch/, /sh/, /th/, /th/, /qu/, /ou/, /oi/, /ue/, /er/, and /ar/.

Tricky words
- Explain that some words are not written exactly as they sound, and that we call these words "tricky words."
- We also use this term to describe words that have alternative spellings that have not yet been taught.
- To remember how to spell these words, the students have to look for, and remember, the "tricky bits."
- Introduce the tricky words: *the, he, she, me, we, and be*. The students look at these words in the flowers on the *Phonics Student Book* page.
- Point out that the /ee/ sound at the end of each word is written with only one ‹e›, even though it sounds like there should be two.
- The students might find it helpful to underline the ‹e› at the end of each of these words in purple, to remind them that this is the "tricky bit."
- Whilst the sound /th/ is written ‹th›, the tricky word *the*, has an ‹e› on the end. Point out that the students must remember to add the ‹e› when writing the tricky word *the*.

Look, copy, cover, write, check
- Look at the first word, *the*, with the students.
- Say the letter names (not the letter sounds) in this word.
- The students write over the dotted word *the*.
- Then the students cover up all instances of the word *the* on their page and try writing the word in the next column.
- Once the students have had one try at writing *the*, they check their spelling.
- Then they cover up all instances of the word *the* again, and have another go at writing *the* in the final column.
- Repeat these steps with the other words.

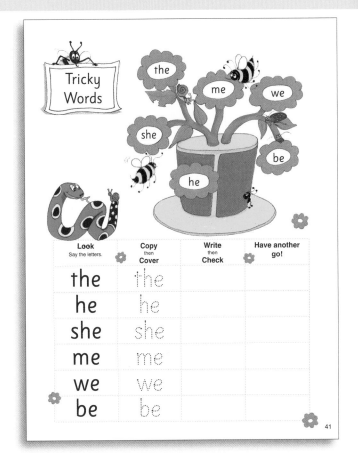

Further blending practice
- Write the following list of words on the board and blend them with the students: *joint, winner, cartoon, thorn, sound.*

Reading sentences
- Write the following sentences on the board, pointing out the tricky words and blending any unknown words with the students.
  1. The dog jumps on the cat.
  2. She is sleeping in the barn.
  3. We must not drop litter.
  4. The king had a red cloak.

Reading and Writing Activities

Flash cards

- Practice some of the basic 42 sounds:
  /s/, /a/, /t/, /i/, /p/, /n/, /c/, /k/, /e/, /h/, /r/, /m/, /d/,
  /g/, /o/, /u/, /l/, /f/, /b/, /ai/, /j/, /oa/, /ie/, /ee/, /or/,
  /z/, /w/, /ng/, /v/, /oo/, /oo/, /y/, /x/, /ch/, /sh/, /th/,
  /th/, /qu/, /ou/, /oi/, /ue/, /er/, and /ar/.
- Use the flash cards, or the *Tricky Word Wall Flowers*, to practice the tricky words *the, he, she, me, we,* and *be.*

Reading words with short vowels

- The students read the words in the picture frames.
- They draw a picture underneath each word to illustrate it.
- The words are: *ant, van, cup.*

Writing short words

- The students look at each picture, say the word and listen for the sounds.
- The students might need some help hearing each individual sound.
- For the first row of pictures, the students write over the dotted letters and fill in the missing sounds.
- For the next two rows of pictures, the students are expected to listen for the sounds and write the whole word on the lines provided.
- A line is provided for each sound in the words.
- A longer line indicates a digraph is needed.
- The pictures are:

  mixer, queen, chin
  hen, sun, ant
  wood, six, ring

Further blending practice

- Write the following list of words on the board and blend them with the students:
  quit, throat, rubbish, ostrich, mix.

Reading sentences

- Write the following sentences on the board, pointing out the tricky words and blending any unknown words with the students.
1. He can finish the job next week.
2. This will be the best toolbox.
3. The rocket zooms up and up.
4. Can we feed the ducks?

Tricky Words

Flash cards
- Practice some of the basic 42 sounds already learned.
- Use the flash cards, or the *Tricky Word Wall Flowers*, to practice the tricky words *the, he, she, me, we,* and *be.*

Tricky words
- Introduce the new tricky words: *I, was, to, do, are,* and *all*. The students look at these words in the flowers on the pages.
- Explain that the letter ‹i› is shy, so when it appears on its own as the tricky word *I*, it puffs itself up and uses its capital letter.
- When introducing the tricky word *was*, say it first by blending its sounds and tell the students that *was* (pronouncing it to rhyme with *mass*), says /woz/.
- Point out that *to* and *do* both have an /oo/ sound at the end, but they are written with only one ‹o›.
- The students might find it helpful to underline the ‹o› at the end of these two words in purple, to remind them that this is the "tricky bit."
- Point out that the sound /ar/ is written ‹ar›, but the tricky word *are* has an ‹e› at the end.
- When the students can read the word *all*, they can also read words with ‹all› at the end, such as *ball* and *call*.

Look, copy, cover, write, check
- Look at the first word, *I*, with the students.
- Say the letter names (not the letter sounds) in this word, and point out the capital letter.
- The students write over the dotted word *I*.
- Then the students cover up all instances of the word *I* on their page and try writing the word in the next column.
- Once the students have had one try at writing *I*, they check their spelling.

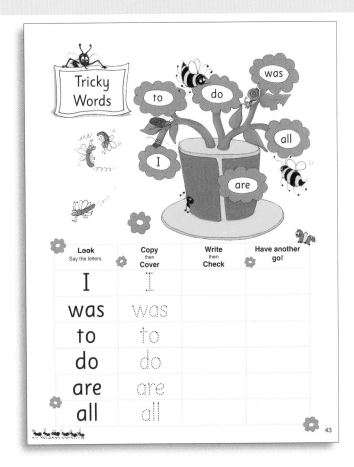

- Then they cover up all instances of the word *I* again, and have another go at writing *I* in the final column.
- Repeat these steps with the other words.

Further blending practice
- Write the following list of words on the board and blend them with the students:
took, toadstool, dinner, coin, sharper.

Reading sentences
- Write the following sentences on the board, pointing out the tricky words and blending any unknown words with the students.
1. I can do the dishes in the morning.
2. All the fish are in the pond.
3. She went to the park.
4. He sat on the picnic rug.

Reading and Writing Activities

Flash cards

- Practice some of the basic 42 sounds:
/s/, /a/, /t/, /i/, /p/, /n/, /c/, /k/, /e/, /h/, /r/, /m/, /d/,
/g/, /o/, /u/, /l/, /f/, /b/, /ai/, /j/, /oa/, /ie/, /ee/, /or/,
/z/, /w/, /ng/, /v/, /oo/, /**oo**/, /y/, /x/, /ch/, /sh/, /th/,
/**th**/, /qu/, /ou/, /oi/, /ue/, /er/, and /ar/.
- Use the flash cards, or the *Tricky Word Wall Flowers*, to practice the tricky words *the, he, she, me, we, be, I, was, to, do, are,* and *all.*

Digraph and consonant blend words

- Look at the pictures with the students, and say the word for each one.
- The students listen for the sounds in each word, and write the words underneath the pictures.
- A line is provided for each sound in the words.
- A longer line indicates a digraph is needed.
- The pictures are:
  > *moth, tree, star,*
  > *snail, flag, nest,*
  > *fish, boat, moon.*

Reading and illustrating sentences

- Many tricky words are very common words and it is difficult to read or write a sentence that does not have a tricky word in it.
- Although so far, the emphasis has been on teaching the lower-case letters, point out to the students that sentences start with a capital letter.
- Point to the capitals *T* and *I* on this page, and refer the students to the capital letters on the /t/ and /i/ pages in their *Student Books.*
- Point out that each sentence ends with a period.
- The students read each sentence, and illustrate the sentences in the picture frames.
- The sentences are:
  > *This is me.*
  > *I can run.*

Look at the pictures and write the words underneath.

Read the sentences and draw a picture in each frame.

This is me.   I can run.

44

Further blending practice

- Write the following list of words on the board and blend them with the students:
  > *thanks,*
  > *quick,*
  > *footsteps,*
  > *yes,*
  > *toffee.*

Reading sentences

- Write the following sentences on the board, pointing out the tricky words and blending any unknown words with the students.
  1. We can all sing the songs.
  2. I do not need the stool.
  3. He was good at tennis.
  4. We are clever.

Tricky Words

Flash cards

· Practice some of the basic 42 sounds:
/s/, /a/, /t/, /i/, /p/, /n/, /c/, /k/, /e/, /h/, /r/, /m/, /d/,
/g/, /o/, /u/, /l/, /f/, /b/, /ai/, /j/, /oa/, /ie/, /ee/, /or/,
/z/, /w/, /ng/, /v/, /oo/, /oo/, /y/, /x/, /ch/, /sh/, /th/,
/th/, /qu/, /ou/, /oi/, /ue/, /er/, and /ar/.

· Use the flash cards, or the *Tricky Word Wall Flowers*, to practice the tricky words *the, he, she, me, we, be, I, was, to, do, are,* and *all.*

Reading CVC words

· Look at the words and pictures at the top of the page with the students.
· Read the first word, *cat*, to the students.
· Point out that it is joined to the picture of the cat.
· The students read the remaining words and join each word to the corresponding picture.
· All the words are CVC words (consonant-vowel-consonant words), and have short vowel sounds.
· Once the students have joined each word to the right picture, they can color the pictures.

Tricky words word search

· Look at the tricky word flowers surrounding the word search and read the tricky words with the students.
· The students have to find each tricky word in the word search, and lightly shade the squares blue.
· As they find each tricky word, the students cross out the corresponding flower.

Further blending practice

· Write the following list of words on the board and blend them with the students:
sheet, think, bumper, blend, sack.

Read the words and join each word to the right picture. Color the pictures.

hat · dog · net · log · fan · cat · bed · bus

Read the tricky words and then try to find them in the wordsearch.

to · be · me · do · are · we · was · he · the · all · she

y	v	a	l	l	b
u	s	r	d	w	e
t	h	e	c	a	f
o	e	b	p	s	g
n	l	h	e	m	e
a	j	d	o	i	r

45

Reading sentences

· Write the following sentences on the board, pointing out the tricky words and blending any unknown words with the students.
1. The snail left a long trail.
2. Do not groan or moan.
3. We all had fun.
4. The dog was wagging his tail.

79

Reading and Writing Activities

Flash cards
- Practice some of the basic 42 sounds:
/s/, /a/, /t/, /i/, /p/, /n/, /c/, /k/, /e/, /h/, /r/, /m/, /d/, /g/, /o/, /u/, /l/, /f/, /b/, /ai/, /j/, /oa/, /ie/, /ee/, /or/, /z/, /w/, /ng/, /v/, /oo/, /oo/, /y/, /x/, /ch/, /sh/, /th/, /th/, /qu/, /ou/, /oi/, /ue/, /er/, and /ar/.
- Use the flash cards, or the *Tricky Word Wall Flowers*, to practice the tricky words *the, he, she, me, we, be, I, was, to, do, are,* and *all*.

Sentence reading
- Look at the sentences underneath the picture frames with the students.
- Read the first sentence to the students:
    He can sing.
- Point out the capital letter at the beginning of this sentence, and the period at the end.
- The students illustrate the sentence in the picture frame above it.
- The students read the remaining sentences, and then draw a picture in each frames to illustrate the sentence.
- The sentences are:
    He can sing.
    She is sad.
    I can jump.
    We can hop.
    The sun is hot.
    Drums are loud.

Further blending practice
- Write the following list of words on the board and blend them with the students:
    windmill,
    foghorn,
    weep,
    zigzag,
    wedding.

Read each sentence and draw a picture in the frame to illustrate it.

He can sing. She is sad.

I can jump. We can hop.

The sun is hot. Drums are loud.

46

Reading sentences
- Write the following sentences on the board, pointing out the tricky words and blending any unknown words with the students.
    1. Bring all the books to me.
    2. We are to sit and wait on the bench.
    3. I ran to the helicopter.
    4. We are all about to jump in the pool.

Reading and Writing Activities

Flash cards

- Practice some of the basic 42 sounds: /s/, /a/, /t/, /i/, /p/, /n/, /c/, /k/, /e/, /h/, /r/, /m/, /d/, /g/, /o/, /u/, /l/, /f/, /b/, /ai/, /j/, /oa/, /ie/, /ee/, /or/, /z/, /w/, /ng/, /v/, /oo/, /oo/, /y/, /x/, /ch/, /sh/, /th/, /th/, /qu/, /ou/, /oi/, /ue/, /er/, and /ar/.
- Use the flash cards, or the *Tricky Word Wall Flowers*, to practice the tricky words *the, he, she, me, we, be, I, was, to, do, are,* and *all*.

Missing words

- The students read each sentence and write the missing word in the gap. The adjacent picture provides the clue.
- The sentences (with missing words in brackets) are:

  The (pie) is hot.
  The (frog) is green.
  The (tent) is big.
  The (bee) flies.

- On the second half of the page the students not only have to fill in the missing words, but also have to color the picture so that it corresponds to the sentence.
- The sentences (with missing words in brackets) are:

  The (car) is red.
  I see the green (tree).
  The (fish) is pink.
  The (pen) is blue.

Further blending practice

- Write the following list of words on the board and blend them with the students:
  cooker, sharp, plain, float, steer.
- Write the following sentences on the board, pointing out the tricky words and blending any unknown words with the students.
  1. He must be a twin.
  2. We all need to bring our food.
  3. His footprints are big.
  4. I must not crash the car.

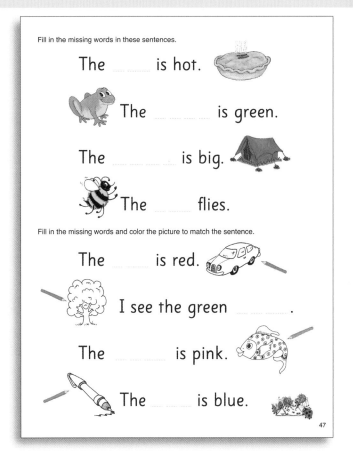

Practice page

- Page 48 is a practice page for the students.
- The students read the tricky words in the flowers.
- Then they trace inside the outline letters and digraphs.

Teaching with
Phonics Student Book 2

In *Phonics Student Book 1*, the basic 42 sounds were introduced and the students were taught one way of writing each of these sounds. Towards the end of *Phonics Student Book 1*, the students were taught how to read and spell the first twelve tricky words. The basic letter-sound skills taught in *Phonics Student Book 1* enable the students to tackle their first reading books. Once *Phonics Student Book 1* has been completed, any students who are able to decode regular words independently and know the first twelve tricky words can start reading decodable books. If the *Jolly Phonics Readers* are available, these more able students can be given books from the Red Level.

If the *Jolly Readers*, or similar decodable books, are not available, the students can practice their blending skills by reading the further blending practice words and the reading sentences provided in the lesson plans.

The exercises in *Phonics Student Book 2* provide the students with numerous opportunities to practice reading and writing the letter sounds they have learned. *Phonics Student Book 2* also introduces some of the common alternative spellings for these sounds, as well as teaching the capital letters and introducing more tricky words. The blending activities in *Phonics Student Book 2* encourage the students towards greater fluency in their reading and the various writing activities help them to become independent and confident writers.

Like *Phonics Student Book 1*, *Phonics Student Book 2* is designed so that each page is a complete lesson. The teaching covered in each lesson follows a pattern and the following types of activities are covered on a regular basis.

Alternatives

- In *Phonics Student Book 1,* one way of writing each sound was introduced. However, in the English language there are often a number of ways to write an individual sound and these alternative spellings also need to be taught.

- To begin with, the students should only be expected to recognize these alternative letter-sound spellings when reading; they should not be expected to use the correct alternative letter-sound spellings consistently in their writing.

- The students need to practice the alternative letter-sound spellings frequently. The further blending practice words give the students the opportunity to practice blending words containing these alternatives.

- The alternative letter-sound spellings that are introduced in *Students Book 2* are as follows:

  ‹y› making an /**ee**/ sound at the end of a word, as in *holly*

  ‹ck› making a /**ck**/ sound in words with a short vowel sound, as in *back*

  double letters in words with short vowels, as in *rabbit*

  "**hop-over e**" digraphs, as in the words *cake, eve, kite, rope, mule*

  ‹ay› spelling for the /**ai**/ sound, as in *day*

  ‹oy› spelling for the /**oi**/ sound, as in *boy*

  ‹ea› making the /**ee**/ sound, as in *leaf*

  ‹y› making the /**ie**/ sound, as in *my*

  ‹ow› making the /**oa**/ sound in *snow,* and the /**ou**/ sound in *owl*

  ‹ir› and ‹ur› making the /**er**/ sound, as in *bird* and *curl*

Handwriting and dictation

- In *Phonics Student Book 2,* dictation and handwriting activities are covered on the same page.

Dictation

- The teacher calls out the dictation words provided in the lesson plan. The students listen for each sound in the words and then write the words on the lines in their books. For more information about dictation, see page 25 of the introduction.

Handwriting

- The handwriting exercises in *Phonics Student Book 2* concentrate first on the formation capital letters and later on the practice of certain types of letter: for example, tall letters, tail letters, and letters that start with a "caterpillar c".

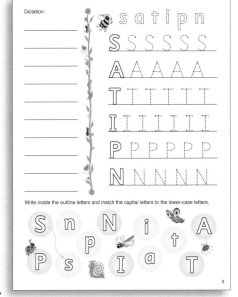

- The students trace inside the outline letters and write over the line of dotted letters.
- On the pages where there are starting dots above the line, the students have to write the letters by themselves.
- The students need to remember to start each letter at the dots and ensure that all their letters sit on the line.
- When the capital letters are being introduced, teachers should explain how each letter is formed before the students start writing.
- Letter formation is very important and it is worth taking the time to ensure it is correct. For more information, see pages 13 to 15 of the introduction for the section on letter formation.
- When students are learning the capital letters, they need to be taught the letter names as well as the sound each letter makes.

Tricky words
- These pages introduce the students to more of the tricky words and help them to review the tricky words that have already been taught.
- For more information, see pages 30 to 33 of this book for the section on tricky words.
- The following tricky words are introduced in *Phonics Student Book 2*:

> *you, your, come, some, said, here,*
> *there, they, go, no, so my*
>   (yellow words)
> *one, by, only, old, like, have,*
> *live, give, little, down, what, when*
>   (red words)
> *why, where, who, which*
>   (green words)

Comprehension
- There are a number of reading activities in *Phonics Student Book 2*, which aim to improve the students' blending and comprehension skills.
- Teachers can also improve students' levels of comprehension by discussing the further blending practice words and sentences and explaining any words the students do not understand.

Words and sentences

- These pages help the students to start writing independently. To begin with, students need plenty of help and guidance when writing.
- The guided writing pages provide the students with a writing topic and a model sentence to get them started.
- The teacher uses the picture to help initiate a class discussion.
- The teacher selects some key words from the discussion to write on the board, pointing out any alternative spelling patterns in these words.
- The teacher uses the model sentence provided in the Daily Guidance as an opportunity to explain basic sentence structure.

- The following things can be pointed out as the teacher writes the model sentence on the board:
    - All sentences start with a capital letter and end with a period.
    - Leave a space between words.
    - Read what you have written and make sure that it makes sense.
- All the students copy the model sentence from the board and try to write some more sentences by themselves.
- Some students will be able to write independently at an early stage, but others may take more time.

The more able students can move on to the Yellow Level of *Jolly Readers* when the have learned the tricky words up to and including *they*, and once they know that ‹y› can make the /ee/ sound when it comes at the end of a word. This knowledge is covered on pages 1 to 17 of *Phonics Student Book 2*.

Alternatives: ⟨y⟩ Making an /ee/ Sound

Flash cards
- Practice some of the basic 42 sounds.

Alternatives: ⟨y⟩ as /ee/
- Explain that the letter ⟨y⟩ only says the sound /y/ when it comes at the beginning of a word (as in the words *yummy, yellow, yoghurt*), or sometimes in the middle (as in the word *beyond*). When a ⟨y⟩ comes at the end of the word it makes an /ee/ sound.
- Remind the students that, when two letters making the same sound are next to each other, the sound is only said once.
- Read the words at the top of the page:
    jolly, daisy, muddy, teddy,
    sunny, funny, daddy, spotty.
- Point out the letter that is making the /ee/ sound at the end of the words (the letter ⟨y⟩).
- The sound made by the ⟨y⟩ may vary slightly according to accent.

Note 1: double letters
- The blending words with short vowel sounds have double consonant letters after the vowel. When two letters that make the same sound are next to each other, the sound is only said once.
- Consonant letters are often doubled after a short vowel sound so that the "magic" from any subsequent vowels cannot "hop back" over the consonants and change the short vowel into a long vowel.
- For example, when one consonant is removed from the word *holly* (which has a short vowel sound, /o/, followed by two consonants), it leaves *holy* (which has a long vowel sound /oa/, and one consonant).
- As the ⟨y⟩ is replacing a vowel sound in the reading words, it has borrowed the "magic" of a vowel. So, if the consonants after the short vowel were not doubled, the ⟨y⟩ at the end of the word would change the short vowel sound into a long vowel.
- There are, however, some exceptions to this rule; in the words *body, lily,* and *copy,* the consonant is not doubled.

On this page, the ⟨y⟩ at the end of each word makes an /ee/ sound.

jolly   daisy   muddy   teddy
sunny   funny   daddy   spotty

Read the words in the logs. Match each word to the right picture.

sunny
body
puppy
teddy
sandy
holly

Word and picture matching
- The students read the words in the logs. They join each word to the frog containing the corresponding picture. The students can then color the pictures.
- The pictures, from top to bottom, are:

(left)	(right)
holly,	*sandy,*
teddy,	*puppy,*
body,	*sunny.*

Reading sentences
- Write the following sentences on the board, pointing out the tricky words, and blending any unknown words with the students.
1. Do sheep sleep in beds?
2. The farmyard is a mess.
3. The shark swam in the reef.
4. Did she do her job well?

Handwriting and Dictation

Flash cards
- Practice some of the basic 42 sounds that were introduced in *Phonics Student Book 1*.

Dictation words
- Dictate the following words:
     cat,
     dog,
     hen,
     step,
     drum,
     chin,
     than,
     sheep,
     rain,
     cobweb.
- The students write these words on the lines in their *Phonics Student Books*.

The alphabet
- Look at a copy of the alphabet with the students.
- Say the alphabet, pointing to each letter as you say it, and pausing between each group: A-E, F-M, N-S, T-Z.

Handwriting
- Practice the sounds and formation for the letters ‹s›, ‹a›, ‹t›, ‹i›, ‹p›, and ‹n›.
- Teach the students how to write the capital letters: ‹S›, ‹A›, ‹T›, ‹I›, ‹P›, and ‹N›.
- All capital letters start at the top.
- The students trace inside the outline letters, and then write over the dotted letters, saying the letter names as they do so.

Capitals and lower-case letters
- The students join each capital letter to its corresponding lower-case letter.
- Then they trace inside the outline letters using a different color for each pair of letters.

Write inside the outline letters and match the capital letters to the lower-case letters.

Further blending practice
- Write the following list of words on the board, and blend them with the students:
     sandwich,
     barn,
     weekend,
     skunk,
     limping.

Reading sentences
- Write the following sentences on the board, pointing out the tricky words, and blending any unknown words with the students.
1. We do not jump on the bed.
2. The big dog has black spots.
3. Her coat was pink and blue.
4. He brushes his teeth in the morning.

Tricky Words

Flash cards
- Use the flashcards, or *Tricky Word Wall Flowers*, to practice the tricky words that were introduced in *Phonics Student Book 1*.

Tricky words
- Introduce the two new tricky words: *you*, and *your*.
- The students look at the two words in yellow flowers at the top of the page: *you*, and *your*.
- Point out that *your* is the same as *you*, but it has a letter ⟨r⟩ at the end.
- The students write inside the outline letters using a yellow pen or pencil.

Look, copy, cover, write, check
- Look at the first word, *you*, with the students.
- Say the letter names (not the letter sounds) in that word. The students write over the dotted word *you*.
- Then the students cover up all instances of the word *you* on their page, and try writing the word in the next column.
- Once the students have had one try at writing *you*, they check their spelling. Then they cover up all instances of the word *you* again, and have another go at writing the word in the final column.
- Repeat these steps with the word *your*, reminding the students that *your* is the same as *you*, but with an ⟨r⟩ at the end.

Short vowels
- Explain that the five vowel letters are ⟨a⟩, ⟨e⟩, ⟨i⟩, ⟨o⟩, and ⟨u⟩. These letters have a short vowel sound, which the students know.
- The students look at the outline letters at the side of their page.
- Say the short vowel sounds with the students.
- The students write inside the outline letters using a blue pencil.
- Then the students look at the letters in the grid.
- They find all the vowel letters, and color these squares blue.

Further blending practice
- Write the following list of words on the board, and blend them with the students:
  - *black,*
  - *paid,*
  - *soak,*
  - *street,*
  - *fork.*

Reading sentences
- Write the following sentences on the board, pointing out the tricky words, and blending any unknown words with the students.
1. Is your jumper red or green?
2. You must stop at the kerb to cross the road.
3. This is the bin for your rubbish.
4. You will get your wish.

Words and Sentences

Flash cards
- Practice some of the basic 42 sounds, plus ‹y› as /ee/.

Words and sentences
- Discuss the hen picture with the students.
- Ask a student to say one sentence about the picture. For example, "I can see a hen." "The chick is on the hen's back." "The hen is on the nest."
- Choose some words to blend, and write them on the board; examples could be: *hen, nest, her, eggs, chicks.*
- Some words will be straightforward to spell by listening for the sounds, but others will need some guidance:
- *Eggs*: explain that the ‹s› on the end of a plural often makes a /z/ sound.
- *Chicks*: explain that in short words with a short vowel followed by a /c/ sound, the /c/ is often spelled ‹ck›; as in the words *sack, neck* and *chick.*
- Write the sentence:

    A hen just sits on her nest.
- Discuss it as you write, saying:
- Sentences start with a capital letter.
- Capital letters are always tall.
- Listen for the sounds in the words.
- Leave a space between each word.
- Don't forget the period.
- All the students copy the sentence. Those students who can write independently can try to write some more sentences on their own.
- At this stage, the students only know one way of writing each sound, so their spelling will not always be accurate, but their work will be readable. Spelling gradually improves through reading many books, and learning the alternative letter-sound spellings.

Short vowels
- Review the five vowel letters and their sounds: ‹a›, ‹e›, ‹i›, ‹o›, and ‹u›.
- The students look at the grid at the bottom of the page.

Choose one of the short vowel sounds, /a/, /e/, /i/, /o/, or /u/, to make the words.

f u n	h p	r d	b g
m n	p t	c p	m p
s ck	sh p	cl p	qu ck

- Each word is missing a short vowel.
- The students look at the first word: f_n.
- Encourage them to try saying this word using all the different short vowel sounds, *fan, fen, fin, fon, fun.*
- Point out that the words *fun, fin,* and *fan* all make sense. The students write over the dotted ‹u› to make the word *fun.*
- The students complete all the other words in the same way. When they come across a sound that makes sense in the word, like the ‹u› in *fun,* they write the vowel in the gap.
- There may be several different correct answers for each word:

    f_n: *fan, fin, fun*; **h_p:** *hip, hop*;

    r_d: *red, rid, rod*; **b_g:** *bag, beg, big, bug*;

    m_n: *man, men*; **p_t:** *pat, pet, pit, pot*;

    c_p: *cap, cop, cup*; **m_p:** *map, mop*;

    s_ck: *sack, sick, sock, suck*; **sh_p:** *ship, shop*;

    cl_p: *clap, clip, clop*; **qu_ck:** *quack, quick*.

Short Vowels

Flash cards
• Practice some of the basic 42 sounds, plus ‹y› as /ee/.

Reading short vowel words
• Remind the students that the short vowel sounds are: /a/, /e/, /i/, /o/, and /u/.
• Together with the students, read the short vowel words at the top of the page.
• The words are: *bag, net, bin, box,* and *mug.*
• Point out the position of Inky Mouse in the pictures above the short vowel words.
• Inky is: **a**gainst the b**a**g,
      r**e**sting on the **e**dge of the n**e**t,
      in the b**i**n,
      on t**o**p of the b**o**x,
      under the m**u**g.
• Emphasize the short vowels as you say where Inky is in each picture.
• The students trace inside the outline vowel letters.

Writing short vowel words
• The students look at the picture of the box.
• Say the word *box,* and ask the students to listen out for the short vowel sound, /o/.
• Point out that, in the line of short vowels above the picture of the box, the ‹o› has been circled.
• The students write over the dotted word, *box,* underneath the picture.
• Then the students look at the rest of the pictures.
• They say each word to themselves, listening first for the short vowel sound, which they ring, and then for all the sounds in the word, which they write on the lines underneath the picture.
• The pictures are:
      box, bus, frog,
      duck, nest, ring,
      hat, shell, crab.
• When the students have finished writing, they can color the pictures.

Further blending practice
• Write the following list of words on the board, and blend them with the students:
      noisy,
      starting,
      groan,
      pail,
      street.

Reading sentences
• Write the following sentences on the board, pointing out the tricky words, and blending any unknown words with the students.
1. Your jumper is not too big for you.
2. He had a train set in his room.
3. You must be good at the shops.
4. I went to the dentist.

Handwriting and Dictation

Flash cards
· Practice some of the basic 42 sounds, plus ‹y› as /ee/.

Dictation words
· Dictate the following words:

cap,
dot,
men,
stop,
drip,
boat,
chip,
thin,
shoot,
nutmeg.

· The students write these words on the lines in their *Phonics Student Books*.

The alphabet
· Look at a copy of the alphabet with the students.
· Say the alphabet, pointing to each letter as you say it, and pausing between each group: A-E, F-M, N-S, T-Z.

Handwriting
· Practice the sounds and formation for the letters ‹c›, ‹k›, ‹e›, ‹h›, ‹r›, ‹m›, and ‹d›.
· Teach the students how to write the capital letters: ‹C›, ‹K›, ‹E›, ‹H›, ‹R›, ‹M›, and ‹D›.
· All capital letters start at the top.
· The students trace inside the outline letters, and then write over the dotted letters, saying the letter names as they do so.

Capitals and lower-case letters
· The students join each capital letter to its corresponding lower-case letter.
· Then they trace inside the outline letters, using a different color for each pair of letters.

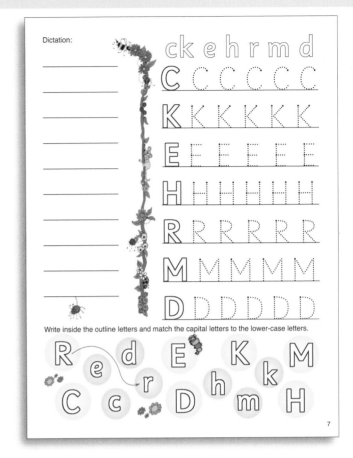

Further blending practice
· Write the following list of words on the board, and blend them with the students:

barbecue,
foggy,
louder,
happy,
handstand.

Reading sentences
· Write the following sentences on the board, pointing out the tricky words, and blending any unknown words with the students.
1. You must be hungry.
2. The car went north along the road.
3. Your hat is floppy.
4. Can you help me?

Tricky Words

Flash cards
- Use the flashcards, or *Tricky Word Wall Flowers*, to practice the tricky words already taught, including *you*, and *your*.

Tricky words
- Introduce the two new tricky words: *come*, and *some*.
- The students look at the two words in yellow flowers at the top of the page: *come*, and *some*.
- Point out that *some* is the same as *come*, but it has a letter ‹s› at the beginning.
- The students might find it helpful to underline the ‹o_e› at the end of these two words in purple, to remind them that this is the "tricky bit."
- The students write inside the outline letters using a yellow pen or pencil.

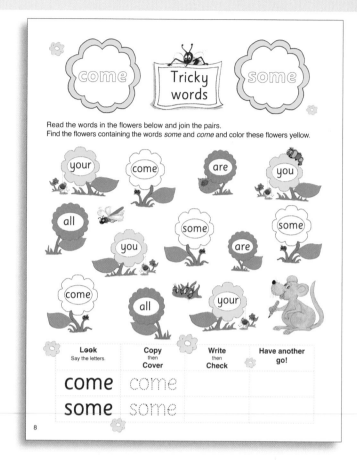

Tricky word flowers
- The students read all the tricky words inside the flowers, and join the matching pairs.
- Then the students find the flowers containing the words *some* and *come*, and color these flowers yellow.

Look, copy, cover, write, check
- Look at the first word, *come*, with the students.
- Say the letter names (not the letter sounds) in that word. The students write over the dotted word *come*.
- Then the students cover up all instances of the word *come* on their page, and try writing the word in the next column.
- Once the students have had one try at writing *come*, they check their spelling. Then they cover up all instances of the word *come* again, and have another go at writing the word in the final column.
- Repeat these steps with the word *some*.

Further blending practice
- Write the following list of words on the board, and blend them with the students:
  - *sandy,*
  - *lorry,*
  - *family,*
  - *soapy,*
  - *berry.*

Reading sentences
- Write the following sentences on the board, pointing out the tricky words, and blending any unknown words with the students.
1. Your dog has muddy feet.
2. Some cats are greedy.
3. Can we come to your party?
4. His fingers are all sticky.

Words and Sentences

Flash cards
· Practice some of the basic 42 sounds, plus ‹y› as /ee/.

Words and sentences
· Discuss the park picture with the students.
· Ask a student to say one sentence about the picture. For example, "I can see a dog." "The boy is throwing the ball."
· Choose some words to blend, and write them on the board; examples could be: *boy, dog, ball, park.*
· Some words will be straightforward to spell by listening for the sounds, but others will need some guidance:
· *Boy*: point that the /oi/ sound in this word is written ‹oy›.
· Explain that ‹y› often replaces ‹i› at the end of a word. Tell the students that the letter ‹i› is shy and does not like to be at the end of a word in English, so its cousin "toughy ‹y›" takes its place.
· *Park*: point out that the /ck/ sound at the end of *park* is spelled with a "kicking k."
· Explain that when a short word ending in a /ck/ sound does not have short vowel sound, the /ck/ sound is usually spelled ‹k›, as in the words *week, rook, oak,* and *park.*
· Write the sentence:
    I can see a big dog.
· Discuss it as you write, saying:
· Sentences start with a capital letter.
· Capital letters are always tall.
· Listen for the sounds in the words.
· Leave a space between each word.
· Don't forget the period.
· All the students copy the sentence. Those students who can write independently can try to write some more sentences on their own.
· At this stage, the students only know one way of writing each sound, so their spelling will not always be accurate, but their work will be readable. Spelling gradually improves through reading many books, and learning the alternative letter-sound spellings.

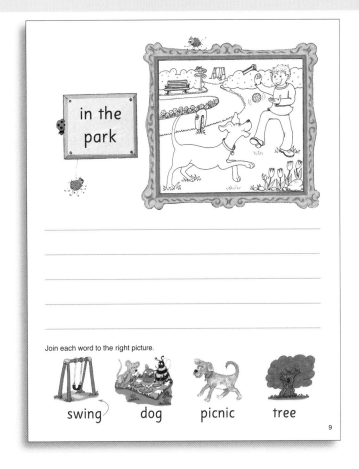

Join each word to the right picture.

swing   dog   picnic   tree

9

Reading words
· The students read each word at the bottom of the page, and join it to the matching picture.

Further blending practice
· Write the following list of words on the board, and blend them with the students:
magpie, fern, roasting, foil, thunderstorm.

Reading sentences
· Write the following sentences on the board, pointing out the tricky words, and blending any unknown words with the students.
1. Did you see the cartoons in that comic book?
2. Some children are painting in the corner.
3. Will you come to the shops with us?
4. The man was rescued in a helicopter.

Alternatives: ‹ck›

Flash cards
•Practice some of the basic 42 sounds, plus ‹y› as /ee/.

Alternatives: ‹ck›
•Remind the students that when two letters that make the same sound are next to each other, the sound is only said once.
•Explain that when a short vowel is followed by a /ck/ sound in short words, the /ck/ sound is spelled ‹ck›; both a "caterpillar c" and a "kicking k" are needed.
•Practice the short vowel sounds: /a/, /e/, /i/, /o/, and /u/.
•The students look at the blending words at the top of the page.
•Read out the first word: *duck*.
•The students listen for, and identify the short vowel sound: /u/.
•Read the other words with the students:
   duck, bricks, sack, peck, black,
   sock, jacket, tick, kick, clock.

Note 1: ‹ck› and ‹k›
•In short words with a short vowel sound followed by a /ck/, the /ck/ sound is spelled with both a ‹c› and a ‹k›, as in the words, *duck,* and *lack.*
•However, in short words where a /ck/ sound follows any other vowel sound (for example, /ai/, /ee/, /ie/, /oa/, /ar/, /er/, or /oo/), then the /ck/ sound is spelled with a ‹k› only, as in the words *rake, peek, look,* and *mark.*

Rockets
•The students look at the dotted words written in the rockets.
•They write over the first dotted word, *stick,* and draw a picture in the rocket to illustrate this word.
•They do the same with the remaining words.
•The words (clockwise from *stick*) are:
   stick, black, socks, rocket,
   duck, brick, neck.

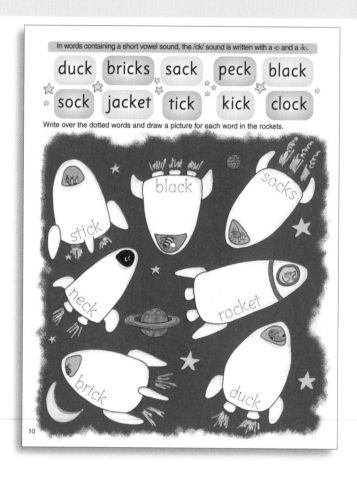

In words containing a short vowel sound, the /ck/ sound is written with a ‹c› and a ‹k›.

duck bricks sack peck black
sock jacket tick kick clock

Write over the dotted words and draw a picture for each word in the rockets.

Further blending practice
•Write the following list of words on the board, and blend them with the students:
   bedroom,
   beetroot,
   cricket,
   haddock,
   packing.

Reading sentences
•Write the following sentences on the board, pointing out the tricky words, and blending any unknown words with the students.
1. I swam ten lengths in the pool.
2. You are very clever indeed.
3. Did you get a book for me?
4. We laid out some nuts for the squirrels.

Handwriting and Dictation

Flash cards
· Practice some of the basic 42 sounds, plus ‹y› as /ee/.

Dictation words
· Dictate the following words:

> *set,*
> *hit,*
> *box,*
> *plum,*
> *snap,*
> *port,*
> *sharp,*
> *chop,*
> *quiz,*
> *redwood.*

· The students write these words on the lines in their *Phonics Student Books.*

The alphabet
· Look at a copy of the alphabet with the students.
· Say the alphabet, pointing to each letter as you say it, and pausing between each group: A-E, F-M, N-S, T-Z.

Handwriting
· Practice the sounds and formation for the letters ‹g›, ‹o›, ‹u›, ‹l›, ‹f›, and ‹b›.
· Teach the students how to write the capital letters: ‹G›, ‹O›, ‹U›, ‹L›, ‹F›, and ‹B›.
· All capital letters start at the top.
· The students trace inside the outline letters, and then write over the dotted letters. Saying the letter names as they do so.

Capitals and lower-case letters
· The students join each upper-case letter to its corresponding lower-case letter.
· Then they trace inside the outline letters, using a different color for each pair of letters.

Further blending practice
· Write the following list of words on the board, and blend them with the students:

> *south,*
> *yummy,*
> *pest,*
> *twig,*
> *hurry.*

Reading sentences
· Write the following sentences on the board, pointing out the tricky words, and blending any unknown words with the students.
1. Pack all your things in the bag.
2. Dad poaches eggs for our lunch.
3. Come and feed ducks with me.
4. She has three pet rabbits.

Comprehension

Flash cards
• Practice some of the basic 42 sounds, plus ⟨y⟩ as /ee/.

Read each phrase and draw a picture in the frame to illustrate it.

a spotty dog   a fluffy cat

a green frog   an oak tree

a big clock   a running man

12

Comprehension: read and draw
• Read the first phrase, *a spotty dog*, with the students.
• Point out that in the word *spotty*, the ⟨y⟩ makes an /ee/ sound.
• The students draw a picture in the picture frame to illustrate this phrase.
• The students read all the other phrases, and draw a picture to illustrate each one.
• The phrases are:
  a spotty dog
  a fluffy cat
  a green frog
  an oak tree
  a big clock
  a running man

Further blending practice
• Write the following list of words on the board, and blend them with the students:
  sleeping,
  waist,
  velvet,
  spooky,
  thump
  socks,
  amber,
  shopping,
  best,
  understand

Reading sentences
• Write the following sentences on the board, pointing out the tricky words, and blending any unknown words with the students.
1. Did he look at the paintings?
2. The clock was on the shelf.
3. We went to the park for a picnic.
4. He had a smart green scarf.
5. Her dog just fell off the bed!
6. She has a blue party dress.
7. Do cats go swimming?
8. The rabbit has black spots.
9. I got some stickers with that comic.
10. Can you come to the shops with us?

Tricky Words

Flash cards

- Practice the tricky words already taught, including *you, your, some,* and *come.*

Tricky words

- Introduce the three new tricky words: *said, here* and *there.* The students look at the words in flowers at the top of the page.
- Point out that *there* is spelled like *here,* but with a letter ‹t› at the beginning.
- The students could underline the ‹ere› at the end of these two words in purple, to remind them that this is the "tricky bit."
- The students write inside the outline letters using a yellow pen or pencil.

Look, copy, cover, write, check

- Look at the first word, *said,* with the students.
- Say the letter names (not the letter sounds) in that word. The students write over the dotted word *said.*
- Then the students cover up all instances of the word *said* on their page and try writing the word in the next column.
- Once the students have had one try at writing *said,* they check their spelling. Then they cover up all instances of the word *said* again, and have another go at writing the word in the final column.
- Repeat these steps for *here,* and *there.*

Writing activities

- Look at the first picture with the students, and say the word, *bed.*
- The students listen for the sounds in the word bed: /b/, /e/, /d/, and write over the dotted word *bed* underneath the picture.
- The students look at the rest of the pictures.
- They say each word to themselves, and identify all the sounds in each word.
- The students write the words on the lines underneath the picture.
- There is a line for each sound in the words.
- The pictures are:
    bed, jam, six, web, fox, dog.

Further blending practice

- Write the following list of words on the board, and blend them with the students:
    clever,
    sorry,
    march,
    toddler,
    seven.

Reading sentences

- Write the following sentences on the board, pointing out the tricky words, and blending any unknown words with the students.
1. There are some happy children here.
2. Dad said that some dogs are silly.
3. There is a teddy on her bed.
4. Here is her blue hat.

Words and Sentences

Flash cards
- Practice some of the basic 42 sounds, plus ⟨y⟩ as /ee/.

Words and sentences
- Look at the picture, and discuss it with the students.
- Ask a child to say one sentence about the picture. For example, "The pond is big." "The duckling quacks at a frog." "I can see a boat."
- Choose some words to blend, and write them on the board; examples could be: *pond, frog, fish, duck.*
- Some words will be straightforward to spell by listening for the sounds, but others will need some guidance.
- Write the sentence:

  A boat sails on the pond.
- Discuss it as you write, saying:
- Sentences start with a capital letter.
- Capital letters are always tall.
- Listen for the sounds in the words.
- Leave a space between each word.
- Don't forget the period.
- All the students copy the sentence.
- Those students who can write independently can try to write some more sentences on their own.
- At this stage, the students only know one way of writing each sound, so their spelling will not always be accurate, but their work will be readable.
- Spelling gradually improves through reading many books, and learning the alternative letter-sound spellings.

Reading words
- The students read each pond-related word at the bottom of the page, and join it to the corresponding picture.

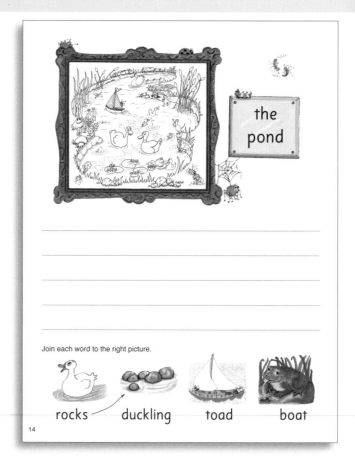

Join each word to the right picture.

rocks   duckling   toad   boat

14

Further blending practice
- Write the following list of words on the board, and blend them with the students:

  sticky,
  tricky,
  rocky,
  dizzy,
  start.

Reading sentences
- Write the following sentences on the board, pointing out the tricky words, and blending any unknown words with the students.
  1. She found some duck eggs.
  2. There is a crack in this egg.
  3. He painted his truck with black paint.
  4. Here is an empty box.

Alternatives: Double Letters

Flash cards
- Practice some of the basic 42 sounds, plus ⟨y⟩ as /ee/.

Alternatives: double letters
- Remind the students that when two letters that make the same sound are next to each other, the sound is only said once.
- Consonants are often doubled after a short vowel sound so that the "magic" from any subsequent vowels cannot "hop back" over the consonants and change the short vowel into a long vowel.
- The students look at the blending words at the top of the page.
- Read out the first word: *parrot*.
- The students listen for, and identify the first short vowel sound: /a/.
- The second vowel letter ⟨o⟩ makes a schwa sound in this word.
- Point out the double ⟨r⟩ in this word.
- Read the other words with the students:
  > *parrot, egg, bell, jazz, button,*
  > *kitten, huff, bill, doll, miss.*

Double letters rabbit
- Read the word in the first of the rabbit's patches: *rabbit*.
- Point out the short vowel, and the double ⟨b⟩ in this word.
- The students color the picture of the rabbit.
- Then they read the words in the rest of the rabbit's patches, and draw a picture in the patches to illustrate each word.
- The words (clockwise from *rabbit*) are:
  > *rabbit, dress, shell, carrot, puppet, duck.*

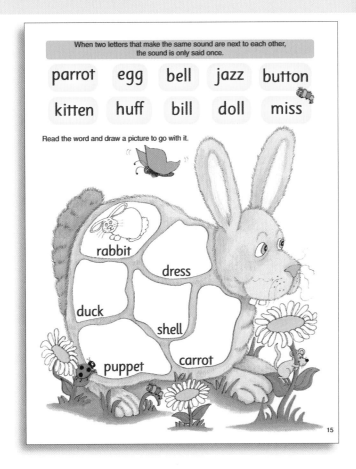

When two letters that make the same sound are next to each other, the sound is only said once.

parrot egg bell jazz button
kitten huff bill doll miss

Read the word and draw a picture to go with it.

rabbit / dress / duck / shell / puppet / carrot

15

Further blending practice
- Write the following list of words on the board, and blend them with the students:
  > *cannot,*
  > *puppet,*
  > *hiccup,*
  > *sniff,*
  > *tick.*

Reading sentences
- Write the following sentences on the board, pointing out the tricky words, and blending any unknown words with the students.
1. Your hands are very grubby.
2. She has a scarf around her neck.
3. There are green bugs on this log.
4. Here is a red toadstool.

Handwriting and Dictation

Flash cards
· Practice some of the basic 42 sounds, plus ⟨y⟩ as /ee/.

Dictation words
· Dictate the following words:

bat,
let,
cup,
swim,
flat,
much,
coin,
loud,
teeth,
herself.

· The students write these words on the lines in their *Phonics Student Books.*

The alphabet
· Look at a copy of the alphabet with the students.
· Say the alphabet, pointing to each letter as you say it, and pausing between each group: A-E, F-M, N-S, T-Z.

Handwriting
· Practice the sounds and formation of the letter ⟨j⟩, and the digraphs ⟨ai⟩, ⟨oa⟩, ⟨ie⟩, ⟨ee⟩, ⟨or⟩.
· Teach the students how to write the capital letter ⟨J⟩.
· The students trace inside the outline letters and then write over the dotted letters.
· Practice writing the digraphs ⟨ai⟩, ⟨oa⟩, ⟨ie⟩, ⟨ee⟩, and ⟨or⟩.
· The students trace inside the outline letters.

Capitals and lower-case letters
· Practice writing the capital letters: S, A, T, I, P, N, C, K, E, H, R, M, D, G, O, U, L, F, B and J.
· The students trace inside the outline letters and then join the capital letters around the edge to the lower-case letters in the middle.

Further blending practice
· Write the following list of words on the board, and blend them with the students:

hissing,
explain,
froth,
snap,
finish.

Reading sentences
· Write the following sentences on the board, pointing out the tricky words, and blending any unknown words with the students.
1. There are some big animals at the zoo.
2. She said that she missed her train.
3. Your cat has such a long tail.
4. The bees buzz happily.

Tricky Words

Flash cards
- Use the flashcards, or *Tricky Word Wall Flowers*, to practice the tricky words already taught, including *you, your, some, come, said, here,* and *there*.

Tricky words
- Introduce the new tricky word: *they*.
- The students look at the word in the yellow flower at the top of the page: *they*.
- The students write inside the outline letters using a yellow pen, or pencil.

Look, copy, cover, write, check
- Look at the word *they* with the students.
- Say the letter names (not the letter sounds) in that word. The students write over the dotted word *they*.
- Then the students cover up all instances of the word *they* on their page, and try writing the word in the next column.
- Once the students have had one try at writing *they*, they check their spelling. Then they cover up all instances of the word *they* again, and have another go at writing the word in the final column.

Choose the correct word
- Look at the first picture with the students.
- Read the words underneath the picture: *met, mat, man*. Ask the students if the picture illustrates *met, mat,* or *man*.
- The students choose the correct word, and write over the dotted word *mat* underneath the picture.
- The students look at the remaining pictures.
- They read the three words under each picture, and decide which word matches that picture.
- They write this word on the lines underneath.
- The pictures are:
  mat, dog, cup, egg, net, ant, tree, book, jar.

Further blending practice
- Write the following list of words on the board, and blend them with the students:
  flatter,
  traffic,
  letter,
  plum,
  umbrella.

Reading sentences
- Write the following sentences on the board, pointing out the tricky words, and blending any unknown words with the students.
  1. They do not drop litter.
  2. They all had pies for supper.
  3. The farmer was digging in the soil.
  4. I found all the pens in the box.

101

Words and Sentences

Flash cards
- Practice some of the basic 42 sounds, plus ⟨y⟩ as /ee/.

Words and sentences
- Look at the picture, and discuss it with the students.
- Ask a student to say one sentence about the picture. For example, "The bat is flying." "The moon and stars are shining." "I can see a fox."
- Choose some words to blend, and write them on the board; examples could be: *fox, moon, tree.*
- Some words will be straightforward to spell by listening for the sounds, but others will need some guidance.
- Write the sentence:
    The fox looks up at the moon.
- Discuss it as you write, saying:
- Sentences start with a capital letter.
- Capital letters are always tall.
- Listen for the sounds in the words.
- Leave a space between each word.
- Don't forget the period.
- All the students copy the sentence.
- Those students who can write independently can try to write some more sentences on their own.
- At this stage, the students only know one way of writing each sound, so their spelling will not always be accurate, but their work will be readable.
- Spelling gradually improves through reading many books, and learning the alternative letter-sound spellings.

Reading words
- The students read each word at the bottom of the page, and join it to the corresponding picture.

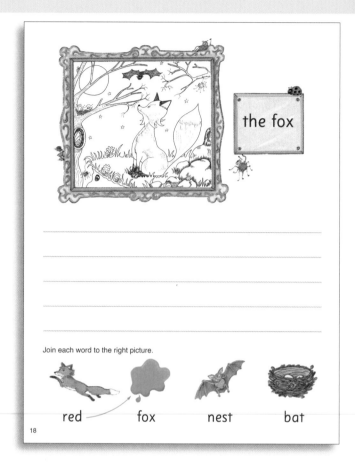

Join each word to the right picture.

red — fox   nest   bat

18

Further blending practice
- Write the following list of words on the board, and blend them with the students:
    jester,
    windy,
    empty,
    filling,
    sweeps.

Reading sentences
- Write the following sentences on the board, pointing out the tricky words, and blending any unknown words with the students.
1. We need butter and flour for our cooking.
2. The moth flaps its wings.
3. The trip to the zoo was fun.
4. Three men went out in a boat.

Alternatives: Hop-Over ‹e› Digraphs

Flash cards
- Practice some of the basic 42 sounds, plus ‹y› as /ee/.

Alternatives: hop-over ‹e› digraphs
- Explain to the students that, when a word has more than one vowel, the "magic" from the second vowel can sometimes hop back over one letter, and change the first short vowel into a long vowel.
- Point out that the "magic" can only hop back over one consonant.
- Encourage the students to say, "When two vowels go walking, the first does the talking."
- This saying explains both the vowel digraphs that the students already know, like ‹ai›, ‹ee›, ‹ie› ‹oa›, and ‹ue›, and the split digraphs like the ‹i_e› in *bike*.
- The students look at the blending words at the top of the page.
- Read the first word to the students: *smoke*.
- The students listen for, and identify, the long vowel sound: /oa/.
- Point out the letters that make the /oa/ sound in the word *smoke*, ‹o_e›.
- Read the other words with the students:
    smoke, use, game, eve, mule,
    hive, these, joke, shave, side.
- Point out to the students that they know one way of writing the long vowels: ‹ai›, ‹ee›, ‹ie›, ‹oa›, and ‹ue›.
- Explain to the students that there are other ways to write these long vowel sounds.
- Write ‹a_e›, ‹e_e›, ‹i_e›, ‹o_e›, and ‹u_e› on the board, and get the students to say each letter sound as you point to it.

Vowel forest trees
- The students look at the words written in the leaves.
- Read out the first word: *Pete*.
- The students listen for, and identify, the long vowel sound: /ee/.
- Ask the students which letters are making the /ee/ sound in this word.

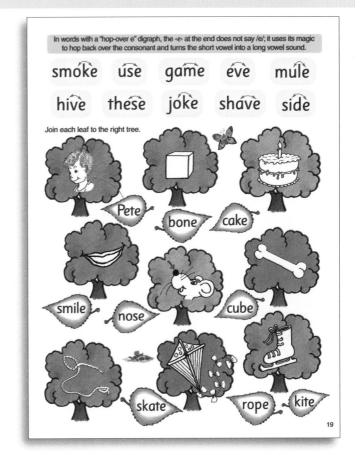

- They should say the ‹e_e› digraph.
- The students circle the letters making the /ee/ sound.
- Point out that the word *Pete* is joined to the tree containing the picture of *Pete*. The students color in this picture.
- The students read the remaining words. They circle the letters making the long vowel sound in each word, and then join the word to the matching picture.
- When they have joined all the words to the correct pictures, the students can color the pictures.

Reading sentences
- Write the following sentences on the board, pointing out the tricky words, and blending any unknown words with the students.
1. Do not argue with the queen.
2. We made a cake with blackberry jam.
3. She lent me her skates.
4. There are a hundred bees in the hive.

Handwriting and Dictation

Flash cards
· Practice the basic 42 sounds, plus ‹y› as /ee/.

Dictation words
· Dictate the following words:

    hid,
    hum,
    ant,
    from,
    slip,
    shed,
    them,
    chain,
    harp,
    mushroom.

· The students write these words on the lines in their *Phonics Student Books.*

The alphabet
· Look at a copy of the alphabet with the students.
· Say the alphabet, pointing to each letter as you say it, and pausing between each group.

Handwriting
· Practice writing the capital letters:
S, A, T, I, P, N, C, K, E, H, R, M, D.
· The students trace inside the outline letters in the boxes.
· If the outline letter is a lower-case letter, the students write the corresponding capital letter in the second half of the box, as with the example, ‹S›. If the outline letter is a capital letter, the students write the corresponding lower-case letter in the second half of the box.
· At the bottom of the page, the students practice writing the lower-case letters ‹z›, ‹w› and ‹v›.
· Teach the students how to write the capital letters ‹Z›, ‹W› and ‹V›. The students trace inside the outline letters, and write over the dotted letters.

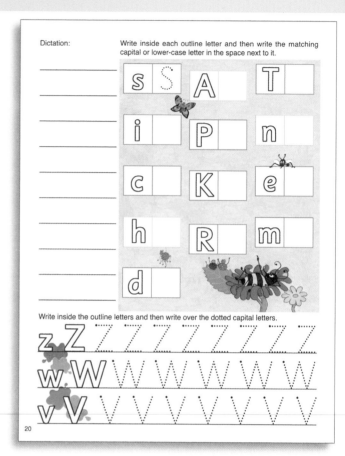

Further blending practice
· Write the following list of words on the board, and blend them with the students:

    spoon,
    sour,
    tenth,
    eggshell,
    throat.

Reading sentences
· Write the following sentences on the board, pointing out the tricky words, and blending any unknown words with the students.
1. I can fix the bench in the shed.
2. She hangs up her coat on the peg.
3. This is a long road.
4. She points to the clouds.

Tricky Words

Flash cards
- Practice the tricky words already taught, including *you, your, some, come, said, here, there,* and *they*.

Tricky words
- Introduce the three new tricky words: *go, no,* and *so*. The students look at these words in the yellow flowers at the top of the page.
- Point out that, judging from their spelling, these words should have the short vowel sound, /o/ at the end, but they actually have the long vowel sound /oa/.
- Encourage the students to say:
 "If one way doesn't work, try the other."
- The students should first say the words as they are spelled, and if this pronunciation does not make sense, they should try saying the word with the long vowel sound instead.
- The students could underline the ‹o› at the end of each of these words in purple, to remind them that this is the "tricky bit."
- The students write inside the outline letters using a yellow pen or pencil.

Word search
- The students read the tricky words written in the yellow flowers surrounding the grid.
- They search for each word in the grid and circle the word when they find it.

Look, copy, cover, write, check
- Look at the first word, *go,* with the students.
- Say the letter names (not the letter sounds) in that word. The students write over the dotted word *go*.
- Then the students cover up all instances of the word *go* on their page, and try writing the word in the next column.
- Once the students have had one try at writing *go*, they check their spelling. Then they cover up all instances of the word *go* again, and have another go at writing the word in the final column.
- Repeat these steps with the words *no,* and *so*.

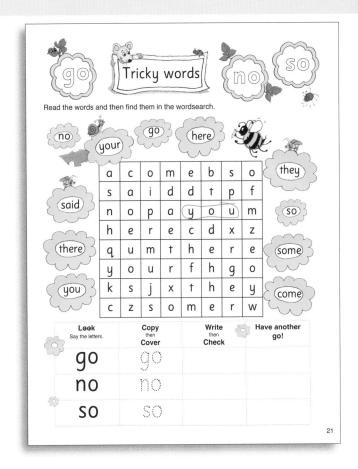

Further blending practice
- Write the following list of words on the board, and blend them with the students:

sprain,	*shame,*
feel,	*theme,*
like,	*truck,*
flick,	*smell,*
cherry,	*poppy.*

Reading sentences
- Write the following sentences on the board, pointing out the tricky words, and blending any unknown words with the students.
1. It is so hilly here.
2. They will go and ring the bells soon.
3. No, you cannot go out alone.
4. They can go to the farm in March.

Words and Sentences

Flash cards

- Practice some of the basic 42 sounds, plus ⟨y⟩ as /ee/, ⟨a_e⟩, ⟨e_e⟩, ⟨i_e⟩, ⟨o_e⟩, ⟨u_e⟩.

Words and sentences

- Look at the picture, and discuss it with the students.
- Ask a student to say one sentence about the picture. For example, "I can see a crab." "The fish is swimming." "There is a shell in the weeds."
- Choose some words to blend. Write them on the board; examples could be: *fish, crab, weeds.*
- Some words will be straightforward to spell by listening for the sounds, but others will need some guidance.
- Write the sentence:

  That fish has a long tail.
- Discuss it as you write, saying:
- Sentences start with a capital letter.
- Capital letters are always tall.
- Listen for the sounds in the words.
- Leave a space between each word.
- Don't forget the period.
- All the students copy the sentence.
- Those students who can write independently can try to write some more sentences on their own.
- At this stage, the students only know one way of writing each sound, so their spelling will not always be accurate, but their work will be readable.
- Spelling gradually improves through reading many books, and learning the alternative letter-sound spellings.

Reading words

- The students read each word at the bottom of the page, and join it to the corresponding fish picture.
- If the students have trouble with this activity, encourage them to join up the words they know, and then see what they are left with.

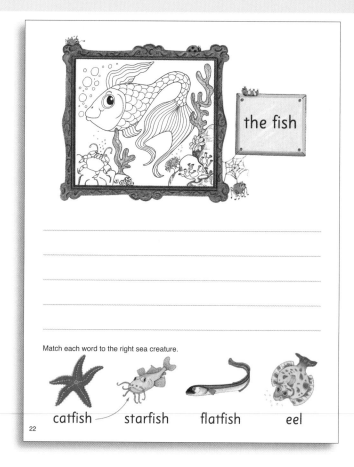

the fish

Match each word to the right sea creature.

catfish   starfish   flatfish   eel

22

Further blending practice

- Write the following list of words on the board, and blend them with the students:

  stale,

  stile,

  milkshake,

  cloth,

  mole.

Reading sentences

- Write the following sentences on the board, pointing out the tricky words, and blending any unknown words with the students.

  1. The boat is so strong.
  2. We must go and sort out the books.
  3. The roof shook in the storm.
  4. There are no fish in this pond.

Handwriting and Dictation

Flash cards
• Practice some of the basic 42 sounds, plus ⟨y⟩ as /ee/, ⟨a_e⟩, ⟨e_e⟩, ⟨i_e⟩, ⟨o_e⟩, ⟨u_e⟩.

Dictation words
• Dictate the following words:

> van,
>
> jug,
>
> yes,
>
> west,
>
> jump,
>
> shin,
>
> thud,
>
> cheep,
>
> quilt,
>
> starfish.

• The students write these words on the lines in their *Phonics Student Books*.

The alphabet
• Look at a copy of the alphabet with the students.
• Say the alphabet, pointing to each letter as you say it, and pausing between each group.

Outline letters
• At the bottom of the page, practice writing the lower-case letters ⟨y⟩, ⟨x⟩ and ⟨q⟩.
• Teach the students how to write the capital letters ⟨Y⟩, ⟨X⟩ and ⟨Q⟩.
• The students trace inside the outline letters and write over the dotted letters, making sure that they start each letter at the dot.

Handwriting
• Practice writing the capital letters: G, O, U, L, F, B, J, Z, W, V, Y, X, Q. The students trace inside the outline letters in the boxes.
• If the outline letter is a capital letter, the students write the corresponding lower-case letter in the second half of the box, as with the example, ⟨g⟩.

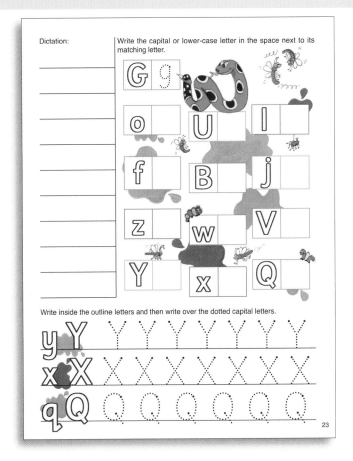

• If the outline letter is a lower-case letter, the students write the corresponding capital letter in the second half of the box.

Further blending practice
• Write the following list of words on the board, and blend them with the students:
raincoat, shouting, fire, shade, charming.

Reading sentences
• Write the following sentences on the board, pointing out the tricky words, and blending any unknown words with the students.
1. This foal was born in the spring.
2. She spoke so quickly.
3. The thorn on this twig is very sharp.
4. This popcorn is too sweet.

Tricky Words

Flash cards

- Use the flashcards, or *Tricky Word Wall Flowers*, to practice the tricky words already taught, including *you, your, some, come, said, here, there, they, go, no,* and *so.*

Tricky words

- Introduce the three new tricky words: *my, one,* and *by.*
- The students look at the words in flowers at the side of the page: *my, one,* and *by.*
- Point out that the word *by* is the same as *my,* but with a ‹b› at the beginning.
- The students could underline the ‹y› at the end of both of these words in purple, to remind them that this is the "tricky bit."
- The students write inside the word *my* using a yellow pencil, and the words *one* and *by* using a red pencil.

Look, copy, cover, write, check

- Look at the first word, *my,* with the students.
- Say the letter names (not the letter sounds) in that word. The students write over the dotted word *my.*
- Then the students cover up all instances of the word *my* on their page, and try writing the word in the next column.
- Once the students have had one try at writing *my,* they check their spelling. Then they cover up all instances of the word *my* again, and have another go at writing the word in the final column.
- Repeat these steps with the words *one,* and *by.*

Writing activities

- Look at the first picture with the students, and say the word, *cue.*
- The students listen for the sounds in the word *cue*: /c/, /ue/.
- They write over the dotted word *cue* underneath the picture.
- The students look at the rest of the pictures. They say each word to themselves, and identify all the sounds in each word.

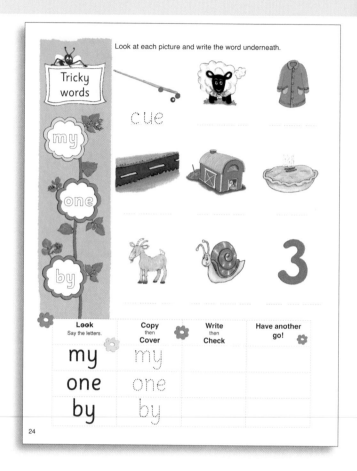

- The students write the words on the lines underneath the picture.
- There is a line for each sound in the words.
- A longer line indicates that a digraph is needed.
- The pictures are:
  cue, sheep, coat,
  road, barn, pie,
  goat, snail, three.

Further blending practice

- Write the following list of words on the board, and blend them with the students:
  smoke, hive, kite, date, perfume.
- Write the following sentences on the board, pointing out the tricky words, and blending any unknown words with the students.
  1. My garden is bigger than this one.
  2. They go by train to the theme park.
  3. You can take one cake with you.
  4. Did you invite my sister as well?

Words and Sentences

Flash cards
· Practice some of the basic 42 sounds, plus ‹y› as /ee/, ‹a_e›, ‹e_e›, ‹i_e›, ‹o_e›, ‹u_e›.

Words and sentences
· Look at the picture, and discuss it with the students.
· Ask a student to say one sentence about the picture. For example, "A bat is flying." "A moon shines in the dark." "I can see an owl."
· Choose some words to blend, and write them on the board; examples could be: *owl, moth, tree.*
· Some words will be straightforward to spell by listening for the sounds, but others will need some guidance:
· *Owl*: point out that the /ou/ sound at the beginning of this word is written ‹ow›.
· Write the sentence:
    The moth is on the tree.
· Discuss it as you write, saying:
· Sentences start with a capital letter.
· Capital letters are always tall.
· Listen for the sounds in the words.
· Leave a space between each word.
· Don't forget the period.
· All the students copy the sentence.
· Those students who can write independently can try to write some more sentences on their own.
· At this stage, the students only know one way of writing each sound, so their spelling will not always be accurate, but their work will be readable.
· Spelling gradually improves through reading many books, and learning the alternative letter-sound spellings.

Reading words
· The students read each night time word at the bottom of the page, and join it to the corresponding picture.

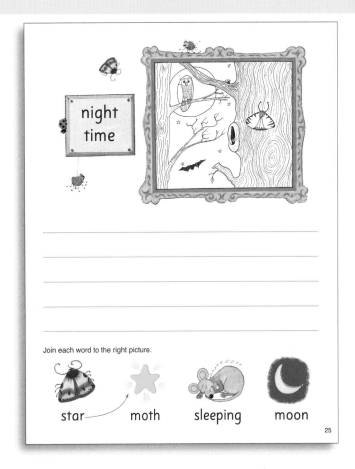

night time

Join each word to the right picture.

star   moth   sleeping   moon

25

Further blending practice
· Write the following list of words on the board, and blend them with the students:
    file,
    inflate,
    athlete,
    flagpole,
    liquid.

Reading sentences
· Write the following sentences on the board, pointing out the tricky words, and blending any unknown words with the students.
1. We can sweep up with this broom.
2. They run by the river.
3. My dog has a blue collar.
4. In this tank there are twenty fish, one squid and three lobsters.

Alternatives: ‹ay› and ‹oy›

Flash cards
- Practice some of the basic 42 sounds, plus ‹y› as /ee/, ‹a_e›, ‹e_e›, ‹i_e›, ‹o_e›, ‹u_e›.

Alternatives: ‹ay› as /ai /
- When an /ai/ sound comes at the end of a word, it is usually written ‹ay›.
- Say the word *stay*.
- Ask the students what sound they hear at the end of this word. The students should say an /ai/ sound.
- Ask them how an /ai/ sound is usually written. The students should say with an ‹a› and an ‹i›.
- Explain that the letter ‹i› is shy, and does not like to come at the end of words in English, so its cousin, "toughy ‹y›" takes its place.
- Explain that when the /ai/ sound is at the end of a word it is usually written ‹ay›, as in the words *day* and *pay*.
- The students write inside the outline digraphs ‹ai› and ‹ay› on their page.

Alternatives: ‹oy› as /oi/
- When an /oi/ sound comes at the end of a word, it is usually written ‹oy›.
- Say the word *joy*.
- Ask the students what sound they hear at the end of this word. The students should say an /oi/ sound.
- Ask them how an /oi/ sound is usually written. The students should say with an ‹o› and an ‹i›.
- Remind the students that the letter ‹i› is shy, and does not like to come at the end of words in English, so its cousin, "toughy ‹y›" takes its place.
- Explain that when the /oi/ sound is at the end of a word it is usually written ‹oy›, as in the words *annoy* and *boy*.
- The students write inside the outline digraphs ‹oi› and ‹oy› on their page.

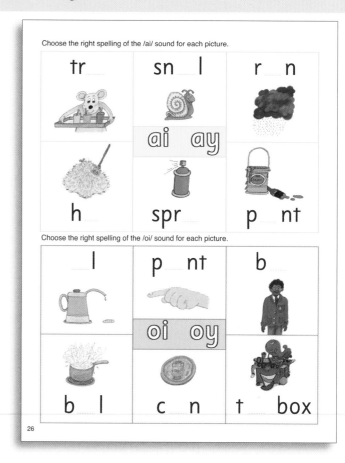

Choose the spelling:
- Look at the pictures with the students.
- Say the word *tray*, so that the students can listen for where the /ai/ sound comes in the word.
- The students decide how tray is spelled and write either ‹ai› or ‹ay› in the space.
- The students continue with the rest of the words, listening for the position of the /ai/ and /oi/ sounds and completing the each word by writing the correct spellings of the /ai/ and /oi/ sounds on the lines.
- The words are:
    tray, snail, rain,
    hay, spray, paint;

    oil, point, boy,
    boil, coin, toy box.

Handwriting and Dictation

Flash cards
- Practice some of the basic 42 sounds, plus ‹y› as /ee/, ‹a_e›, ‹e_e›, ‹i_e›, ‹o_e›, ‹u_e›.

Dictation words
- Dictate the following words:

  log,
  jam,
  bat,
  loft,
  hunt,
  shut,
  chest,
  tooth,
  tree,
  oilcan.
- The students write these words on the lines in their *Phonics Student Books*.

The alphabet
- Look at the alphabet with the students.
- Say the alphabet, pointing to each letter as you say it, and pausing between each group.

Handwriting
- The students practice writing the capital letters.
- On this page, the capital letters are in alphabetical order. The students write inside the outline letters, using a red pencil for the letters A-E, a yellow pencil for the letters F-M, a green pencil for the letters N-S, and a blue pencil for the letters T-Z.

Capitals and lower-case letters
- The students write the lower-case letter next to each capital letter.

Further blending practice
- Write the following list of words on the board, and blend them with the students:

  sometimes,
  dragonflies,
  choke,
  crane,
  tunes.

Reading sentences
- Write the following sentences on the board, pointing out the tricky words, and blending any unknown words with the students.
1. He felt unwell and had to go home.
2. She made a bee costume for the party.
3. My cat had one kitten.
4. The ducklings jumped into the pond one by one.

Tricky Words

Flash cards
· Practice the tricky words already taught, including *you, your, some, come, said, here, there, they, go, no, so, my, one,* and *by.*

Tricky words
· Introduce the two new tricky words: *only,* and *old*. The students look at the words in red flowers at the top of the page: *only,* and *old.*
· The students write inside the outline letters using a red pencil.

Look, copy, cover, write, check
· Look at the first word, *only*, with the students.
· Say the letter names (not the letter sounds) in that word. The students write over the dotted word *only*.
· Then the students cover up all instances of the word *only* on their page, and try writing the word in the next column.
· Once the students have had one try at writing *only*, they check their spelling. Then they cover up all instances of the word *only* again, and have another go at writing the word in the final column.
· Repeat these steps with the word *old.*

Animal anagrams
· Look at the first picture with the students, and say the word, *ant.*
· The students listen carefully and try to work the sounds in this word, and the order in which the sounds come.
· The students look at the letters at the side of the picture, and decide which order the letters should be placed in the word.
· The students write the word on the lines underneath the picture of the ant.
· The students solve the remaining anagrams in the same way.
· There is a line for each sound in the word. The slightly longer lines indicate a digraph is needed.
· The pictures are: *ant, snail, goat, sheep, shark, crab, yak, chick, fox.*

Further blending practice
· Write the following list of words on the board and blend them with the students:
> *wife,*
> *lake,*
> *choke,*
> *plane,*
> *safely.*

Reading sentences
· Write the following sentences on the board, pointing out the tricky words and blending any unknown words with the students.
1. My old teddy is lonely.
2. I only need some wire.
3. She only gave me five grapes.
4. Inside the shell is an old crab.

112

Words and Sentences

Flash cards
- Practice some of the basic 42 sounds, plus ‹y› as /ee/, ‹a_e›, ‹e_e›, ‹i_e›, ‹o_e›, ‹u_e›, ‹ay›, ‹oy›.

Words and sentences
- Discuss the ducks picture with the students.
- Ask a students to say one sentence about the picture. For example, "The ducks are quacking." "The man has caught a fish." "I can see some ducks."
- Choose some words to blend and write them on the board; examples could be: *ducks, quack, fisherman.*
- Some words will be straightforward to spell by listening for the sounds, but others will need some guidance.
- Write the sentence:
    The ducks on the pond are quacking.
- Discuss it as you write, saying:
- Sentences start with a capital letter.
- Capital letters are always tall.
- Listen for the sounds in the words.
- Leave a space between each word.
- Don't forget the period.
- All the students copy the sentence.
- Those students who can write independently can try to write some more sentences on their own.
- At this stage, the students only know one way of writing each sound, so their spelling will not always be accurate, but their work will be readable.
- Spelling gradually improves through reading many books, and learning the alternative letter-sound spellings.

Animal anagrams
- Look at the first picture with the students, and say the word, *duck.*
- The students listen carefully and try to work the sounds in the word, and the order in which the sounds come.
- The students look at the letters at the side of the picture, and decide which order the letters should be placed in the word.

Animal anagrams: put the letters in the right order.

c u d k   g r o f   sh i f

29

- The students write the word on the lines underneath the picture of the duck.
- The students solve the remaining anagrams in the same way.
- There is a line for each sound in the word. The slightly longer lines indicate that digraph is needed.
- The pictures are: *duck, frog, fish.*

Further blending practice
- Write the following list of words on the board, and blend them with the students:
    daytime, toys, employ, playing, pays.
- Write the following sentences on the board, pointing out the tricky words, and blending any unknown words with the students.
    1. He was such a good boy on Tuesday.
    2. We made pots from clay.
    3. The plane is still on the runway.
    4. The snail left a silver trail.

Alternatives: ‹ee› and ‹ea›

Flash cards

- Practice some of the basic 42 sounds, plus ‹y› as /ee/, ‹a_e›, ‹e_e›, ‹i_e›, ‹o_e›, ‹u_e›, ‹ay›, ‹oy›.

Alternatives: ‹ea› as /ee/

- Say the word *free,* and ask the students what sound they can hear at the end of this word. The students should say an /ee/ sound.
- Ask the students how an /ee/ sound is usually written; they should say ‹ee›.
- Write *free* on the board, and point out the ‹ee› at the end.
- Now say the word *eve,* and ask the students what sound they can hear at the beginning of this word. The students should say an /ee/ sound.
- Write *eve* on the board, and point out the ‹e_e› digraph that makes the /ee/ sound in this word.
- Remind the students that the /ee/ sound can be written in more than one way.
- Point to the words *free* and *eve* on the board, and tell the students that they already know two ways to write the /ee/ sound, ‹ee› and ‹e_e›.
- Now say the word *leap,* and ask the students what sound they can hear in the middle of this word. Again, the students should say an /ee/ sound.
- Tell the students that, in the word *leap,* the /ee/ sound is not written ‹ee› or ‹e_e›, but ‹ea›.
- Write *leap* on the board, and point out the ‹ea› in the middle.
- Blend all three words with the students, pointing to the letters as you say each sound.
- The students look at the blending words at the top of their page.
- Read the blending words with the students, and point out the letters making the ‹ee› sound in each word.
- The words are:
  three, teeth, tree,
  leaf, feet, sheep,
  seal, bee, sea.

Word and picture matching

- The students look at the pictures in the grid at the bottom of the page.
- They read each blending word again, and write it in the grid, on the lines underneath the corresponding picture.
- There is a line for each of the sounds in the word. A longer line indicates that a digraph is needed.

Reading sentences

- Write the following sentences on the board, pointing out the tricky words, and blending any unknown words with the students.
  1. There are some old bikes in this shed.
  2. We can only cross the sea in the boats.
  3. This hill is far too steep.
  4. I made some tea for my sister.

Handwriting and Dictation

Flash cards
- Practice some of the basic 42 sounds, plus ‹y› as /ee/, ‹a_e›, ‹e_e›, ‹i_e›, ‹o_e›, ‹u_e›, ‹ay›, ‹oy›.

Dictation words
- Dictate the following words:
    big,
    bag,
    men,
    sand,
    belt,
    wish,
    north,
    lunch,
    sort,
    without.
- The students write these words on the lines in their *Phonics Student Books.*

The alphabet
- Look at the alphabet with the students.
- Say the alphabet, pointing to each letter as you say it, and pausing between each group.

| A B C D E |
| F G H I J K L M |
| N O P Q R S |
| T U V W X Y Z |

Handwriting
- The students practice writing the capital letters for the first half of the alphabet.
- Take down, or cover, any visible copies of the alphabet so that the students have to remember how the capital letters are written.
- The students write inside each lower-case outline letter, and then write the corresponding capital letter next to it.
- They use a red pencil for the letters A-E, and a yellow pencil for the letters F-M.

Writing: ‹b› and ‹d›
- These two letters are often confused.
- One way to help prevent confusion is to remind the students how these letters are formed.

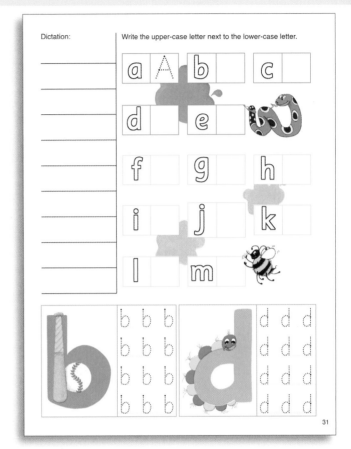

- Tell the students to remember that the letter ‹b› starts at the top with a down stroke (the bat), and then bounces up and round for the ball.
- Then say that the letter ‹d› is a "caterpillar c" letter, so it starts in the middle with a ‹c› shape.
- The students write over the letters ‹b› and ‹d› making sure that they start at the starting dots.

Further blending practice
- Write the following list of words on the board, and blend them with the students:
  railway, Sunday, joy, annoy, yesterday.
- Write the following sentences on the board, pointing out the tricky words, and blending any unknown words with the students.
  1. She had some toys in her bag.
  2. The boy only needs one pen.
  3. They spent the day at the park.
  4. The old man is very rich indeed.

Tricky Words

Flash cards
- Use the flashcards, or *Tricky Word Wall Flowers*, to practice the tricky words already taught, including *one, by, only,* and *old.*

Tricky words
- Introduce the two new tricky words: *like,* and *have.*
- The students look at the words in red flowers at the side of the page: *like,* and *have.*
- Point out that *like* is not really tricky because the students now know that ‹i_e› says /ie/.
- Explain that English words ending in a /v/ sound do not end with a letter ‹v›, but have a silent ‹e› added to the end.
- Point out the ‹e› at the end of the word *have.*
- The students write inside the outline letters using a red pencil.

Look, copy, cover, write, check
- Look at the first word, *like,* with the students.
- Say the letter names (not the letter sounds) in that word. The students write over the dotted word *like.*
- Then the students cover up all instances of the word *like* on their page, and try writing the word in the next column.
- Once the students have had one try at writing *like,* they check their spelling. Then they cover up all instances of the word *like* again, and have another go at writing the word in the final column.
- Repeat these steps with the word *have.*

Reviewing ‹b› and ‹d›
- Practice the formation of the letters ‹b› and ‹d›.
- The students look at the pictures.
- Say the first word, *bed,* to the children.
- The students listen for the sounds /b/ and /d/.
- They trace over the dotted ‹b› and ‹d› in the word *bed,* making sure that they start at the starting dots.
- The students say the remaining ‹b› and ‹d› words to themselves, and add the correct letters to each word.

Further blending practice
- Write the following list of words on the board, and blend them with the students:
  - *crayons,*
  - *joystick,*
  - *underneath,*
  - *neaten,*
  - *shampoo.*

Reading sentences
- Write the following sentences on the board, pointing out the tricky words, and blending any unknown words with the students.
1. We like to have a holiday in May.
2. The boys like to play with toy cars.
3. They have a long playtime.
4. Do you like tea or coffee?

Words and Sentences

Flash cards

- Practice some of the basic 42 sounds, plus ‹y› as /ee/, ‹a_e›, ‹e_e›, ‹i_e›, ‹o_e›, ‹u_e›, ‹ay›, ‹oy›, ‹ea›.

Words and sentences

- Look at the picture, and discuss it with the students.
- Ask a student to say one sentence about the picture. For example, "I can see a queen." "She has a long cloak." "The queen waves."
- Choose some words to blend, and write them on the board; examples could be: *queen, cloak, wave.*
- Some words will be straightforward to spell by listening for the sounds, but others will need some guidance:
- *Wave*: point out that the /ai/ sound in the word *wave* is spelt ‹a_e›.
- Write the sentence:

    The queen has a red cloak.

- Discuss it as you write, saying:
- Sentences start with a capital letter.
- Capital letters are always tall.
- Listen for the sounds in the words.
- Leave a space between each word.
- Don't forget the period.
- All the students copy the sentence. Those students who can write independently can try to write some more sentences on their own.
- At this stage, the students only know one way of writing each sound, so their spelling will not always be accurate, but their work will be readable. Spelling gradually improves through reading many books, and learning the alternative letter-sound spellings.

Reviewing ‹b› and ‹d›

- Remind the students that the letter ‹b› starts at the top with a down stroke (the bat), and then bounces up and around for the ball, whilst the letter ‹d› is a "caterpillar c" letter, so it starts in the middle with a ‹c› shape.
- The students write inside the outline letters ‹b› and ‹d›, and trace over the dotted letters, ensuring that they start at the starting dots.

Practice writing ‹b› and ‹d›.

Further blending practice

- Write the following list of words on the board, and blend them with the students:

    peanuts,
    sunshine,
    salute,
    speaking,
    seagull.

Reading sentences

- Write the following sentences on the board, pointing out the tricky words, and blending any unknown words with the students.
1. Our teacher likes us to be good.
2. Do you like peaches?
3. Have you got a torch?
4. We have toads and frogs in the stream in our garden.

Alternatives: ‹ie›, ‹y›, and ‹i_e›

Flash cards
• Practice some of the basic 42 sounds, plus ‹y› as /ee/, ‹a_e›, ‹e_e›, ‹i_e›, ‹o_e›, ‹u_e›, ‹ay›, ‹oy›, ‹ea›.

Alternatives: ‹ie›, ‹y›, and ‹i_e› as /ie/
• Say the word *pie,* and ask the students what sound they can hear at the end of this word. The students should say an /ie/ sound.
• Ask the students how an /ie/ sound is usually written; they should say ‹ie›.
• Write the word *pie* on the board.
• Explain that the /ie/ sound can be written in a number of different ways.
• Write the different spellings for the /ie/ sound on the board: ‹ie› as in *pie,* ‹y› as in *my,* and ‹i_e› as in *like.*
• Remind the students that they already know the ‹ie› spelling for the /ie/ sound, and they know that a "hop-over e" turns a short vowel into a long vowel, so they can also read words containing ‹i_e›.
• Remind the students of the tricky words *my* and *by.* Point out that, in these words, the ‹y› makes an /ie/ sound.
• The students look at the words at the top of their page.
• Read the words with the students, and point out the letters making the /ie/ sound in each word.
• The words are:
> *pie, lie, tried, cries, tie, die;*
> *line, time, sunshine, drive, slide;*
> *my, flying, shy, sky, drying, try.*

Reading activities
• The students read the words in the stars, and draw a picture to illustrate them in the adjoining moons.
• The words in the stars are:
> *tie, pie, fly, sky,*
> *bike, kite, slide, crying.*

The /ie/ sound can be written ‹ie›, ‹i_e›, or ‹y›.

pie   lie   line   time   my   flying
tried   cries   sunshine   shy   sky
tie   die   drive   slide   drying   try

Read the words in the stars and draw pictures in the moons to illustrate each word.

tie   pie
fly   sky
bike   kite
slide   crying

34

Further blending practice
• Write the following list of words on the board, and blend them with the students:
> *nylon,*
> *satisfy,*
> *spy,*
> *pylon,*
> *sly.*

Reading sentences
• Write the following sentences on the board, pointing out the tricky words, and blending any unknown words with the students.
1. We must eat the crusts too.
2. The roses have thorns on the stem.
3. I like the green socks best.
4. The boy is unhappy about the hole in his jumper.

Handwriting and Dictation

Flash cards
- Practice some of the basic 42 sounds, plus ‹y› as /ee/, ‹a_e›, ‹e_e›, ‹i_e›, ‹o_e›, ‹u_e›, ‹ay›, ‹oy›, ‹ea›.

Dictation words
- Dictate the following words:
  - *dug,*
  - *mix,*
  - *leg,*
  - *help,*
  - *soft,*
  - *rang,*
  - *this,*
  - *shout,*
  - *coach,*
  - *raindrop.*
- The students write these words on the lines in their *Phonics Student Books.*

The alphabet
- Look at the alphabet with the students.
- Say the alphabet, pointing to each letter as you say it, and pausing between each group.

Handwriting
- The students practice writing the capital letters for the second half of the alphabet.
- Take down, or cover, any visible copies of the alphabet so that the students have to remember how the capital letters are written.
- The students write inside each lower-case outline letter, and then write the corresponding capital letter next to it.
- They use a green pencil for the letters N-S, and a blue pencil for the letters T-Z.

Read and draw
- The students read each sentence, and illustrate it in the frame above.
- The sentences are:
  The sun is hot.   She is running.

Dictation:

Write the upper-case letter next to the lower-case letter.

Read each sentence and draw a picture in the frame to illustrate it.

The sun is hot.   She is running.

35

Further blending practice
- Write the following list of words on the board, and blend them with the students:
  - *bedtime,*
  - *meaning,*
  - *flashing,*
  - *flicking,*
  - *amused.*

Reading sentences
- Write the following sentences on the board, pointing out the tricky words, and blending any unknown words with the students.
1. We have a set of silver teaspoons at home.
2. The king and queen have a throne each.
3. Dad cooks shrimps on the grill.
4. I like my blue dress best.

Tricky Words

Flash cards
· Use the flashcards, or *Tricky Word Wall Flowers*, to practice the tricky words already taught, including *one, by, only, old, like,* and *have.*

Tricky words
· Introduce the two new tricky words: *live,* and *give.*
· The students look at the words in red flowers at the top of the page: *live,* and *give.*
· Remind the students that English words ending in a /v/ sound do not end with a letter ‹v›, but have a silent ‹e› added to the end.
· Point out the ‹e› at the end of the words *live* and *give.*
· The students write inside the outline letters using a red pencil.

Tricky flowers
· The students write over the dotted words *like, have, live,* and *give,* and color the flowers red.

Look, copy, cover, write, check
· Look at the first word, *live,* with the students.
· Say the letter names (not the letter sounds) in that word. The students write over the dotted word *live.*
· Then the students cover up all instances of the word *live* on their page, and try writing the word in the next column.
· Once the students have had one try at writing *live,* they check their spelling. Then they cover up all instances of the word *live* again, and have another go at writing the word in the final column.
· Repeat these steps with the word *give.*

Word and picture matching
· Look at the first picture with the students, and read the two words written underneath, *cub* and *cube.*
· Ask the students if the picture shows a *cub* or a *cube.*
· They should say a *cube.*

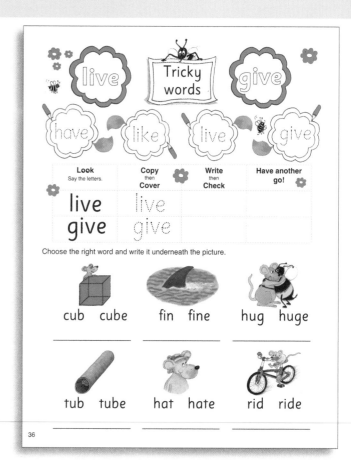

· The students write this word on the line underneath the picture.
· The students repeat these steps with the remaining words and pictures, writing the correct word on the line each time.
· Point out that the ‹g› in the word *huge* makes a /j/ sound
· The words are:
> *cub,* **cube**; **fin**, *fine;* **hug**, *huge;*
> *tub,* **tube**; **hat**, *hate;* *rid,* **ride**.
· The words in bold type are the correct answers.

Reading sentences
· Write the following sentences on the board, pointing out the tricky words, and blending any unknown words with the students.
1. They live near the beach.
2. Can you give me some teabags?
3. Your teacher will give you a book to read.
4. Three slugs live underneath this rock.

Words and Sentences

Flash cards

- Practice some of the basic 42 sounds, plus ‹y› as /ee/ and /ie/, ‹a_e›, ‹e_e›, ‹i_e›, ‹o_e›, ‹u_e›, ‹ay›, ‹oy›, ‹ea›.

Words and sentences

- Look at the picture, and discuss it with the students.
- Ask a student to say one sentence about the picture. For example, "Some sharks swim in the sea." "The man digs in the sand." "I see a sunset."
- Choose some words to blend, and write them on the board; examples could be: *sea*, or *pirate*.
- Some words will be straightforward to spell by listening for the sounds, but others will need some guidance:
- *Pirate*: tell the students that the ‹i› in this word makes a long /ie/ sound. Remind them of the saying, "If the short vowel doesn't work, try the long vowel."
- It may help the students to use the "say it as it sounds" technique when spelling *pirate*. Encourage the students to pronounce the word as *pie-rat*, and tell them not to forget to put an ‹e› at the end.
- *Sea*: point out that the /ee/ sound in this word is spelled ‹ea›.
- Write the sentence:

  He went south and then north.

- Discuss it as you write, saying:
- Sentences start with a capital letter.
- Capital letters are always tall.
- Listen for the sounds in the words.
- Leave a space between each word.
- Don't forget the period.
- All the students copy the sentence. Those children who can write independently can try to write some more sentences on their own.
- At this stage, the students only know one way of writing each sound, so their spelling will not always be accurate, but their work will be readable. Spelling gradually improves through reading many books, and learning the alternative letter-sound spellings.

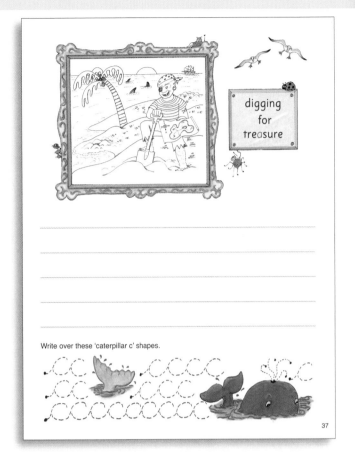

Write over these 'caterpillar c' shapes.

37

Letter Formation:

- Forming the "caterpillar c" letters can prove difficult for students.
- The students trace over the lines of "caterpillar c" shapes to complete the sea picture.
- Remind the students to stop at the top of the wave and come back round for the ‹c› shape.

Further blending practice

- Write the following list of words on the board, and blend them with the students: *bringing, jester, messy, windmill, easy.*
- Write the following sentences on the board, pointing out the tricky words, and blending any unknown words with the students.
1. Give your sister some lemonade.
2. The bonfire made the ground all black.
3. Do you live here?
4. Some tadpoles live in this pond.

Alternatives: ‹ow›

Flash cards
• Practice some of the basic 42 sounds, plus ‹y› as /ee/ and /ie/, ‹a_e›, ‹e_e›, ‹i_e›, ‹o_e›, ‹u_e›, ‹ay›, ‹oy›, ‹ea›.

Alternatives: ‹ow› as /oa/ and /ou/
• The digraph ‹ow› can make two sounds: the /oa/ sound, as in *yellow*, and the /ou/ sound, as in *owl*.
• Remind the students of the rule, "If one way doesn't work, try the other," which can help them to read words containing ‹ow›.
• Say the word *yellow,* and ask the students what sound they can hear at the end of this word. They should say an /oa/ sound.
• Ask the students how an /oa/ sound is usually written. They should say ‹oa›.
• Write the word *yellow* on the board. Explain that the /oa/ sound can also be written ‹ow› and point to the ‹ow› at the end of the word *yellow*.
• Now say the word *owl,* and ask the students what sound they can hear at the beginning of this word. They should say an /ou/ sound.
• Ask the students how an /ou/ sound is usually written. They should say ‹ou›.
• Write the word *owl* on the board. Explain that the /ou/ sound can also be written ‹ow›, and point to the ‹ow› at the beginning of the word *owl*.
• Explain to the students that the digraph ‹ow› has two sounds: it can make an /oa/, as in *yellow*, or /ou/, as in *owl*.
• When the students are reading words with an ‹ow› digraph, they should first try one pronunciation of ‹ow› to see if it makes a word. If it does not make a word, they should try reading the word with the other pronunciation of ‹ow›.
• The students look at the blending words on their page. First, read the /ou/ sound words with the students. Point out the letters making the /ou/ sound in each word.
• The /ou/ words are:
    shout, south, mouse, flour,
    town, brown, owl, flower.

• Now read the /oa/ sound words with the students. Point out the letters making the /oa/ sound in each word.
• The /oa/ words are:
    coat, toad, oak, soap,
    grow, borrow, yellow, slow.

Read and draw: clouds and boats
• The students read the words in the clouds and boats, and draw a picture to illustrate each one.
• The words are:
cloud, crown, owl (in clouds);
boat, arrow, snow (in boats).

Further blending practice
• Write the following list of words on the board, and blend them with the students:
shallow, drown, sparrow, shower, rainbow.

Handwriting and Dictation

Flash cards
- Practice some of the basic 42 sounds, plus ⟨y⟩ as /ee/ and /ie/, ⟨a_e⟩, ⟨e_e⟩, ⟨i_e⟩, ⟨o_e⟩, ⟨u_e⟩, ⟨ay⟩, ⟨oy⟩, ⟨ea⟩.

Dictation words
- Dictate the following words:

  run,   bad,
  lip,   just,
  melt,   moth,
  sang,   porch,
  rescue,   magpie.

- The students write these words on the lines in their *Phonics Student Books*.

The alphabet

- Look at the alphabet with the students.
- Say the alphabet, pointing to each letter as you say it and pausing between each group.

Handwriting
- The students practice writing the letters that start with a "caterpillar c" shape: ⟨c⟩, ⟨a⟩, ⟨d⟩, ⟨o⟩, ⟨g⟩, ⟨q⟩.

Writing activities
- Look at the first picture with the students, and say the word, *moon*.
- The students listen for the sounds in the word: /m/, /oo/, /n/.
- The students write the word on the lines underneath the picture.
- There is a line for each sound in the word. A longer line indicates that a digraph is needed.
- The students look at the rest of the pictures. They say each word to themselves, and identify all the sounds in each word.
- The pictures are: *moon, drum, queen*.
- When the students have finished writing, they can color the pictures.

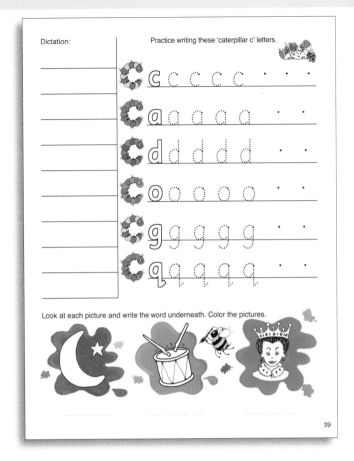

Further blending practice
- Write the following list of words on the board, and blend them with the students:

  caterpillar,
  beaming,
  away,
  stocky,
  flea.

Reading sentences
- Write the following sentences on the board, pointing out the tricky words, and blending any unknown words with the students.
1. Give me those beaten eggs.
2. Did you give your toys to her?
3. Do sheep live in houses or on farms?
4. We went on the bumper cars at the theme park.

Tricky Words

Flash cards
- Use the flashcards, or *Tricky Word Wall Flowers*, to practice the tricky words already taught, including *one, by, only, old, like, have, live,* and *give.*

Tricky words
- Introduce the two new tricky words: *little,* and *down.*
- The students look at the words in red flowers at the top of the page: *little,* and *down.*
- Point out that *down* is not really tricky, because the students now know that ‹ow› can say /ou/.
- The students write inside the outline letters using a red pencil.

Word search
- The students read the tricky words written in the red and yellow flowers surrounding the grid.
- They search for each word in the grid and circle the word when they find it.

Look, copy, cover, write, check
- Look at the first word, *little,* with the students.
- Say the letter names (not the letter sounds) in that word. The students write over the dotted word *little.*
- Then the students cover up all instances of the word *little* on their page, and try writing the word in the next column.
- Once the students have had one try at writing *little,* they check their spelling. Then they cover up all instances of the word *little* again, and have another go at writing the word in the final column.
- Repeat these steps with the word *down.*

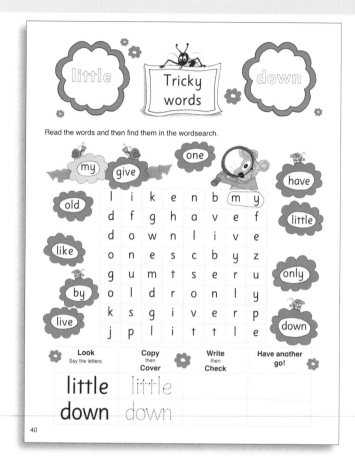

Further blending practice
- Write the following list of words on the board, and blend them with the students:
    - *frowning,*
    - *blow,*
    - *crowded,*
    - *mown,*
    - *how.*

Reading sentences
- Write the following sentences on the board, pointing out the tricky words, and blending any unknown words with the students.
  1. The little boy ran down the hill.
  2. We went up and down in the lift.
  3. Show me that little book.
  4. The little mole lives deep down underground.

Words and Sentences

Flash cards
- Practice some of the basic 42 sounds, plus ‹y› as /ee/ and /ie/, ‹a_e›, ‹e_e›, ‹i_e›, ‹o_e›, ‹u_e›, ‹ay›, ‹oy›, ‹ea›, ‹ow› as /oa/ and /ou/.

Words and sentences
- Look at the picture, and discuss it with the students.
- Ask a student to say one sentence about the picture. For example, "I can see a shark." "The shark is swimming." "The ship has sunk."
- Choose some words to blend, and write them on the board; examples could be: *shark, ship, wreck.*
- Some words will be straightforward to spell by listening for the sounds, but others will need some guidance:
- *Shark*: because *shark* has a long vowel sound, /ar/, only a ‹k› is needed to make the /ck/ sound at the end.
- *Wreck*: the word *wreck* has a silent ‹w› at the beginning. The /ck/ sound in *wreck* is spelled ‹ck› because *wreck* has the short vowel sound /e/.
- Write the sentence:
  The strong shark swam in and around the ship.
- Discuss it as you write, saying:
- Sentences start with a capital letter.
- Capital letters are always tall.
- Listen for the sounds in the words.
- Leave a space between each word.
- Don't forget the period.
- All the students copy the sentence.
- Those students who can write independently can try to write some more sentences on their own.
- At this stage, the students only know one way of writing each sound, so their spelling will not always be accurate, but their work will be readable. Spelling gradually improves through reading many books, and learning the alternative letter-sound spellings.

Reading words
- The students read each word at the bottom of the page, and join it to the matching picture.

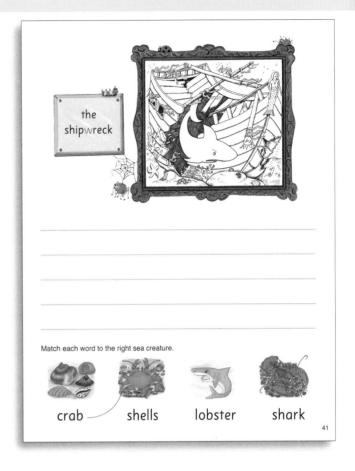

Match each word to the right sea creature.

crab   shells   lobster   shark

41

Further blending practice
- Write the following list of words on the board, and blend them with the students:
  allow,
  below,
  sunflower,
  throw,
  bowl.

Reading sentences
- Write the following sentences on the board, pointing out the tricky words, and blending any unknown words with the students.
1. The rude little clown was very funny.
2. Do you have a little sister?
3. The little frog jumps up and down.
4. There are some foxes outside.

Alternatives: ‹er›, ‹ir›, and ‹ur›

Flash cards
- Practice some of the basic 42 sounds, plus ‹y› as /ee/ and /ie/, ‹a_e›, ‹e_e›, ‹i_e›, ‹o_e›, ‹u_e›, ‹ay›, ‹oy›, ‹ea›, ‹ow› as /oa/ and /ou/.

Alternatives: ‹er›, ‹ir›, and ‹ur› as /er/
- Say the word *summer,* and ask the students what sound they can hear at the end of this word.
- They should say an /er/ sound.
- Ask the students how an /er/ sound is usually written.
- They should say ‹er›.
- Write the word *summer* on the board, and point to the ‹er› at the end.
- Explain to the students that the /er/ sound can also be written as ‹ir› or ‹ur›.
- Now say the word *bird,* and ask the students what sound they can hear in the middle of this word.
- They should say an /er/ sound.
- Write the word *bird* on the board.
- Explain that, in this word, the /er/ sound is spelled ‹ir›, and point to the ‹ir› in the middle of the word *bird.*
- Now say the word *burn,* and ask the students what sound they can hear in the middle of this word.
- Again, they should say an /er/ sound.
- Write the word *burn* on the board.
- Explain that, in this word, the /er/ sound is spelled ‹ur›, and point to the ‹ur› in the middle of the word *burn.*

Read and draw
- The students read the /er/ words in the gingerbread men, birds, and turkeys, and draw a picture to illustrate each one.
- The words are:
  summer, winter (in gingerbread men);
  skirt, shirt (in birds);
  purple, purse (in turkeys).

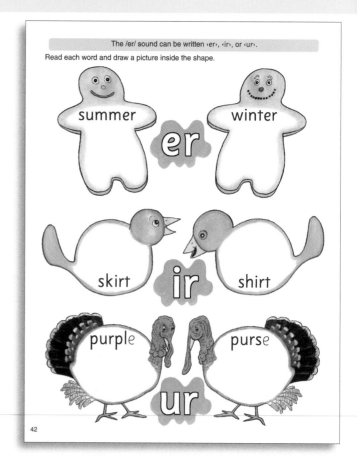

The /er/ sound can be written ‹er›, ‹ir›, or ‹ur›.

Read each word and draw a picture inside the shape.

summer winter **er**

skirt **ir** shirt

purple **ur** purse

42

Further blending practice
- Write the following list of words on the board, and blend them with the students:
  thirteen,
  burst,
  thirsty,
  turnip,
  first.

Reading sentences
- Write the following sentences on the board, pointing out the tricky words, and blending any unknown words with the students.
1. Your little skirt is much too short.
2. I had a surprise party on my birthday.
3. We had a barbecue and Dad burnt all the burgers.
4. My cat's fur is black and brown.

Handwriting and Dictation

Flash cards

· Practice some of the basic 42 sounds, plus ‹y› as /ee/ and /ie/, ‹a_e›, ‹e_e›, ‹i_e›, ‹o_e›, ‹u_e›, ‹ay›, ‹oy›, ‹ea›, ‹ow› as /oa/ and /ou/.

Dictation words

· Dictate the following words:

> *can,*
> *hen,*
> *pit,*
> *best,*
> *went,*
> *wing,*
> *chart,*
> *three,*
> *tried,*
> *toadstool.*

· The students write these words on the lines in their *Phonics Student Books*.

The alphabet

· Look at the alphabet with the students.
· Say the alphabet, pointing to each letter as you say it, and pausing between each group.

Handwriting

· The students practice writing the tall letters: ‹b›, ‹d›, ‹h›, ‹k›, ‹l›, ‹t›.

Finish the alphabet

· If you think the students will be able to remember the alphabet, cover any visible copies of the alphabet around the classroom before the students start this activity.
· The students fill in the missing capital letters to complete the alphabet.
· They use a red pencil to write the letters A-E, a yellow pencil for the letters F-M, a green pencil for the letters N-S, and a blue pencil for the letters T-Z.

Further blending practice

· Write the following list of words on the board, and blend them with the students:

> *powder,*
> *marrow,*
> *vowel,*
> *fellow,*
> *arrow.*

Reading sentences

· Write the following sentences on the board, pointing out the tricky words, and blending any unknown words with the students.
1. Did you throw that pillow at me?
2. There is a spooky shadow by that window.
3. My grandad grows carrots and marrows.
4. That little dog howls all day long.

Tricky Words

Flash cards
- Use the flashcards, or *Tricky Word Wall Flowers*, to practice the tricky words already taught, including *one, by, only, old, like, have, live, give, little,* and *down.*

Tricky words
- Introduce the three new tricky words: *what, when,* and *why.*
- The students look at the words in red and green flowers at the top of the page.
- Explain that the ‹wh› at the beginning of each of these words makes a /w/ sound.
- The students could underline the ‹wh› at the beginning of each of these words in purple, to remind them that this is the "tricky bit."
- Point out that *what, when,* and *why* are all words that we use to ask questions.
- The students write inside the words *what* and *when* using a red pencil, and the word *why* using a green pencil.

Look, copy, cover, write, check
- Look at the first word, *what,* with the students.
- Say the letter names (not the letter sounds) in that word. The students write over the dotted word *what.*
- Then the students cover up all instances of the word *what* on their page, and try writing the word in the next column.
- Once the students have had one try at writing *what,* they check their spelling. Then they cover up all instances of the word *what* again, and have another go at writing the word in the final column.
- Repeat these steps with the words *when* and *why.*

Word and picture matching
- The students read the words at the bottom of the page, and look at the pictures in the leaves around the edge.
- The words are:
  lie, snail, tree, soap,
  nail, road, leek, pie.

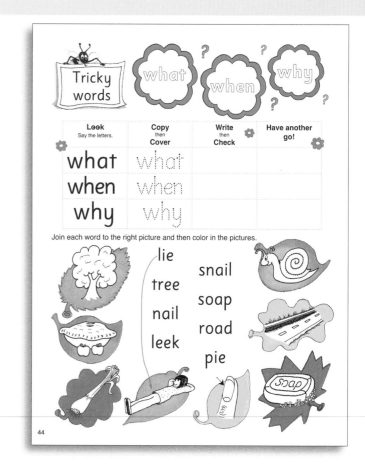

- The students join each word to the corresponding picture, and then color the pictures.

Further blending practice
- Write the following list of words on the board, and blend them with the students:
  curly,
  stirring,
  Saturn,
  sir,
  hurting.

Reading sentences
- Write the following sentences on the board, pointing out the tricky words, and blending any unknown words with the students.
  1. When did Dad lay the turf in the garden?
  2. There is a bird's nest in our fir tree.
  3. What is the first thing you remember?
  4. Why are there muddy footprints on the rug?

Words and Sentences

Flash cards
· Practice some of the basic 42 sounds, plus ‹y› as /ee/ and /ie/, ‹a_e›, ‹e_e›, ‹i_e›, ‹o_e›, ‹u_e›, ‹ay›, ‹oy›, ‹ea›, ‹ow› as /oa/ and /ou/, ‹ir›, and ‹ur›.

Words and sentences
· Look at the picture, and discuss it with the students.
· Ask a student to say one sentence about the picture. For example, "I can see a car." "The boy is helping his Dad." "They are putting oil in the car."
· Choose some words to blend, and write them on the board; examples could be: *boy, Dad, oil, car*.
· Some words will be straightforward to spell by listening for the sounds, but others will need some guidance:
· *Boy*: remind the students that the /oi/ sound is usually spelled ‹oy› when it comes at the end of the word.
· Write the sentence:
    He helps to check the oil in the car.
· Discuss it as you write, saying:
· Sentences start with a capital letter.
· Capital letters are always tall.
· Listen for the sounds in the words.
· Leave a space between each word.
· Don't forget the period.
· All the students copy the sentence.
· Those students who can write independently can try to write some more sentences on their own.
· At this stage, the students only know one way of writing each sound, so their spelling will not always be accurate, but their work will be readable.
· Spelling gradually improves through reading many books, and learning the alternative letter-sound spellings.

Reading words
· The students read each word at the bottom of the page, and join it to the corresponding vehicle.

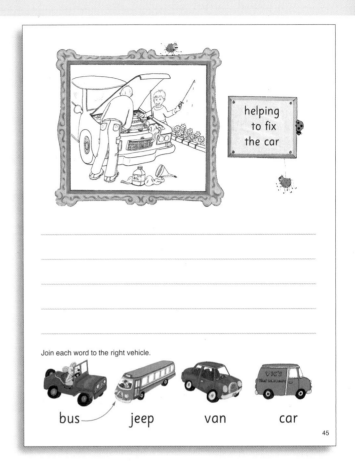

Join each word to the right vehicle.

bus   jeep   van   car

45

Further blending practice
· Write the following list of words on the board, and blend them with the students:
    burglary,
    firmly,
    further,
    twirl,
    churn.

Reading sentences
· Write the following sentences on the board, pointing out the tricky words, and blending any unknown words with the students.
1. When is the next train?
2. What is that blue stuff on his shirt?
3. Why do the leaves on the trees turn brown?
4. When is granny visiting?

129

Handwriting and Dictation

Flash cards

- Practice some of the basic 42 sounds, plus ‹y› as /ee/ and /ie/, ‹a_e›, ‹e_e›, ‹i_e›, ‹o_e›, ‹u_e›, ‹ay›, ‹oy›, ‹ea›, ‹ow› as /oa/ and /ou/, ‹ir› and ‹ur› as /er/.

Dictation words

- Dictate the following words:

  rub,
  man,
  get,
  land,
  test,
  long,
  mouth,
  bench,
  yard,
  toothbrush.

- The students write these words on the lines in their *Phonics Student Books.*

The alphabet

- Look at the alphabet with the students.
- Say the alphabet, pointing to each letter as you say it and pausing between each group.

Handwriting

- The students practice writing the tail letters: ‹g›, ‹j›, ‹p›, ‹q›, and ‹y›.

Finish the alphabet

- If you think the students will be able to remember the alphabet, cover any visible copies of the alphabet around the classroom before the students start this activity.
- The students fill in the missing capital letters to complete the alphabet.
- They can use a red pencil to write the letters A-E, a yellow pencil for the letters F-M, a green pencil for the letters N-S, and a blue pencil for the letters T-Z.

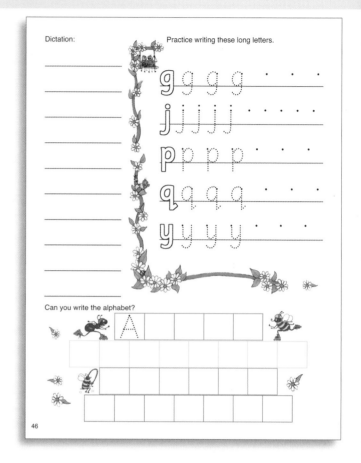

Further blending practice

- Write the following list of words on the board, and blend them with the students:

  hamster,
  Thursday,
  continue,
  sensible,
  storybook.

Reading sentences

- Write the following sentences on the board, pointing out the tricky words, and blending any unknown words with the students.

1. Why is the snow melting?
2. He went down the lane by himself.
3. What did you borrow from Pete?
4. Why is my shadow so long?

Tricky Words

Flash cards
- Practice the tricky words already taught.

Tricky words
- Introduce the three new tricky words: *where, who,* and *which.* The students look at the words in green flowers at the top of the page.
- Explain that the ‹wh› at the beginning of the words *where* and *which* makes a /w/ sound, but the ‹wh› at the beginning of *who* makes a /h/ sound.
- The students could underline the ‹wh› at the beginning of each of these words in purple, to remind them that this is the "tricky bit."
- Point out that *where, who,* and *which* are all words that we use to ask questions.
- The students write inside the outline letters using a green pencil.

Look, copy, cover, write, check
- Look at the first word, *where,* with the students.
- Say the letter names (not the letter sounds) in that word. The students write over the dotted word *where.*
- Then the students cover up all instances of the word *where* on their page, and try writing the word in the next column.
- Once the students have had one try at writing *where,* they check their spelling. Then they cover up all instances of the word *where* again, and have another go at writing the word in the final column.
- Repeat these steps with the words *who* and *which.*

Reading activities
- The students read each sentence, and illustrate it in the picture frame above.
- The sentences are:
  I see the moon and stars.
  A boy is asleep in bed.
  A duck is swimming on the pond.
  The girl has a green dress.

Further blending practice
- Write the following list of words on the board, and blend them with the students:
  blanket,
  untrue,
  playground,
  yogurt,
  return.

Reading sentences
- Write the following sentences on the board, pointing out the tricky words, and blending any unknown words with the students.
  1. Where shall we go today?
  2. Who will come with us?
  3. Who left all this brown paint on the mat?
  4. Which of these cupcakes do you like best?

Words and Sentences

Flash cards

- Practice some of the basic 42 sounds, plus ⟨y⟩ as /ee/ and /ie/, ⟨a_e⟩, ⟨e_e⟩, ⟨i_e⟩, ⟨o_e⟩, ⟨u_e⟩, ⟨ay⟩, ⟨oy⟩, ⟨ea⟩, ⟨ow⟩ as /oa/ and /ou/, ⟨ir⟩ and ⟨ur⟩.

Words and sentences

- Look at the picture, and discuss it with the students.
- Ask a student to say one sentence about the picture. For example, "I can see a statue." "The man has a lamb." "The sun shines."
- Choose some words to blend, and write them on the board; examples could be: *statue, lamb, bird, sunshine.*
- Some words will be straightforward to spell by listening for the sounds, but others will need some guidance:
- *Bird*: remind the students that the /er/ sound in *bird* is spelled ⟨ir⟩.
- *Lamb*: the word *lamb* has a silent ⟨b⟩ at the end.
- *Sunshine*: the /ie/ sound in the word *sunshine* is written with a ⟨i_e⟩ digraph.
- Write the sentence:

    The statue has a hat and coat.

- Discuss it as you write, saying:
- Sentences start with a capital letter.
- Capital letters are always tall.
- Listen for the sounds in the words.
- Leave a space between each word.
- Don't forget the period.
- All the students copy the sentence. Those students who can write independently can try to write some more sentences on their own.
- At this stage, the students only know one way of writing each sound, so their spelling will not always be accurate, but their work will be readable.
- Spelling gradually improves through reading many books, and learning the alternative letter-sound spellings.

Reading words

- The students read each word at the bottom of the page, and join it to the matching picture.

Join each word to the right picture.

tie   lamb   bird   boot

48

Further blending practice

- Write the following list of words on the board, and blend them with the students:

    creamy,
    lower,
    broomstick,
    smirk,
    dreaming.

Reading sentences

- Write the following sentences on the board, pointing out the tricky words, and blending any unknown words with the students.
1. Who likes peanut butter sandwiches?
2. Where are all the tennis balls?
3. What is the quickest way to the pool?
4. Which bird is bigger, a sparrow, or an ostrich?

Teaching with Phonics Student Book 3

In *Phonics Student Book 3*, the students continue to build upon the reading and writing skills learned in *Phonics Student Books 1* and *2*. The exercises in *Phonics Student Book 3* give the students a greater understanding of the alternative letter-sound spellings and introduce them to the remaining tricky words. The students are also encouraged to write with increasing independence in *Phonics Student Book 3* and many of the activities are designed to improve the students' comprehension skills as well as their reading and writing skills. In *Phonics Student Book 3*, the teaching covered during each lesson follows a pattern and the following activities are covered on a regular basis.

Alternatives

- In *Phonics Student Book 3*, the students are gradually encouraged to apply their knowledge of alternative letter-sound spellings to writing as well as reading. However, at this early stage, the students cannot be expected to use the correct alternative letter-sound spellings consistently in their work.
- The students are taught number of rules that relate to the letter-sound spellings. For example, they are taught that ‹i› is "too shy" to come at the end of a word and is replaced by ‹y›. This means that when the /ai/ sound comes at the end of a word it is spelled ‹ay›.
- Rules like these can help the students to choose the correct letter-sound spellings when writing a word.
- The students are also introduced to the following alternative letter-sound spelling in *Phonics Student Book 3*:
    ‹**ph**› making an /**f**/ sound, as in *phonic*
    soft ‹**c**›: when ‹**c**› is followed by ‹e›, ‹i›, ‹y›, it makes a /**s**/ sound
    soft ‹**g**›: when ‹**g**› is followed by ‹e›, ‹i›, ‹y›, it makes a /**j**/ sound
    ‹**igh**› making the /**ie**/ sound
    ‹**ew**› making the /**ue**/ sound
    ‹**air**›, ‹**are**›, and ‹**ear**› making the /**air**/ sound, as in *fairy*
- The following alternatives are reviewed in *Phonics Student Book 3*:
    ‹**ai**›, ‹**ay**›, and ‹**a_e**› making the /**ai**/ sound
    ‹**ee**›, ‹**ea**›, and ‹**e_e**› making the /**ee**/ sound
    ‹**ie**›, ‹**y**›, and ‹**i_e**› making the /**ie**/ sound
    ‹**oa**›, ‹**ow**›, and ‹**o_e**› making the /**oa**/ sound
    ‹**ue**›, and ‹**u_e**› making the /**ue**/ sound

‹ou›, and ‹ow› making the /ou/ sound
‹oi›, and ‹oy› making the /oi/ sound
‹er›, ‹ir›, and ‹ur› making the /er/ sound

Tricky words
- In *Phonics Student Book 2*, dictation and tricky words are covered on the same page.

Tricky words

- These pages introduce the students to more of the tricky words as well as helping them to review the tricky words that have already been taught.
- For more information, see pages 30 to 33 of this book for the section on tricky words.
- The following tricky words are introduced in *Phonics Student Book 3*:

    any, many, more, before, other, were, because, want
        (green words)
    saw, put, could, should, would, right, two, four, goes, does, made, their
        (pink words)
    once, upon, always, also, of, eight, love, cover, after, every, mother, father
        (brown words)

Dictation
- In *Phonics Student Book 3* the students begin to write sentences from dictation. The dictation sentences, provided in the lesson plans, give the students a chance to practice spelling tricky words as well as phonetically regular words. For more information about dictation, see page 25 of this book.

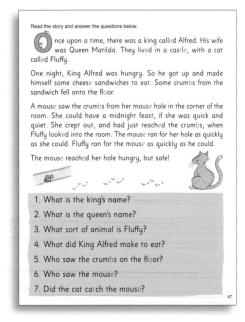

Comprehension

- The comprehension pages in *Phonics Student Book 3* cover arange of activities, all of which aim to improve the students' blending abilities as well as their comprehension skills.
- There is a greater emphasis on comprehension in *Phonics Student Book 3*.

Words and sentences

- In *Phonics Student Book 3*, the students are given the opportunity to write with an increasing amount of freedom.
- The students are no longer provided with a model sentence to copy, or with a discussion picture to write about. Instead, they are provided with the title for their piece of writing and a blank picture box in which they can illustrate their writing.
- The teacher initiates a class discussion about the given topic, or about a theme of the teacher's own choosing.
- The teacher selects some key words from the discussion to write on the board, pointing out any alternative spelling patterns in these words.

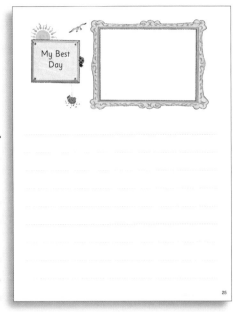

- Then the students write freely and independently about the class discussion topic and illustrate their writing in the picture frame.
- At this stage, the students' spelling will not always be accurate, but their work will be readable. Spelling gradually improves through reading many books and learning the alternative letter-sound spellings.
- Teachers should feel free to set their own writing subject. The title of the writing exercise does appear on the *Phonics Student Book* pages, but the picture frame is empty and the lines are blank. It may be that the students would like to write about a recent holiday they have celebrated, or a story they have heard. If this is the case, teachers can set their own title and guide the students' writing accordingly.

The more able students can move on to the Green Level of *Jolly Phonics Readers* when they have learned the tricky words up to and including *which* and once they have been introduced to the "hop-over e" digraphs found in words like *shake*, *these*, *bike*, *rose* and *cube*. This knowledge is covered by the end of *Phonics Student Book 2*.

Alternatives: ‹ph›

Flash cards

• Practice some of the letter sounds introduced in *Phonics Student Books 1* and *2*.

Alternatives: ‹ph› as /f/

• Say the word *phone* and ask the students what sound they can hear at the beginning of this word. They should say a /f/ sound.
• Write the word *phone* on the board.
• Explain that, in some words, the /f/ sound is written ‹ph›. This is because these words originally come from the Greek language.
• Point to the ‹ph› at the beginning of the word *phone*.
• Tell the students that, when they come across a word with a ‹p› and an ‹h› next to each other, they need to say /f/, and not /p-h/ to read the word.
• The students look at the blending words on the page. Read the words with the students.
• The words are:
    elephant, dolphin, graphic,
    microphone, phantom, photograph,
    alphabet, telephone.

Letter formation

• The students write over the dotted ‹ph› digraphs at the top of the page.

Read and draw: elephants

• The students read the words underneath each elephant.
• They draw a picture inside the elephant to illustrate each word.
• The words are:
    elephant, dolphin,
    phone, phantom.

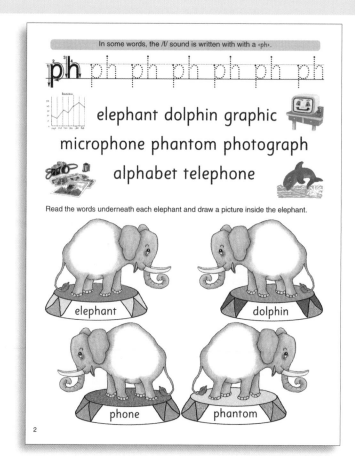

In some words, the /f/ sound is written with with a ‹ph›.

elephant dolphin graphic
microphone phantom photograph
alphabet telephone

Read the words underneath each elephant and draw a picture inside the elephant.

elephant

dolphin

phone

phantom

Further blending practice

• Write the following list of words on the board, and blend them with the students:
    phonic,
    buttercup,
    orphan,
    phrase,
    philosopher.

Reading sentences

• Write the following sentences on the board, pointing out the tricky words, and blending any unknown words with the students.
    1. The elephants at the zoo had long trunks.
    2. Who can say the alphabet?
    3. Dolphins live in the sea.
    4. Grandad spoke to me on the telephone.

Tricky Words and Dictation

Flash cards

- Use the flashcards, or *Tricky Word Wall Flowers*, to practice some of the tricky words taught so far.

Tricky words

- Introduce the two new tricky words: *any*, and *many*.
- The students look at the words in green flowers at the top of the page: *any*, and *many*.
- Point out that the word *many* is like the word *any*, but with an ‹m› at the beginning.
- The students write inside the words *any,* and *many* using a green pencil.

Filling in the gaps

- The students trace inside the outline letters in the word *any*, saying the letter names as they do so.
- Then the students cover up all instances of the word *any* on their page, and try to complete a line of this word, by tracing over the dotted letters and filling in the missing letters.
- The students repeat these steps for the word *many*.

Complete the sentences

- Read the first sentence, pausing at the gap:
  Have you got ___ milk?
- Ask the students whether they think they should write *any,* or *many* in this gap.
- Read the sentence back to the students, including their chosen word, and ask them if they think the sentence makes sense with this word.
- The students write the correct word in the gap in their *Phonics Student Books*.
- The students read the next sentence by themselves and decide which of the tricky words completes the sentence.
- They write this tricky word on the line in the sentence.

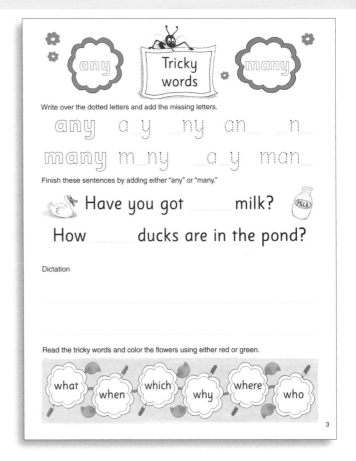

Dictation sentences

- Dictate the following sentences:
  We look to see if any fish are left.
  A shark has many sharp teeth.
- The students write these sentences on the lines in their *Phonics Student Books*.

Tricky word flowers

- The students look at the tricky words flowers at the bottom of their page.
- Read each tricky word with the students.
- The words are: *what, when, which, why, where, who.*
- The students color the flowers using either red, or green.

Further blending practice

- Write the following list of words on the board, and blend them with the students:
  muffin, dustbin, morning, frosty, cliff.

Short or Long Vowel?

Flash cards
- Practice some of the alternative letter-sound spellings taught so far, including ⟨ph⟩.

The vowel hand
- Remind the children that the vowel letters, ⟨a⟩, ⟨e⟩, ⟨i⟩, ⟨o⟩, ⟨u⟩, can make a short sound, or long sound.
- Usually, when these vowel letters are on their own, they make a short vowel sound.
- The students trace inside the outline letters for short vowels, saying each sound as they do so.
- Remind the students of the saying, "When two vowels go walking, the first one does the talking."
- Explain that when two vowels are together in a word, they usually make the long vowel sound of the first vowel letter. For example, the ⟨ea⟩ digraph in the word *sea* makes the long /e/ sound, /ee/.
- The students trace inside the outline letters for the vowel digraphs, saying the long vowels sounds as they do so.
- If the students know the short and long sound each vowel can make, they can use the rule, "If one way doesn't make a word, try the other." This is an extremely useful rule for reading.
- Teach the students to point to their fingertips when saying the short vowel sounds and to the base of each finger when saying the long vowel sounds, as in the picture on the students' page.
- Remind the students that the ⟨ue⟩ digraph sometimes makes a long /oo/ sound. Encourage them to say, "If /u/ doesn't work, try /ue/, or /oo/."

Short or long vowel?
- The students look at the first picture.
- Read the two words above this picture: *ran,* and *rain.*
- These two words differ in their vowel sounds only; *ran* has a short vowel sound, and *rain* has a long vowel sound.

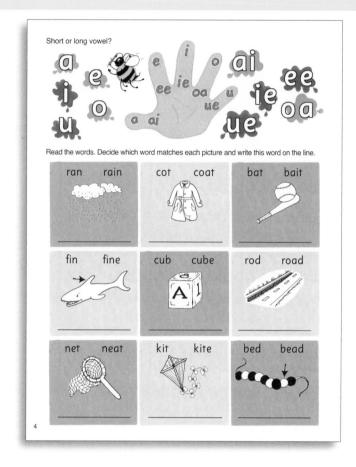

- Ask the students whether the picture illustrates the word *ran,* or the word *rain*?
- They should say *rain.*
- The students write the correct word on the line underneath the picture.
- The students repeat these steps for the rest of the pictures, reading the words to themselves, and writing the correct words underneath each picture.
- The pictures are:
     rain, coat, bat,
     fin, cube, road,
     net, kite, bead.
- When the students have finished writing, they can color the pictures.

Further blending practice
- Write the following list of words on the board, and blend them with the students:
petticoat, crocodile, birdseed, curtain, seashell.

Comprehension

Flash cards
- Practice some of the alternative letter-sound spellings taught so far, including ‹ph›.

Comprehension: the sea
- The students look at the empty sea scene on their page.
- They read the list of items underneath the scene, and add each thing to their picture.
- The students should add:
  1. six fish,
  2. a big crab,
  3. a flying seagull,
  4. a starfish,
  5. a shark with big teeth,
  6. three red shells,
  7. a boat,
  8. a man in the boat,
  9. a yellow sun in the sky.

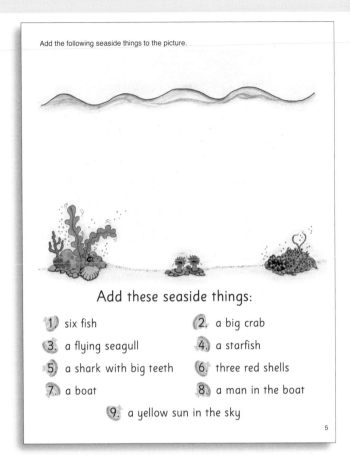

Add the following seaside things to the picture.

Add these seaside things:

1. six fish
2. a big crab
3. a flying seagull
4. a starfish
5. a shark with big teeth
6. three red shells
7. a boat
8. a man in the boat
9. a yellow sun in the sky

5

Further blending practice
- Write the following list of words on the board, and blend them with the students:

  seaside,
  freezing,
  crunchy,
  slipping,
  quicker,
  chimpanzee,
  trapeze,
  quite,
  envelope,
  seaweed.

Reading sentences
- Write the following sentences on the board, pointing out the tricky words, and blending any unknown words with the students.

1. The king and queen live in the royal tower.
2. How many yogurts are left?
3. The king has a silver crown.
4. The snail is very slow.
5. Is a dolphin a fish?
6. Mom and I had a picnic at the beach.
7. Are there any girls in the cricket club?
8. When can we try growing some beans?
9. We can read many phrases.
10. Can you throw the ball?

Alternatives: Soft ‹c›

Flash cards
- Practice some of the alternative letter-sound spellings taught so far, including ‹ph›.

Alternatives: soft ‹c›
- Explain that if the letter ‹c› is followed by ‹e›, ‹i›, or ‹y›, it tends to make a /s/ sound. This is called the soft ‹c› sound.
- The students look at the soft ‹c› words at the top of their page.
- Point out the faint letter ‹e› at the end of some of the words.
- Tell the students that these ‹e› letters are faint because they make no sound.
- Read the words with the students.
- The words are:
  excellent, ice, fence, face, circle, pencil, circus, cylinder, cycle, cygnet.

Read and match: circus tents
- The students look the list of words surrounded by circus tents.
- Point out that the first word, *ice-cream*, is written in dotted letters underneath the circus tent containing the ice-cream.
- The students write over the dotted word, *ice-cream.*
- Then they read the remaining words, and write each word underneath the circus tent containing the corresponding picture.
- Once the students have finished writing, they can color the pictures.
- The pictures (clockwise from ice-cream) are:
  ice-cream, fence, circle, circus tent, cycle, pencil, cygnets, face.

Further blending practice
- Write the following list of words on the board, and blend them with the students:
nice, concern, celery, excite, centipede.

Reading sentences
- Write the following sentences on the board, pointing out the tricky words, and blending any unknown words with the students.
1. The mice ran away from the cat.
2. My uncle lives in the city.
3. I have been ill since Sunday.
4. Did you get the parcel I sent?
5. He is not good at running.
6. Can we go to the bookshop now?

Tricky Words and Dictation

Flash cards

· Use the flashcards, or *Tricky Word Wall Flowers*, to practice some of the tricky words taught so far, including *any,* and *many.*

Tricky words

· Introduce the two new tricky words: *more,* and *before.*
· The students look at the words in green flowers at the top of the page: *more,* and *before.*
· Point out the ‹ore› at the end of both words makes an /or/ sound.
· The students could underline the ‹ore› at the end of each of these words in purple, to remind them that this is the "tricky bit."
· The students write inside the words *more,* and *before* using a green pencil.

Filling in the gaps

· The students trace inside the outline letters in the word *more,* saying the letter names as they do so.
· Then the students cover up all instances of the word *more* on their page, and try to complete a line of this word, by tracing over the dotted letters and filling in the missing letters.
· The students repeat these steps for the word *before.*

Complete the sentences

· Read the first sentence, pausing at the gap:
  I went swimming ___ lunch.
· Ask the students whether they think they should write *more* or *before* in this gap.
· Read the sentence back to the students, including their chosen word, and ask them if they think the sentence makes sense with this word. The students write the correct word in the gap in their *Phonics Student Books.*
· The students read the next sentence by themselves and decide which of the tricky words completes the sentence.
· They write this tricky word on the line in the sentence.

Dictation sentences

· Dictate the following sentences:
  I had some more crisps.
  We ran before the picnic.
· The students write these sentences on the lines in their *Phonics Student Books.*

Tricky word flowers

· The students look at the tricky words flowers at the bottom of their page.
· Read each tricky word with the students.
· The words are: *which, why, where, who, any, many.*
· The students color the flowers green.

Further blending practice

· Write the following list of words on the board, and blend them with the students:
  December, balance, dice, cleaning, teapot.

Words and Sentences

Flash cards
- Practice some of the alternative letter-sound spellings taught so far.

Words and sentences
- Write the title on the board, *This is me.*
- Read the title with the students.
- Ask a student to say one sentence about himself or herself. For example, "My name is…" "I am five years old." "I have a brown eyes." "I like running."
- You may need to stop the student at the end of their sentence, as most students will try to carry on.
- Ask some other students to say a sentence about themselves. Encourage the students to say a different sentence each.

Writing
- The students copy the title, *This is me*, onto the top line.
- They write as much as they can about themselves on the remaining lines.

Picture
- The students draw a picture of themselves in the picture frame.

Note 1: spelling
- At this stage, the students' spelling will not always be accurate, but their work will be readable. Spelling gradually improves through reading many books, and learning the alternative letter-sound spellings.

Note 2: title
- Teachers should feel free to set their own writing subject. The title of the writing exercise does appear on the *Phonics Student Book* pages, but the picture frame is empty, and the lines are blank. It may be that the students would like to write about a recent holiday they have celebrated, or a story they have heard. If this is the case, teachers can set their own title, and guide the students' writing accordingly.

This is me.

8

Further blending practice
- Write the following list of words on the board, and blend them with the students:
    reach,
    year,
    enjoys,
    stays,
    squeaking.

Reading sentences
- Write the following sentences on the board, pointing out the tricky words, and blending any unknown words with the students.
1. Dad said that there are no more grapes.
2. The farmer raced to rescue his sheep.
3. May we have some more rice?
4. You must clean your face before you go to bed.

Comprehension

Flash cards
· Practice some of the alternative letter-sound spellings taught so far, including ‹ph›, and soft ‹c›.

Yes or No?
· Read the sentence underneath the first picture, *The cat is sleeping.*
· Ask the students to look at the picture above the sentence and decide whether this sentence is true or false.
· The students should say that the sentence is true. They write over the dotted word *yes* on the line.
· The students read each of the remaining sentences, looking at the picture to decide whether the sentence is true, or false.
· If the sentence is true, the students write *yes* on the line, and if the sentence is false, they write *no*.
· The sentences are:

The cat is sleeping.	(yes)
Rabbits are good at hopping.	(yes)
There are five red socks.	(no)
It is three o'clock.	(yes)
The dragon has ten eggs.	(no)
The magpie has a hat.	(no)

Further blending practice
· Write the following list of words on the board, and blend them with the students:

photocopy,
rainbow,
apply,
butterfly,
concern,
cabin,
phoneme,
confidence,
certificate,
stir.

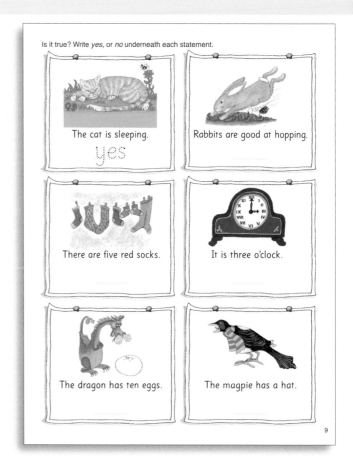

Is it true? Write *yes*, or *no* underneath each statement.

The cat is sleeping. yes

Rabbits are good at hopping.

There are five red socks.

It is three o'clock.

The dragon has ten eggs.

The magpie has a hat.

9

Reading sentences
· Write the following sentences on the board, pointing out the tricky words, and blending any unknown words with the students.
1. I spy some more insects under that tree.
2. Who came first in the hopping race?
3. How many mice are in the shed?
4. May I have one more toffee?
5. The spaceman went to the moon in a rocket.
6. We must smarten up before our photograph.
7. Can we play more games today?
8. How many boys came to the party?
9. Did you count all the coins?
10. Read the book before you give it back.

Alternatives: Soft ‹g›

Flash cards
- Practice some of the alternative letter-sound spellings taught so far, including ‹ph›, and soft ‹c›.

Alternatives: soft ‹g›
- Explain that if the letter ‹g› is followed by ‹e›, ‹i›, or ‹y›, it tends to make a /j/ sound. This is called the soft ‹g› sound.
- The students look at the soft ‹g› words at the top of their page. Read the words with the students. The words are:

    oranges, large, vegetable, germ,
    giraffe, giant, ginger, magic,
    gypsy, gym, gymnast, dingy.

Vegetables
- Read the first soft ‹g› word, *oranges*, again.
- Point out that the ‹g› is making a /j/ sound because it is followed by an ‹e›.
- Point out the outline letters ‹ge› in the cauliflower.
- The students write the word *oranges* in the cauliflower.
- Then the students pick out all the other soft ‹g› words where the ‹g› is followed by an ‹e›, and write these words in the cauliflower.
- Point out the outline letters ‹gi› in the potato.
- The students pick out all the soft ‹g› words where the ‹g› is followed by an ‹i›, and write these words in the potato.
- Point out the outline letters ‹gy› in the carrot.
- The students pick out all the soft ‹g› words where the ‹g› is followed by an ‹y›, and write these words in the carrot.
- In the word *ginger* the first soft ‹g› is followed by an ‹i›, and the second is followed by an ‹e›, so the students need to write this word in both the cauliflower, and the potato.
- Ask the students which word fits in two of the vegetables.

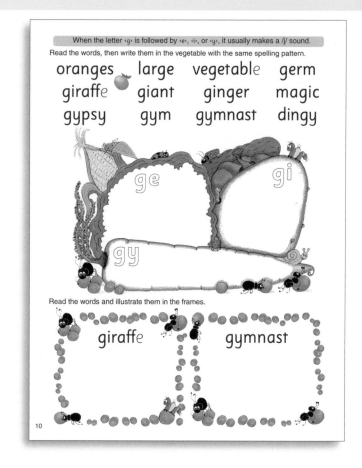

Read and draw
- The students read the soft ‹g› words, and illustrate them in the vegetable frames.
- The words are: *giraffe, gymnast*.

Further blending practice
- Write the following list of words on the board, and blend them with the students:

    gentle,
    stage,
    space,
    price,
    pancake.

Reading sentences
- Write the following sentences on the board, pointing out the tricky words, and blending any unknown words with the students.
  1. What do you call this vegetable?
  2. We had such fun at the magic show.
  3. All my pencils are broken.
  4. Are many girls going to camp?

Tricky Words and Dictation

Flash cards

- Use the flashcards, or *Tricky Word Wall Flowers*, to practice some of the tricky words taught so far, including *any, many, more,* and *before*.

Tricky words

- Introduce the two new tricky words: *other,* and *were*.
- The students look at the words in green flowers at the top of the page: *other,* and *were*.
- Teach the students to use the "say it as it sounds" technique, when spelling the word *other*.
- When writing *other*, the students should try to say it with an /o/ sound at the beginning, as though the word rhymes with *bother*.
- Point out that the ‹ere› at the end of the word *were* is the same as the ending of some other tricky words, such as, *here, there,* and *where*.
- The students write inside the words *other,* and *were* using a green pen, or pencil.

Filling in the gaps

- The students trace inside the outline letters in the word *other*, saying the letter names as they do so.
- Then the students cover up all instances of the word *other* on their page, and try to complete a line of this word, by tracing over the dotted letters, and filling in the missing letters.
- The students repeat these steps for the word *were*.

Complete the sentences

- Read the first sentence, pausing at the gap:
  We ___ skipping in the park.
- Ask the students whether they think they should write *other,* or *were* in this gap.
- Read the sentence back to the students, including their chosen word, and ask them if they think the sentence makes sense with this word.
- The students write the correct word in the gap in their *Phonics Student Books*.

- The students read the next sentence by themselves, and decide which of the tricky words completes the sentence.
- They write this tricky word on the line in the sentence.

Dictation sentences

- Dictate the following sentences:
  The other car was quicker.
  There were a hundred sheep in the barn.
- The students write these sentences on the lines in their *Phonics Student Books*.

Tricky word flowers

- The students look at the tricky words flowers at the bottom of their page.
- Read each tricky word with the students.
- The words are: *where, who, any, many, more, before*.
- The students color the flowers green.

Words and Sentences

Flash cards
• Practice some of the alternative letter-sound spellings taught so far.

Words and sentences
• Write the title on the board, *My Family*.
• Read the title with the students.
• Ask a student to say one sentence about his or her family. For example, "There are four people in my family." "Everyone in my family has brown hair." "I have a little brother."
• You may need to stop the student at the end of their sentence, as most students will try to carry on.
• Ask some other students to say a sentence about their family. Encourage the students to say a different sentence each.

Writing
• The students copy the title, *My Family*, onto the top line.
• They write as much as they can about their family on the remaining lines.

Picture
• The students draw a picture of their family in the picture frame.

Note 1: spelling
• At this stage, the students' spelling will not always be accurate, but their work will be readable. Spelling gradually improves through reading many books, and learning the alternative letter-sound spellings.

Note 2: title
• Teachers should feel free to set their own writing subject. The title of the writing exercise does appear on the *Phonics Student Book* pages, but the picture frame is empty, and the lines are blank. It may be that the students would like to write about a recent holiday they have celebrated, or a story they have heard. If this is the case, teachers can set their own title, and guide the students' writing accordingly.

Further blending practice
• Write the following list of words on the board, and blend them with the students:
> *wage,*
> *badger,*
> *bridges,*
> *mummy,*
> *daddy.*

Reading sentences
• Write the following sentences on the board, pointing out the tricky words, and blending any unknown words with the students.
1. My other sister is nine years old.
2. I have a digital clock.
3. Were you at the fancy dress party?
4. The other children were at the park.

Alternatives: ‹ai›, ‹ay›, and ‹a_e›

Flash cards
- Practice some of the alternative letter-sound spellings taught so far, including ‹ph›, soft ‹c›, and soft ‹g›.

Alternatives: the /ai/ sound
- Remind the students of the three main ways to write the /ai/ sound: ‹ai›, ‹ay›, and ‹a_e›.
- Remind the students that the ‹ay› spelling usually comes at the end of a word.
- Tell them that this is because the letter ‹i› is too shy to go at the end of a word, so its cousin, "toughy ‹y›" takes its place.
- The students look at the /ai/ words on their page.
- Point out that the ‹wh› at the beginning of the word *whale* makes a /w/ sound.
- Read these words with the students.
- The words are:
    whale, paint, play, snake, train, tray, name, may, cake, tail, snail, hail.

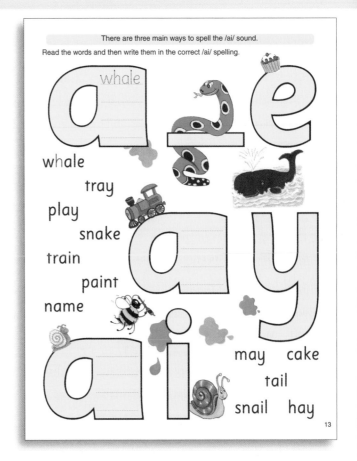

There are three main ways to spell the /ai/ sound.

Read the words and then write them in the correct /ai/ spelling.

whale • tray • play • snake • train • paint • name • may • cake • tail • snail • hay

‹ai›, ‹a_e›, or ‹ay›?
- Read the first /ai/ word, *whale*, again.
- Ask the students whether the /ai/ sound is spelled ‹ai›, ‹a_e›, or ‹ay› in this word.
- They should say ‹a_e›.
- Using a yellow pencil, the students circle the letters making the /ai/ sound in the word *whale*.
- Then they write over the dotted word *whale* in the large yellow ‹a_e› digraph on their page.
- The students read the remaining words, and circle the letters making the /ai/ sound in each word.
- Then they write the words in the corresponding digraphs on their page.

Further blending practice
- Write the following list of words on the board, and blend them with the students:
  grain, caveman, stray, make, spray.

Reading sentences
- Write the following sentences on the board, pointing out the tricky words, and blending any unknown words with the students.
1. We eat our cornflakes with milk.
2. I made a mistake on the other page.
3. Were you playing with my skates?
4. The goldfish had many scales.
5. Were the oranges nice?
6. The other hamster is still in its cage.

Tricky Words and Dictation

Flash cards

• Use the flashcards, or *Tricky Word Wall Flowers*, to practice some of the tricky words taught so far, including *any, many, more, before, other,* and *were.*

Tricky words

• Introduce the two new tricky words: *want,* and *because.*
• The students look at the words in green flowers at the top of the page.
• Teach the students to use the "say it as it sounds" technique, when spelling the word *want.*
• When writing *want,* the students should try to say it with an /a/ sound in the middle, as though the word rhymes with *pant.*
• For spelling the word *because,* it may help the students to learn this mnemonic:
  Big **e**lephants **c**atch **a**nts **u**nder **s**mall **e**lephants.
• Write the mnemonic on the board.
• Read the words to the students, pointing to the first letter of each word as you say it.
• Point out that if you write down the first letter of each word in this sentence, it spells *because.*
• The students write inside the words *want,* and *because* using a green pencil.

Filling in the gaps

• The students trace inside the outline letters in the word *want,* saying the letter names as they do so.
• Then the students cover up all instances of the word *want* on their page and try to complete a line of this word, by tracing over the dotted letters and filling in the missing letters.
• The students repeat these steps for the word *because.*

Complete the sentences

• Read the first sentence, pausing at the gap:
  Do you ___ to help?
• Ask the students whether they think they should write *want,* or *because* in this gap.
• They should write *want* in the gap.

• The students read the next sentence by themselves and decide which of the tricky words completes the sentence. They write this tricky word on the line in the sentence.

Dictation sentences

• Dictate the following sentences:
  We want more good books.
  I need my coat because it is raining.
• The students write these sentences on the lines in their *Phonics Student Books.*

Mnemonics

• The students read the mnemonic:
  Big **e**lephants **c**atch **a**nts **u**nder **s**mall **e**lephants.
• Remind the students that if they write down the first letter of each word in this sentence, it spells *because.*
• On the students' page, the first letter of each word in this mnemonic is an outline letter.
• The students trace inside these letters to spell *because.*

Words and Sentences

Flash cards
- Practice some of the alternative letter-sound spellings taught so far, including ‹ph›, soft ‹c›, and soft ‹g›.

Words and sentences
- Write the title on the board, *My House*.
- Read the title with the students.
- Some students might not live in a house. This is a good opportunity to discuss the various different types of homes the students have.
- Ask a student to say one sentence about his or her home. For example, "I live in a big apartment." "My house is quite small." "My house has a nice garden."
- You may need to stop the student at the end of their sentence, as most students will try to carry on.
- Ask some other students to say a sentence about their home. Encourage the students to say a different sentence each.

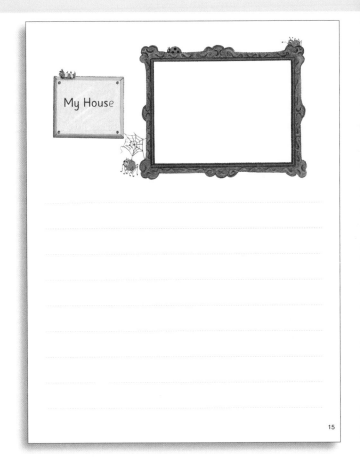

Writing
- The students copy the title, *My House*, onto the top line.
- They write as much as they can about their home on the remaining lines.

Picture
- The students draw a picture of their home in the picture frame.

Note 1: spelling
- At this stage, the students' spelling will not always be accurate, but their work will be readable. Spelling gradually improves through reading many books, and learning the alternative letter-sound spellings.

Note 2: title
- Teachers should feel free to set their own writing subject. The title of the writing exercise does appear on the *Phonics Student Book* pages, but the picture frame is empty, and the lines are blank.

- It may be that the students would like to write about a recent holiday they have celebrated, or a story they have heard. If this is the case, teachers can set their own title, and guide the students' writing accordingly.

Further blending practice
- Write the following list of words on the board, and blend them with the students:
  fragile, cage, waited, sprain, generally.

Reading sentences
- Write the following sentences on the board, pointing out the tricky words, and blending any unknown words with the students.
  1. Do you want the red paint or the green?
  2. She fainted because the room was too hot.
  3. Do you want to help me grate the carrots?
  4. This salad dressing is too oily for me.

Alternatives: ‹ee›, ‹ea›, and ‹e_e›

Flash cards

• Practice some of the alternative letter-sound spellings taught so far, including ‹ph›, soft ‹c›, and soft ‹g›.

Alternatives: the /ee/ sound

• Remind the students of the three main ways to write the /ee/ sound: ‹ee›, ‹ea›, and ‹e_e›.
• Remind the students that the ‹e_e› spelling is not used very often.
• The students look at the /ee/ words on their page.
• Read these words with the students.
• The words are:

> speed, sneeze, toffee, indeed,
> teacher, peanut, peach, seatbelt,
> eve, theme, these, Pete.

‹ee›, ‹e_e›, or ‹ea›?

• Read the first /ee/ word, *feet*, and ask the students whether the /ee/ sound is spelled ‹ee›, ‹e_e›, or ‹ea› in this word.
• They should say ‹ee›.
• Using an orange pencil, the students circle the letters making the /ee/ sound in the word *feet*.
• Then they write over the dotted word *feet* in the large orange ‹ee› digraph on their page.
• The students read the remaining words, and circle the letters making the /ee/ sound in each word.
• Then they write the words in the corresponding digraphs on their page.

Further blending practice

• Write the following list of words on the board, and blend them with the students:

> *seaside,*
> *feeling,*
> *underneath,*
> *sheep,*
> *extremely.*

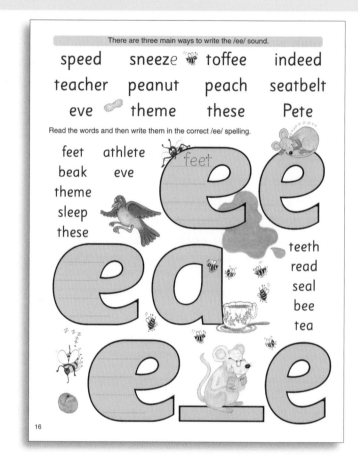

Reading sentences

• Write the following sentences on the board, pointing out the tricky words, and blending any unknown words with the students.
1. I got up because I had a bad dream.
2. The circus performers swing on the trapeze.
3. Do you want to stay for tea?
4. The seagulls fly close to the beach.
5. Are there more elephants than before?
6. You must finish your lunch before you can have an ice-cream.

Tricky Words and Dictation

Flash cards
- Use the flashcards, or *Tricky Word Wall Flowers*, to practice some of the tricky words taught so far, including *any, many, more, before, other, were, want,* and *because.*

Tricky words
- Introduce the two new tricky words: *put,* and *saw.*
- The students look at the words in pink flowers at the top of the page: *put,* and *saw.*
- Teach the students to use the "say it as it sounds" technique, when spelling the word *put.* When writing *put,* the students should try to say it with an /u/ sound in the middle, as though the word rhymes with *shut.*
- The students write inside the words *put,* and *saw* using a pink pencil.

Filling in the gaps
- The students trace inside the outline letters in the word *put,* saying the letter names as they do so.
- Then the students cover up all instances of the word *put* on their page and try to complete a line of this word, by tracing over the dotted letters, and filling in the missing letters.
- The students repeat these steps for the word *saw.*

Complete the sentences
- Read the first sentence, pausing at the gap:
    I ___ my drum back in the toy box.
- Ask the students whether they think they should write *put* or *saw* in this gap.
- Read the sentence back to the students, including their chosen word, and ask them if they think the sentence makes sense with this word. The students write the correct word in the gap in their *Phonics Student Books.*
- The students read the next sentence by themselves, and decide which of the tricky words completes the sentence.
- They write this tricky word on the line in the sentence.

Dictation sentences
- Dictate the following sentences:
    Put the map in the car.
    We saw some frogs in the pond.
- The students write these sentences on the lines in their *Phonics Student Books.*

Tricky word flowers
- The students look at the tricky words flowers at the bottom of their page.
- Read each tricky word with the students.
- The words are:
    more, before, other, were, want, because.
- The students color the flowers green.

Further blending practice
- Write the following list of words on the board, and blend them with the students:
    seesaw, pleasing, creepy, asleep, teabag.

Words and Sentences

Flash cards
•Practice some of the alternative letter-sound spellings taught so far, including ‹ph›, soft ‹c›, and soft ‹g›.

Words and sentences
•Write the title on the board, *My Best Dinner*.
•Read the title with the students.
•Ask a student to say one sentence about his or her favorite meal. For example, "I like cheese sandwiches." "My favorite food is rice and peas." "I like to eat chicken curry for dinner."
•You may need to stop the student at the end of their sentence, as most students will try to carry on.
•Ask some other students to say a sentence about the foods they like most. Encourage the students to say a different sentence each.

Writing
•The students copy the title, *My Best Dinner*, onto the top line.
•They write as much as they can about their favorite meal on the remaining lines.

Picture
•The students draw a picture of their favorite meal in the picture frame.

Note 1: spelling
•At this stage, the students' spelling will not always be accurate, but their work will be readable.

Note 2: title
•Teachers should feel free to set their own writing subject. The title of the writing exercise does appear on the *Phonics Student Book* pages, but the picture frame is empty, and the lines are blank. It may be that the students would like to write about a recent holiday they have celebrated, or a story they have heard. If this is the case, teachers can set their own title, and guide the students' writing accordingly.

My Best Dinner

Further blending practice
•Write the following list of words on the board, and blend them with the students:
evening,
teaspoons,
street,
athlete,
reach.

Reading sentences
•Write the following sentences on the board, pointing out the tricky words, and blending any unknown words with the students.
1. I saw the man put the ladder away.
2. Please put the ice back in the freezer.
3. We saw that little girl win the race.
4. I can put this nice lace on her dress.

152

Comprehension

Flash cards

•Practice some of the alternative letter-sound spellings taught so far, including ‹ph›, soft ‹c›, and soft ‹g›.

Read and draw

•Read the first phrase to the students:

   a rabbit in a hutch.

•Point out the faint letter ‹t› in the word *hutch*.

•Tell the students that this letter ‹t› is faint because it makes no sound.

•The students illustrate this phrase in the picture frame above.

•The students read the remaining phrases, and illustrate them in the picture frames.

•The phrases are:

   a rabbit in a hutch
   a big rainbow in the sky
   a black cat in red boots
   a bat in a tree
   the moon and some stars
   three snails in the rain

Further blending practice

•Write the following list of words on the board, and blend them with the students:

   sprain,
   mean,
   better,
   teeth,
   stealing,
   beehive,
   cleaner,
   steeper,
   yelp,
   stopper.

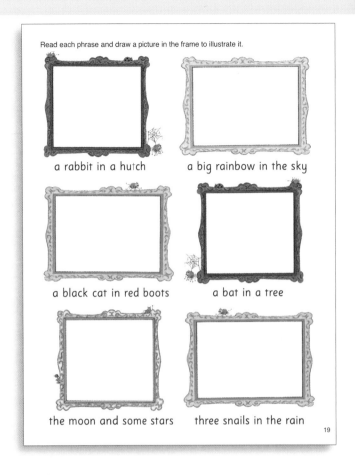

Read each phrase and draw a picture in the frame to illustrate it.

a rabbit in a hutch   a big rainbow in the sky

a black cat in red boots   a bat in a tree

the moon and some stars   three snails in the rain

19

Reading sentences

•Write the following sentences on the board, pointing out the tricky words, and blending any unknown words with the students.

1. One kitten is black and the other is ginger.
2. The elephants at the circus were very large.
3. He wants to come to the baseball game.
4. I need to go now because I am late.
5. The goalkeeper has the ball.
6. They played on the seesaw at the park.
7. I saw her jump on the haystacks in the barn.
8. We completed the jigsaw in no time at all.
9. Put the clean socks in here.
10. He put the peas by the sink.

Alternatives: ‹ie›, ‹y›, ‹i_e›, and ‹igh›

Flash cards
- Practice some of the alternative letter-sound spellings taught so far, including ‹ph›, soft ‹c›, and soft ‹g›.

Alternatives: the /ie/ sound
- Say the word *sight,* and ask the students what vowel sound they can hear in the middle of this word.
- They should say an /ie/ sound.
- Ask the students how an /ie/ sound is written.
- The students should say that /ie/ can be written as ‹ie›, ‹y›, or ‹i_e›.
- Write the word *sight* on the board.
- Explain that the /ie/ sound can also be written ‹igh›, and point to the ‹igh› in the middle of the word *sight.*
- The students look at the /ie/ words on their page.
- Read these words with the students, and point out the letters making the /ie/ sound in each word.
- The words are:

  *light, fly, like, pie, night, prize,
  lie, time, right, thigh, reply,
  my, die, kite, sky, tie.*

‹ie›, ‹i_e›, ‹y› or ‹igh›?
- Read the first /ie/ word, *light,* again.
- Ask the students whether the /ie/ sound is spelled ‹ie›, ‹i_e›, ‹y›, or ‹igh› in this word.
- They should say ‹igh›.
- Using a green pencil, the students circle the letters making the /ie/ sound in the word *light.*
- Then they write over the dotted word *light* in the large green ‹igh› digraph on their page.
- The students read the remaining words, and circle the letters making the /ie/ sound in each word.
- Then they write the words in the corresponding digraphs on their page.

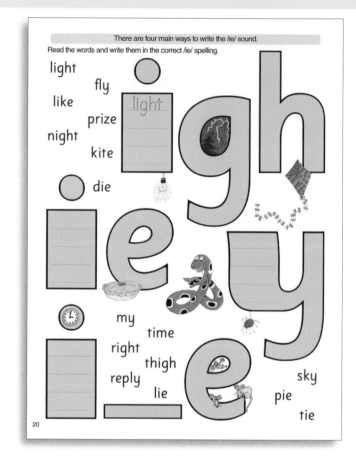

Further blending practice
- Write the following list of words on the board, and blend them with the students:

  *frighten,
  line,
  crying,
  sigh,
  prize.*

Reading sentences
- Write the following sentences on the board, pointing out the tricky words, and blending any unknown words with the students.
1. The butterfly flutters by my bike.
2. The sun shines so brightly.
3. The lighthouse stands on the cliff edge.
4. The moth flies too close to the flame.
5. She cannot eat nuts because she is allergic.
6. I want to have balloons at my party.

Tricky Words and Dictation

Flash cards
• Practice some of the tricky words taught so far.

Tricky words
• Introduce the three new tricky words: *could, should,* and *would.* The students look at the words in pink flowers at the top of the page.
• Point out that the words *could, should,* and *would* all have the same ‹ould› ending.
• Explain that in each of these words the ‹ould› makes an /oo-d/ sound (with the little /oo/).
• Point out that the sounds at the beginning of these words, /c/, /sh/ and /w/, are spelled in the usual way.
• The students could underline the ‹ould› at the end of each of these words in purple, to remind them that this is the "tricky bit."
• The students write inside the words *could, should,* and *would* using a pink pencil.

Filling in the gaps
• The students trace inside the outline letters in the word *could,* saying the letter names as they do so. Then the students cover up all instances of the word *could* on their page, and try to complete a column of this word, by tracing over the dotted letters, and filling in the missing letters.
• The students repeat these steps for the words *should,* and *would.*

Complete the sentences
• Read the first sentence, pausing at the gap:
    ___ you like some more tea?
• Ask the students whether they think they should write *could, should,* or *would* in this gap.
• Read the sentence back to the students, including their chosen word, and ask them if they think the sentence makes sense with this word. The students write the correct word in the gap in their *Phonics Student Books.*
• The students read the next two sentences by themselves, and decide which of the tricky words completes the sentence. They write the correct tricky word on the line in each sentence.

Dictation sentences
• Dictate the following sentences:
    We could sing a song next.
    It should be a good outing.
    It would be fun to go on the swings.
• The students write these sentences on the lines in their *Phonics Student Books.*

Tricky word flowers
• The students look at the tricky words flowers at the bottom of their page.
• Read each tricky word with the students.
• The words are: *other, were, because, want, saw, put.*
• The students color the flowers using a green, or pink pencil.

Further blending practice
• Write the following list of words on the board, and blend them with the students:
intelligent, charges, emergency, excite, cool.

155

Words and Sentences

Flash cards
- Practice some of the alternative letter-sound spellings taught so far, including ‹ph›, soft ‹c›, soft ‹g›, and ‹igh›.

Words and sentences
- Write the title on the board, *The Animal I like Best*.
- Read the title with the students.
- Ask a student to say one sentence about his or her favorite animal. For example, "I like fish best." "I like cats because they are fluffy." 'I love dolphins."
- You may need to stop the student at the end of their sentence, as most students will try to carry on.
- Ask some other students to say a sentence about the animal they like most. Encourage the students to say a different sentence each.

Writing
- The students copy the title, *The Animal I like Best*, onto the top line.
- They write as much as they can about their favorite animal on the remaining lines.

Picture
- The students draw a picture of their favorite animal in the picture frame.

Note 1: spelling
- At this stage, the students' spelling will not always be accurate, but their work will be readable.

Note 2: title
- Teachers should feel free to set their own writing subject. The title of the writing exercise does appear on the *Phonics Student Book* pages, but the picture frame is empty and the lines are blank. It may be that the students would like to write about a recent holiday they have celebrated, or a story they have heard. If this is the case, teachers can set their own title, and guide the students' writing accordingly.

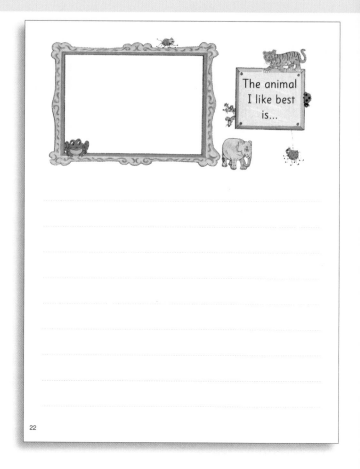

Further blending practice
- Write the following list of words on the board, and blend them with the students:
    hippopotamus,
    giraffe,
    tiger,
    blackbird,
    raccoon.

Reading sentences
- Write the following sentences on the board, pointing out the tricky words, and blending any unknown words with the students.
1. We would like to ride our bikes outside.
2. He should do his chores.
3. Could you teach me how to make tea?
4. They should get away from the angry bees.

Alternatives: ‹oa›, ‹ow›, and ‹o_e›

Flash cards
- Practice some of the alternative letter-sound spellings taught so far, including ‹ph›, soft ‹c›, soft ‹g›, and ‹igh›.

Alternatives: the /oa/ sound
- Remind the students of the three main ways to write the /oa/ sound: ‹oa›, ‹ow›, and ‹o_e›.
- Remind the students that the ‹ow› spelling usually comes at the end of a word.
- The students look at the /oa/ words on their page.
- Read these words with the students.
- The words are:

  toast, coach, coast, raincoat, tadpole, those, home, joke, rainbow, elbow, snow, window.

‹oa›, ‹o_e›, or ‹ow›?
- Read the first /oa/ word, *those*, and ask the children whether the /oa/ sound is spelled ‹oa›, ‹o_e›, or ‹ow› in this word.
- They should say ‹o_e›.
- Using a purple pencil, the students circle the letters making the /oa/ sound in the word *those*.
- Then they write over the dotted word *those* in the large purple ‹o_e› digraph on their page.
- The students read the remaining words, and circle the letters making the /oa/ sound in each word.
- Then they write the words in the corresponding digraphs on their page.

Further blending practice
- Write the following list of words on the board, and blend them with the students:

  *yellow,
  toaster,
  tightrope,
  window,
  flagpole.*

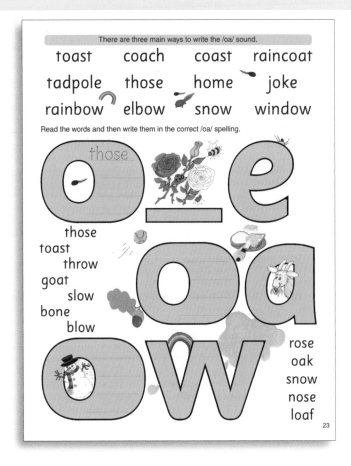

Reading sentences
- Write the following sentences on the board, pointing out the tricky words, and blending any unknown words with the students.
1. Could we have some butter for our toast?
2. That girl should stop moaning.
3. The sea was very shallow at the beach.
4. I wish the snow would melt.
5. May we go home now?
6. The anteater has a very long nose.

Tricky Words and Dictation

Flash cards
- Use the flashcards, or *Tricky Word Wall Flowers*, to practice some of the tricky words taught so far, including *put, saw, could, should,* and *would.*

Tricky words
- Introduce the four new tricky words: *right, two, four,* and *goes.*
- The students look at the words in pink flowers at the top of the page: *right, two, four,* and *goes.*
- Point out that *right* is not really tricky, because the students now know that ‹igh› can say /ie/.
- The students write inside the words *right, two, four,* and *goes* using a pink pencil.

Filling in the gaps
- The students trace inside the outline letters in the word *right,* saying the letter names as they do so.
- Then the students cover up all instances of the word *right* on their page and try to complete a column of this word, by tracing over the dotted letters and filling in the missing letters.
- The students repeat these steps for the words *two, four,* and *goes.*

Complete the sentences
- Read the first sentence, pausing at the gap:
    He got all the sums ___.
- Ask the students whether they think they should write *right, two, four,* or *goes* in this gap.
- Read the sentence back to the students, including their chosen word, and ask them if they think the sentence makes sense with this word. The students write the correct word in the gap in their *Phonics Student Books.*
- The students read the remaining three sentences by themselves, and decide which of the tricky words completes the sentence.
- They write the correct tricky word on the line in each sentence.

Dictation sentences
- Dictate the following sentences:
    He goes to the pool by bus.
    They must count them two by two.
    A dog has four legs.
    We went right then left.
- The students write these sentences on the lines in their *Phonics Student Books.*

Further blending practice
- Write the following list of words on the board, and blend them with the students:
telescope, choke, foaming, throws, toffee.
- Write the following sentences on the board, pointing out the tricky words, and blending any unknown words with the students.
    1. Two sheep and four goats were in the yard.
    2. The swimming pool is on the right.
    3. She goes bowling with her family.
    4. The two tigers were quite frightening.

Words and Sentences

Flash cards
- Practice some of the alternative letter-sound spellings taught so far, including ‹ph›, soft ‹c›, soft ‹g›, and ‹igh›.

Words and sentences
- Write the title on the board, *My Best Day*.
- Read the title with the students.
- Ask a student to say one sentence about his or her best day. For example, "We went to a party." "Dad took me to the beach." "I rode a horse."
- You may need to stop the student at the end of their sentence, as most students will try to carry on.
- Ask some other students to say a sentence about a day they enjoyed. Encourage the students to say a different sentence each.

Writing
- The students copy the title, *My Best Day*, onto the top line.
- They write as much as they can about a day they enjoyed on the remaining lines.

Picture
- The students draw a picture illustrating their best day in the picture frame.

Note 1: spelling
- At this stage, the students' spelling will not always be accurate, but their work will be readable. Spelling gradually improves through reading many books, and learning the alternative letter-sound spellings.

Note 2: title
- Teachers should feel free to set their own writing subject. The title of the writing exercise does appear on the *Phonics Student Book* pages, but the picture frame is empty, and the lines are blank. It may be that the students would like to write about a recent holiday they have celebrated, or a story they have heard. If this is the case, teachers can set their own title, and guide the students' writing accordingly.

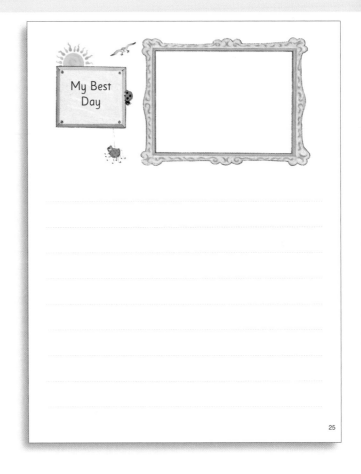

My Best Day

25

Further blending practice
- Write the following list of words on the board, and blend them with the students:
  bonfire,
  coast,
  stroked,
  owner,
  spoken.

Reading sentences
- Write the following sentences on the board, pointing out the tricky words, and blending any unknown words with the students.
1. He goes home on the train.
2. My right foot is slightly bigger than my left.
3. The clock hands were at ten to four.
4. Those two cats ate all the shrimps.

Comprehension

Flash cards
• Practice some of the alternative letter-sound spellings taught so far, including ‹ph›, soft ‹c›, soft ‹g›, and ‹igh›.

Reading and comprehension
• The students look at the sentences and pictures on their page.
• Read the first sentence to the students, pausing at the gap:

> The tall oak ___ is green.

• Ask the students what word they think will fit in this gap. If they struggle to answer, tell them that the picture beside the sentence is a clue.
• The students should say that the missing word is *tree*. They write this word in the lines.
• There is a line for each sound in the missing word.
• A longer line indicates that a digraph is needed.
• Read the completed sentence back to the students:

> The tall oak *tree* is green.

• Ask the students if the tree in the picture is green. They should say that it is not.
• The students color the picture of the tree green, so that it matches the sentence.
• The students read the remaining sentences to themselves.
• They fill in the gaps to complete each sentence, and color the pictures to match.
• The sentences are:

The tall oak (tree) is green.
My (tie) is long and has red and green stripes.
My blue (coat) has a big collar.
The little green (frog) jumped into the pond.
The (moon) shines in the night.
I found a (snail) in the garden.
It had a yellow shell on its back.

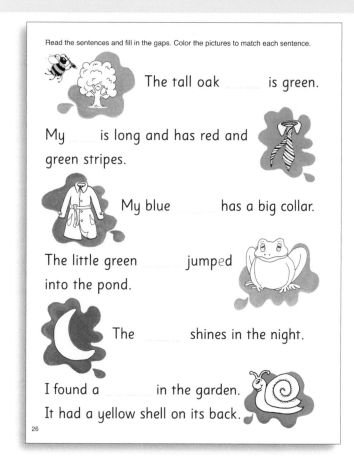

Read the sentences and fill in the gaps. Color the pictures to match each sentence.

The tall oak _____ is green.

My _____ is long and has red and green stripes.

My blue _____ has a big collar.

The little green _____ jumped into the pond.

The _____ shines in the night.

I found a _____ in the garden.
It had a yellow shell on its back.

26

Further blending practice
• Write the following list of words on the board, and blend them with the students:

> *stoke,*
> *roasted,*
> *throwing,*
> *stone,*
> *follows.*

Reading sentences
• Write the following sentences on the board, pointing out the tricky words, and blending any unknown words with the students.
1. Those four boys made that boat.
2. Do not sit on the two broken seats.
3. Which room is the right one?
4. They should not boast so much.

Alternatives: ‹ue›, ‹ew›, and ‹u_e›

Flash cards
- Practice some of the alternative letter-sound spellings taught so far, including ‹ph›, soft ‹c›, soft ‹g›, and ‹igh›.

Alternatives: the /ue/ sound
- Remind the students of the three main ways to write the /ue/ sound: ‹ue›, ‹ew› and ‹u_e›.
- Remind the students that the digraphs ‹ue›, ‹ew›, and ‹u_e› can make a long /oo/ sound as well as a /ue/ sound.
- The students look at the /ue/ words on their page.
- Read these words with the students.
- The words are:

    bluebell, rescue, true, statue,
    ruler, use, excuse, tune,
    news, chew, threw, stew.

‹ue›, ‹u_e›, or ‹ew›?
- Read the first /ue/ word, *cube*, and ask the students whether the /ue/ sound is spelled ‹ue›, ‹u_e›, or ‹ew› in this word.
- They should say ‹u_e›.
- Using a brown pencil, the students circle the letters making the /ue/ sound in the word *cube*.
- Then they write over the dotted word *cube* in the large brown ‹u_e› digraph on their page.
- The students read the remaining words, and circle the letters making the /ue/ sound in each word.
- Then they write the words in the corresponding digraphs on their page.

Further blending practice
- Write the following list of words on the board, and blend them with the students:

    Tuesday,
    June,
    newer,
    excuse,
    screws.

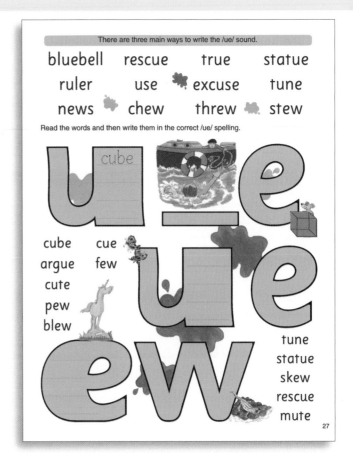

Reading sentences
- Write the following sentences on the board, pointing out the tricky words, and blending any unknown words with the students.
    1. We should let the tea brew before drinking it.
    2. I saw so many bluebells in the wood.
    3. She drew four blue flowers in my book.
    4. They used all the ice cubes.
    5. Should the teapot go on this mat?
    6. Before mathematics, we have singing.

Tricky Words and Dictation

Flash cards

- Use the flashcards, or *Tricky Word Wall Flowers*, to practice some of the tricky words taught so far, including *put, saw, could, should, would, right, two, four,* and *goes*.

Tricky words

- Introduce the three new tricky words: *does, mad,e* and *their*.
- The students look at the words in pink flowers at the top of the page.
- Point out that the letters ‹oe› in the word *does* make an /u/ sound.
- Point out that *made* is not really tricky, because the students now know that ‹a_e› can say /ai/.
- The students write inside the words *does, made,* and *their* using a pink pencil.

Filling in the gaps

- The students trace inside the outline letters in the word *does*, saying the letter names as they do so.
- Then the students cover up all instances of the word *does* on their page and try to complete a column of this word, by tracing over the dotted letters and filling in the missing letters.
- The students repeat these steps for the words *made,* and *their*.

Complete the sentences

- Read the first sentence, pausing at the gap:
     We ___ some cakes yesterday.
- Ask the students whether they think they should write *does, made,* or *their* in this gap.
- Read the sentence back to the students, including their chosen word, and ask them if they think the sentence makes sense with this word. The students write the correct word in the gap in their *Phonics Student Books*.
- The students read the next two sentences by themselves, and decide which of the tricky words completes the sentence.
- They write the correct tricky word on the line in each sentence.

Dictation sentences

- Dictate the following sentences:
     He does not swim with the rest.
     She made a big car with some boxes.
     They hang their coats on the pegs.
- The students write these sentences on the lines in their *Phonics Student Books*.

Tricky word flowers

- The students look at the tricky words flowers at the bottom of their page.
- Read each tricky word with the students.
- The words are: *should, would, right, two, four, goes*.
- The students color the flowers using a pink pencil.

Further blending practice

- Write the following list of words on the board, and blend them with the students:
plum, complete, Saturday, starting, brakes.

Words and Sentences

Flash cards
- Practice some of the alternative letter-sound spellings taught so far, including ‹ph›, soft ‹c›, soft ‹g›, and ‹igh›.

Words and sentences
- Write the title on the board, *My Game*.
- Read the title with the students.
- Ask a student to say one sentence about his or her favorite game. For example, "I love baseball." "I like to play chess." "We play tag."
- You may need to stop the student at the end of their sentence, as most students will try to carry on.
- Ask some other students to say a sentence about their favorite games. Encourage the students to say a different sentence each.

Writing
- The students copy the title, *My Game*, onto the top line.
- They write as much as they can about their game on the remaining lines. The students might like to write about the rules of their game, or about the people they play it with.

Picture
- The students draw a picture illustrating their game in the picture frame.

Note 1: spelling
- At this stage, the students' spelling will not always be accurate, but their work will be readable.

Note 2: title
- Teachers should feel free to set their own writing subject. The title of the writing exercise does appear on the *Phonics Student Book* pages, but the picture frame is empty, and the lines are blank. It may be that the students would like to write about a recent holiday they have celebrated, or a story they have heard. If this is the case, teachers can set their own title, and guide the students' writing accordingly.

My Game

29

Further blending practice
- Write the following list of words on the board, and blend them with the students:
  - *homemade,*
  - *computer,*
  - *chewing,*
  - *ruler,*
  - *tuned.*

Reading sentences
- Write the following sentences on the board, pointing out the tricky words, and blending any unknown words with the students.
1. The clowns did not amuse him.
2. Does she like the pink paint?
3. Their sister made a new floral dress.
4. Does the river flow by their home?

Comprehension

Flash cards
- Practice some of the alternative letter-sound spellings taught so far, including ⟨ph⟩, soft ⟨c⟩, soft ⟨g⟩, and ⟨igh⟩.

Comprehension: at the zoo
- The students look at the picture of the zoo, in the bottom right hand corner of their page.
- Read the first question to the students:
      How many animals are in the tree?
- The students should say that there are three monkeys in the tree.
- They write *three* on the line next to the first question.
- The students read the remaining questions, and write the answers on the lines.
- The questions (with answers in brackets) are:
  1. How many animals are in the tree?
        (three)
  2. Which animal has a trunk?
        (the elephant)
  3. What sort of animal is an ostrich?
        (it is a bird)
  4. Where is the crocodile swimming?
        (in the pool)
  5. Who has black and white stripes?
        (the zebras)
  6. How many giraffes are there?
         (two)

Note 1: spelling
- At this stage, the students' spelling will not always be accurate, but their work will be readable. Spelling gradually improves through reading many books, and learning the alternative letter-sound spellings.

Anagrams
- The students look at the word *elephants* on their page. Point out that a number of other words can be made from the letters of the word *elephants*.
- Say the word *sheep* to the students.
- Point out that all the letters in the word *sheep* can be found in the word *elephants*.

At the zoo: answer the questions by looking at the zoo picture underneath.

1. How many animals are in the tree?
2. Which animal has a trunk?
3. What sort of animal is an ostrich?
4. Where is the crocodile swimming?
5. Who has black and white stripes?
6. How many giraffes are there?

30

Make as many words as you can from the letters in the word:

elephants

sheep

- The students write over the dotted word *sheep*.
- Then they make as many words as they can from the letters in the word *elephants*.
- If plastic, or magnetic letters are available, they can be very useful for this activity.
- The students can move the plastic letters around to try and make words. When they find a word they can copy it into their books.
- Examples of words made from the letters in *elephants* are:
sheep, sleep, please, sea, she, he, pant, heel, peel, pale, sale, seal, plan, nap, tap, lap, heap, leap, help, ants, snap, hen, then, than, lean, pen, pan, let, set, pet, net and *sent*, but there are many more.

Further blending practice
- Write the following list of words on the board, and blend them with the students:
cracking, blend, fewer, further, freezing.

Alternatives: ‹ou› and ‹ow›

Flash cards
· Practice some of the alternative letter-sound spellings taught so far, including ‹ph›, soft ‹c›, soft ‹g›, and ‹igh›.

Alternatives: the /ou/ sound
· Remind the students of the two main ways to write the /ou/ sound: ‹ou›, and ‹ow›.
· The students look at the /ou/ words on their page.
· Read these words with the students.
· The words are:
> flour, about, count,
> mouse, found, sound,
> flower, shower, brown,
> downhill, vowel, clown.

‹ou› or ‹ow›?
· Read the first /ou/ word, *mouse*, and ask the students whether the /ou/ sound is spelled ‹ou› or ‹ow› in this word.
· They should say ‹ou›.
· Using a pink pencil, the students circle the letters making the /ou/ sound in the word *mouse*.
· Then they write over the dotted word *mouse* in the large pink ‹ou› digraph on their page.
· The students read the remaining words, and circle the letters making the /ou/ sound in each word.
· Then they write the words in the corresponding digraphs on their page.

Further blending practice
· Write the following list of words on the board, and blend them with the students:
> greenhouse,
> cowshed,
> however,
> growl,
> found.

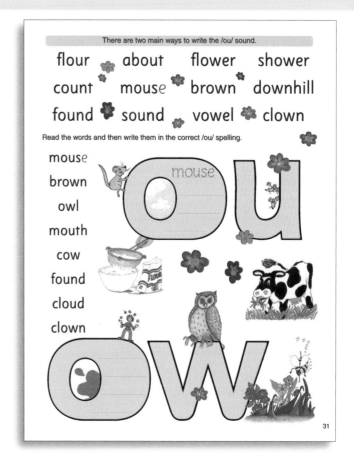

Reading sentences
· Write the following sentences on the board, pointing out the tricky words, and blending any unknown words with the students.
1. Mum had a new blouse for her birthday.
2. There was a large crowd at the festival.
3. There are their hats and coats.
4. He does not want any more sandwiches.
5. We ate a thick stew at their house.
6. They made little statues from modeling clay.

Tricky Words

Flash cards
- Practice some of the tricky words taught so far.

Tricky words
- Introduce the three new tricky words: *once, upon,* and *always.*
- The students look at the words in brown flowers at the top of the page: *once, upon,* and *always.*
- The students write inside the words *once, upon,* and *always* using a brown pencil.

Filling in the gaps
- The students trace inside the outline letters in the word *once,* saying the letter names as they do so.
- Then the students cover up all instances of the word *once* on their page, and try to complete a column of this word, by tracing over the dotted letters, and filling in the missing letters.
- The students repeat these steps for the words *upon,* and *always.*

Complete the Story
- This time, rather than completing sentences, the students have to fill in the gaps, and complete a story.
- Read the first sentence to the students, pausing at the two gaps:

    ___ ___ a time, there was a little house in a big wood.
- Ask the students which of the three tricky words they have just learned might come at the beginning of this sentence.
- Children's stories often begin with the phrase, "Once upon a time..." and, with a bit of encouragement, the students should say *once* and *upon.*
- The students write *once* and *upon* in the first two gaps.
- Now read the first two sentences, including the two words filled in so far, and pause at the remaining gap:

    Once upon a time, there was a little house in a big wood. The wood was ___ dark.

- Ask the students whether they think the remaining tricky word, *always,* might fit in this gap. The students should agree that it does, and write the word *always* in the final gap.
- The students read the two completed sentences again, and finish the story on the remaining lines. They might like to continue their stories on some extra paper, which can then be stuck into their books.

Tricky word flowers
- The students look at the tricky words flowers at the bottom of their page.
- Read each tricky word with the students.
- The words are:
  four, right, goes, does, made, their.
- The students color the flowers using a pink pencil.

Words and Sentences

Flash cards
- Practice some of the alternative letter-sound spellings taught so far, including ‹ph›, soft ‹c›, soft ‹g›, and ‹igh›.

Words and sentences
- Read a story that the students know well and like.
- Write the title of the story on the board.
- Read the title with the students.
- Ask a student to say one sentence about the story. You may need to stop the student at the end of their sentence, as most students will try to carry on.
- Ask some other students to say a sentence about the story. Encourage the students to say a different sentence each.

Writing
- The students copy the title of the story onto the top line, and re-tell the story on the remaining lines.

Picture
- The students draw a picture illustrating the story in the picture frame.

Note 1: spelling
- At this stage, the students' spelling will not always be accurate, but their work will be readable. Spelling gradually improves through reading many books, and learning the alternative letter-sound spellings.

Note 2: title
- Teachers should feel free to set their own writing subject. The title of the writing exercise does appear on the *Phonics Student Book* pages, but the picture frame is empty, and the lines are blank. It may be that the students would like to write about a recent holiday they have celebrated, or a story they have heard. If this is the case, teachers can set their own title, and guide the students' writing accordingly.

Further blending practice
- Write the following list of words on the board, and blend them with the students:

    crown,
    shouted,
    frowning,
    around,
    powder.

Reading sentences
- Write the following sentences on the board, pointing out the tricky words, and blending any unknown words with the students.
1. She is always bouncing up and down.
2. They have only been to the park once.
3. At night, I lay upon my bed.
4. He always sings that song.

Comprehension

Flash cards
- Practice some of the alternative letter-sound spellings taught so far, including ‹ph›, soft ‹c›, soft ‹g›, and ‹igh›.

Comprehension: at the park
- The students look carefully at the picture of the park.
- Discuss the picture with the students.
- Read the first sentence to the students, pausing at the gap:

    The dog is carrying a ___.
- Point out the two words next to the sentence, *stick* and *stuck*.
- Ask the students whether the dog in the picture is carrying a *stick,* or a *stuck.*
- The students should say a *stick.*
- The students circle the word *stick,* and write this word in the gap to complete the sentence.
- The students read the remaining sentences to themselves, and complete each sentence by writing the correct word in the gap.
- The completed sentences are:
    1. The dog is carrying a (stick).
    2. There is a cat in the (tree).
    3. The fox is looking at the (rabbit).
    4. The ducks (quack) on the pond.
    5. The boys have a bat and (ball).
    6. The bird is (singing).

Further blending practice
- Write the following list of words on the board, and blend them with the students:

    without,
    sprouting,
    showery,
    about,
    salute,
    outing,
    mounted,
    coaches,
    sunflower,
    power.

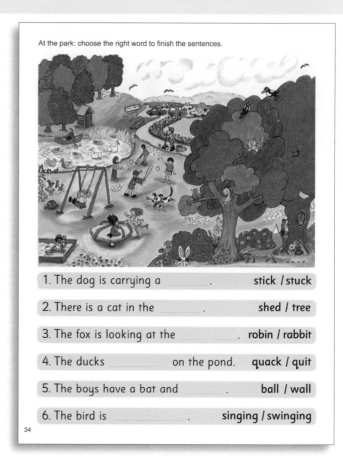

At the park: choose the right word to finish the sentences.

1. The dog is carrying a .	stick / stuck
2. There is a cat in the .	shed / tree
3. The fox is looking at the .	robin / rabbit
4. The ducks on the pond.	quack / quit
5. The boys have a bat and .	ball / wall
6. The bird is .	singing / swinging

34

Reading sentences
- Write the following sentences on the board, pointing out the tricky words, and blending any unknown words with the students.
    1. We always want more vegetables.
    2. We must sift the flour into a bowl.
    3. It is always hot when the sun is out.
    4. Mum and I went camping by the lake once.
    5. Those angry dogs always bark loudly.
    6. Once upon a time, there was a frog who turned into a prince.

Alternatives: ‹oi› and ‹oy›

Flash cards
- Practice some of the alternative letter-sound spellings taught so far, including ‹ph›, soft ‹c›, soft ‹g›, and ‹igh›.

Alternatives: the /oi/ sound
- Remind the students of the two main ways to write the /oi/ sound: ‹oi›, and ‹oy›.
- Remind the students that the ‹oy› spelling usually comes at the end of a word. Tell them that this is because the letter ‹i› is too shy to go at the end of a word, so its cousin, "toughy ‹y›" takes its place.
- The students look at the /oi/ words on their page.
- Read these words with the students.
- The words are:
    royal, boy, annoy, enjoy, toys, joy,
    spoil, coin, oil, point, join, boil.

‹oi› or ‹oy›?
- Read the first /oi/ word, *point*, and ask the students whether the /o/ sound is spelled ‹oi› or ‹oy› in this word.
- They should say ‹oi›.
- Using a gray pencil, the students circle the letters making the /oi/ sound in the word *point*.
- Then they write over the dotted word *point* in the large gray ‹oi› digraph on their page.
- The students read the remaining words, and circle the letters making the /oi/ sound in each word.
- Then they write the words in the corresponding digraphs on their page.

Further blending practice
- Write the following list of words on the board, and blend them with the students:
    spoilt,
    royalty,
    ointment,
    flowerpot,
    joystick.

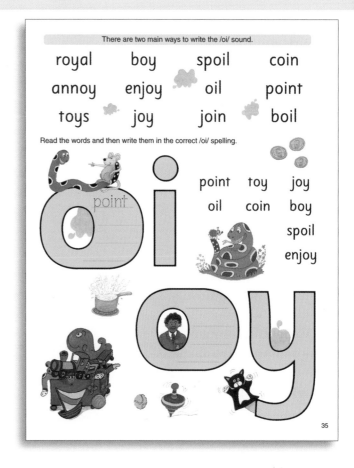

Reading sentences
- Write the following sentences on the board, pointing out the tricky words, and blending any unknown words with the students.
1. We should put tinfoil around this dish.
2. They avoid the deep river.
3. Have you ever eaten oysters?
4. I put the sunflower seeds in the soil.
5. You are one of the noisiest boys here.
6. Her painting is spoilt now.

Tricky Words and Dictation

Flash cards
- Use the flashcards, or *Tricky Word Wall Flowers*, to practice some of the tricky words taught so far, including *once, upon,* and *always*.

Tricky words
- Introduce the three new tricky words: *also, of,* and *eight*.
- The students look at the words in brown flowers at the top of the page: *also, of,* and *eight*.
- The students write inside the words *also, of,* and *eight* using a brown pencil.

Filling in the gaps
- The students trace inside the outline letters in the word *also*, saying the letter names as they do so.
- Then the students cover up all instances of the word *also* on their page, and try to complete a column of this word, by tracing over the dotted letters and filling in the missing letters.
- The students repeat these steps for the words *of,* and *eight*.

Dictation sentences
- Dictate the following sentences:
    She also waits for the bus.
    They counted eight hundred ants.
    She put a pinch of nutmeg in the mix.
- The students write these sentences on the lines in their *Phonics Student Books*.

Complete the sentences
- Read the first sentence, pausing at the gap:
    There are lots ___ sheep on the farm.
- Ask the students whether they think they should write *also, of,* or *eight* in this gap.
- Read the sentence back to the students, including their chosen word, and ask them if they think the sentence makes sense with this word.
- The students write the correct word in the gap in their *Phonics Student Books*.

- The students read the next two sentences by themselves, and decide which of the tricky words completes the sentence.
- They write the correct tricky word on the line in each sentence.

Tricky word flowers
- The students look at the tricky words flowers at the bottom of their page.
- Read each tricky word with the students.
- The words are:
  does, made, their, once, upon, always.
- The students color the flowers using a pink, or brown pencil.

Further blending practice
- Write the following list of words on the board, and blend them with the students:
  enjoying, pointed, destroys, ahoy, employ.

Words and Sentences

Flash cards
· Practice some of the alternative letter-sound spellings taught so far, including ‹ph›, soft ‹c›, soft ‹g›, and ‹igh›.

Words and sentences
· Write the title on the board, *My Best Story*.
· Read the title with the students.
· Pick one student, and ask him or her for the title of their favorite story.
· Ask the student to describe, very briefly, what happens in the story.
· Ask some other students to say a sentence about their favorite stories. Encourage the students to say a different sentence each.

Writing
· The students write the title of their favorite story on the top line.
· They write as much as they can about their favorite stories on the remaining lines.

Picture
· The students draw a picture illustrating their favorite story in the picture frame.

Note 1: spelling
· At this stage, the students' spelling will not always be accurate, but their work will be readable. Spelling gradually improves through reading many books, and learning the alternative letter-sound spellings.

Note 2: title
· Teachers should feel free to set their own writing subject. The title of the writing exercise does appear on the *Phonics Student Book* pages, but the picture frame is empty, and the lines are blank. It may be that the students would like to write about a recent holiday they have celebrated, or a story they have heard. If this is the case, teachers can set their own title, and guide the students' writing accordingly.

Further blending practice
· Write the following list of words on the board, and blend them with the students:

> *plays,*
> *twenty,*
> *squirrel,*
> *film,*
> *coy.*

Reading sentences
· Write the following sentences on the board, pointing out the tricky words, and blending any unknown words with the students.
1. We go on holiday in eight days' time.
2. There are lots of sticks on the ground.
3. Are you afraid of the dark?
4. We also play cricket in the summer.

Comprehension

Flash cards
- Practice some of the alternative letter-sound spellings taught so far.

Comprehension: Moat Farm
- Read the story *Moat Farm* to the students.
- If you have enough copies of the Jolly Reader *Moat Farm*, the students could read the story for themselves. Alternatively, you could write the story on the board for the students to read. The story is as follows:

Moat Farm
This is Moat Farm.
Farmer Green lives on Moat Farm.
Ben and Neb are sheepdogs.
Neb and Ben help on the farm.
This morning, Ben and Neb run up the hill…
…and help round up the sheep.
Farmer Green checks that the sheep are well.
Neb and Ben rest in the back of the truck.

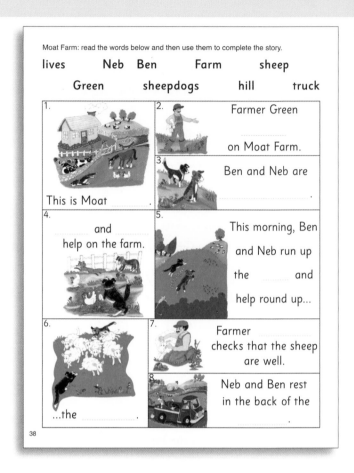

- The students look at the comic strip version of *Moat Farm* on their page.
- Point out that there are a number of words missing from the story. Explain that the missing words are printed at the top of the page.
- Read the first sentence, pausing at the gap:
    This is Moat ___.
- Ask the students which of the words at the top of the page should go in this gap.
- They should say *Farm*. The students write this word in the gap, and cross it out at the top of the page.
- The students read the remaining sentences to themselves and fill in the gaps as follows:
  1. This is Moat (Farm).
  2. Farmer Green (lives) on Moat Farm.
  3. Ben and Neb are (sheepdogs).
  4. (Neb) and (Ben) help on the farm.
  5. This morning, Ben and Neb run up the (hill) and help round up…
  6. …the (sheep).
  7. Farmer (Green) checks that the sheep are well.
  8. Neb and Ben rest in the back of the (truck).

Further blending practice
- Write the following list of words on the board, and blend them with the students:
    tractor,
    farmhouse,
    fence,
    dungarees,
    helping.

Reading sentences
- Write the following sentences on the board, pointing out the tricky words, and blending any unknown words with the students.
  1. Farmer Green has a flock of sheep.
  2. Ben has black fur, but Neb's fur is brown.
  3. Farmer Green also has eight cows.
  4. A fox tried to steal one of the chickens.

Alternatives: ‹er›, ‹ir›, and ‹ur›

Flash cards
- Practice some of the alternative letter-sound spellings taught so far, including ‹ph›, soft ‹c›, soft ‹g›, and ‹igh›.

Alternatives: the /er/ sound
- Remind the students of the three main ways to write the /er/ sound: ‹er›, ‹ir›, and ‹ur›.
- Point out that, when the /er/ sound comes at the end of a word, it is often spelled ‹er›.
- Point out that the /er/ sound in the days of the week, *Saturday* and *Thursday*, is spelled ‹ur›.
- The students look at the /er/ words on their page.
- Read these words with the students.
- The words are:

    helicopter, sister, numbers, cooker,
    girl, thirsty, third, bird,
    Saturday, purple, Thursday, hurt.

‹er›, ‹ir›, or ‹ur›?
- Read the first /er/ word, *dinner*, and ask the students whether the /er/ sound is spelled ‹er›, ‹ir›, or ‹ur› in this word.
- They should say ‹er›.
- Using a blue pencil, the students circle the letters making the /er/ sound in the word *dinner*.
- Then they write over the dotted word *dinner* in the large blue ‹er› digraph on their page.
- The students read the remaining words, and circle the letters making the /er/ sound in each word.
- Then they write the words in the corresponding digraphs on their page.

Further blending practice
- Write the following list of words on the board, and blend them with the students:

    sunburnt,
    thunder,
    thirteen,
    tweezers,
    burger.

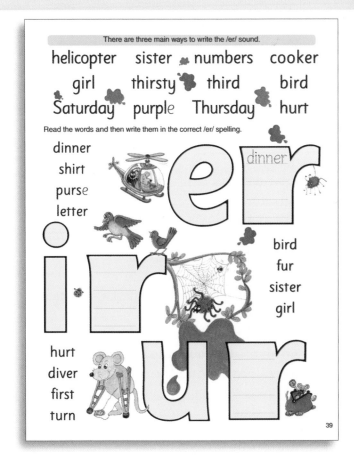

Reading sentences
- Write the following sentences on the board, pointing out the tricky words, and blending any unknown words with the students.
  1. On Thursday we will have supper together.
  2. She is better at swimming than we are.
  3. Some of those stones are quite dirty.
  4. Your new shirt is also very smart.
  5. All spiders have eight legs.
  6. We would also like to join the club.

Tricky Words and Dictation

Flash cards
- Use the flashcards, or *Tricky Word Wall Flowers*, to practice some of the tricky words taught so far, including *also, of,* and *eight.*

Tricky words
- Introduce the three new tricky words: *love, cover,* and *after.*
- The students look at the words in brown flowers at the top of the page.
- Point out that the ‹o› in the words *love* and *cover* makes an /u/ sound.
- The students write inside the words *love, cover* and *after* using a brown pencil.

Filling in the gaps
- The students trace inside the outline letters in the word *love*, saying the letter names as they do so.
- Then the students cover up all instances of the word *love* on their page and try to complete a column of this word, by tracing over the dotted letters and filling in the missing letters.
- The students repeat these steps for the words *cover* and *after.*

Dictation sentences
- Dictate the following sentences:
  We love our dog.
  She has a pink cover on her bed.
  We went out after lunch.
- The students write these sentences on the lines in their *Phonics Student Books.*

Complete the sentences
- Read the first sentence, pausing at the gap:
  I ___ to go swimming.
- Ask the students whether they think they should write *love, cover,* or *after* in this gap.
- Read the sentence back to the students, including their chosen word, and ask them if they think the sentence makes sense with this word.
- The students write the correct word in the gap in their *Phonics Student Books.*

- The students read the next two sentences by themselves, and decide which of the tricky words completes the sentence.
- They write the correct tricky word on the line in each sentence.

Tricky word flowers
- The students look at the tricky words flowers at the bottom of their page.
- Read each tricky word with the students.
- The words are:
  once, upon, always, also, of, eight.
- The students color the flowers using a brown pencil.

Further blending practice
- Write the following list of words on the board, and blend them with the students:
  loyal, squirt, twirling, fur, returns.

Words and Sentences

Flash cards
• Practice some of the alternative letter-sound spellings taught so far, including ‹ph›, soft ‹c›, soft ‹g›, and ‹igh›.

Words and sentences
• Write the title on the board, *Inky's Day Out.*
• Read the title with the students.
• Discuss day trips with the students.
• Ask a student to say one sentence about a recent day out. For example, "We went to the seaside." "Granny took me to the park." "I went on a boat."
• Then ask the students where they think Inky and her friends might go on a day out.
• Encourage the students to say a different sentence each.

Writing
• The students write the title, *Inky's Day Out,* on the top line.
• They write their own story about Inky's day out on the remaining lines.

Picture
• The students illustrate their story about Inky in the picture frame.

Note 1: spelling
• At this stage, the students' spelling will not always be accurate, but their work will be readable. Spelling gradually improves through reading many books, and learning the alternative letter-sound spellings.

Note 2: title
• Teachers should feel free to set their own writing subject. The title of the writing exercise does appear on the *Phonics Student Book* pages, but the picture frame is empty, and the lines are blank. It may be that the students would like to write about a recent holiday they have celebrated, or a story they have heard. If this is the case, teachers can set their own title, and guide the students' writing accordingly.

Inky's Day Out

41

Further blending practice
• Write the following list of words on the board, and blend them with the students:
> *nightingale,*
> *untied,*
> *myself,*
> *brighter,*
> *highest.*

Reading sentences
• Write the following sentences on the board, pointing out the tricky words, and blending any unknown words with the students.
1. I love to make snowmen in winter.
2. Did you remember to cover the cakes?
3. She twirls and spins in her new skirt.
4. We can see the sharks after looking at the dolphins.

Comprehension

Flash cards
• Practice some of the alternative letter-sound spellings taught so far, including ‹ph›, soft ‹c›, soft ‹g›, and ‹igh›.

Crossword
• The students read each crossword clue.
• They write the answer to each clue, starting at the correct square.
• The clues (with answers in brackets) are:
1. This will help you find your way.
   (map)
2. This heats food for you to eat.
   (cooker)
3. A small insect that lives in a nest underground.
   (ant)
4. If you go camping, you may sleep in this.
   (tent)
5. You wash with ___ and water.
   (soap)
6. An animal that hisses.
   (snake)
7. The time of year when it is cold.
   (winter)
8. A chick hatches from this.
   (egg)
9. This is on the end of your arm.
   (hand)
10. A sort of stone.
    (rock)
11. The sky is blue and the trees are ___.
    (green)
12. At night it is ___.
    (dark)

Further blending practice
• Write the following list of words on the board, and blend them with the students:
   one, two, three, four, five, six, seven, eight, nine, ten.

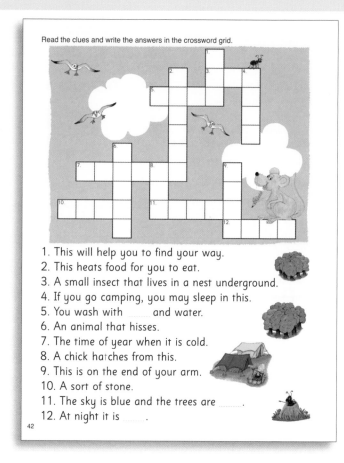

Read the clues and write the answers in the crossword grid.

1. This will help you to find your way.
2. This heats food for you to eat.
3. A small insect that lives in a nest underground.
4. If you go camping, you may sleep in this.
5. You wash with _____ and water.
6. An animal that hisses.
7. The time of year when it is cold.
8. A chick hatches from this.
9. This is on the end of your arm.
10. A sort of stone.
11. The sky is blue and the trees are _____.
12. At night it is _____.

42

Reading sentences
• Write the following sentences on the board, pointing out the tricky words, and blending any unknown words with the students.
1. They cover the food with butter and herbs.
2. I love my Mom and Dad very much.
3. We could have a running race after skipping.
4. Nine comes after eight, but before ten.
5. Cover the pot with this cloth.
6. I would love to come to your party.

Handwriting and Comprehension

Flash cards
- Practice some of the alternative letter-sound spellings taught so far, including ‹ph›, soft ‹c›, soft ‹g›, and ‹igh›.

Handwriting: the alphabet
- The students review writing the capital letters for the alphabet.
- Take down, or cover, any visible copies of the alphabet so that the students have to remember how the capital letters are written.
- The students write inside each lower-case outline letter and then write the corresponding capital letter next to it.
- They use a red pencil for the letters A-E, a yellow pencil for the letters F-M, a green pencil for the letters N-S, and a blue pencil for the letters T-Z.

Comprehension
- The students read each sentence, and complete the picture so that it matches the sentence.
- The first sentence is:
  The boy has a blue drum.
- The students color the boy's drum blue.
- The second sentence is:
  There are six red fish.
- There are five red fish in the picture, and one black and white fish. The students color this fish red.

Further blending practice
- Write the following list of words on the board and blend them with the students:
  sharper,
  neater,
  urban,
  thirsty,
  casserole.

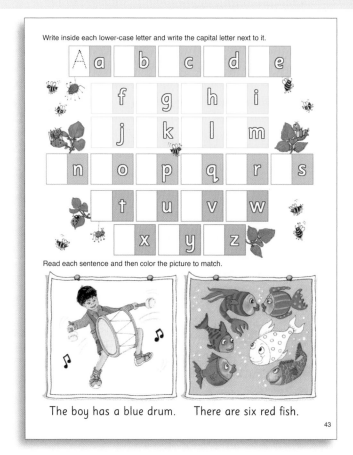

Write inside each lower-case letter and write the capital letter next to it.

A a b c d e
f g h i
j k l m
n o p q r s
t u v w
x y z

Read each sentence and then color the picture to match.

The boy has a blue drum.   There are six red fish.

43

Reading sentences
- Write the following sentences on the board, pointing out the tricky words, and blending any unknown words with the students.
  1. You must look before you cross the road.
  2. Shall we have another game of tennis?
  3. He only cried after he fell off the stool.
  4. The bed cover has purple polka dots.
  5. We should put the ball away after our game.
  6. Who does this phone belong to?

Alternatives: ‹air›, ‹ear›, and ‹are›

Flash cards
- Practice some of the alternative letter-sound spellings taught so far, including ‹ph›, soft ‹c›, soft ‹g›, and ‹igh›.

Alternatives: the /air/ sound
- The /air/ sound, as in the word *fair*, is a new sound for the students.
- The students look at the /air/ words on their page.
- Read these words with the students.
- The words are:

      fairy, stairs, chair, pair,
      bear, wear, tear, pear,
      scarecrow, hare, square, dare.

- Point out the letters making the /air/ sound in each word.
- Explain that the /air/ sound can be spelled ‹air›, ‹ear›, or ‹are›.

‹air›, ‹ear›, or ‹are›?
- The students look at the bears and salmon on their page.
- The students read each word in the salmon, and circle the letters making the /air/ sound.
- The students look at the first bear. The bear has a picture of a pear on its back.
- The students find the salmon containing the word *pear,* and join it to this bear.
- They do the same with the remaining bears.
- When the students have joined all the bears to the correct salmon, they color the /air/ pictures inside the bears.

Further blending practice
- Write the following list of words on the board, and blend them with the students:

      hairy,
      spare,
      wearing,
      rare,
      fairly.

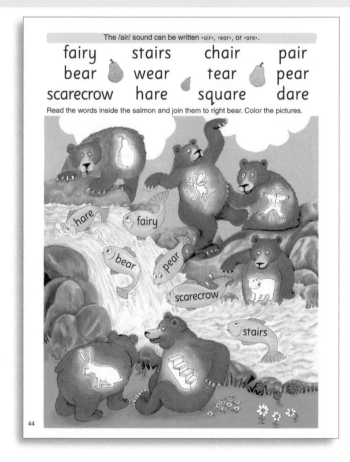

The /air/ sound can be written ‹air›, ‹ear›, or ‹are›.

fairy	stairs	chair	pair
bear	wear	tear	pear
scarecrow	hare	square	dare

Read the words inside the salmon and join them to right bear. Color the pictures.

Reading sentences
- Write the following sentences on the board, pointing out the tricky words, and blending any unknown words with the students.
  1. I love this teddy bear most of all.
  2. They went to the fair without their sister.
  3. I was not scared by the phantom.
  4. The hot-air balloon flew very high.
  5. She has long brown hair.
  6. We should share the puppets with those girls.

Tricky Words and Dictation

Flash cards
• Use the flashcards, or *Tricky Word Wall Flowers*, to practice some of the tricky words taught so far, including *once, upon, always, also, of, eight, love, cover,* and *after.*

Tricky words
• Introduce the three new tricky words: *every, mother,* and *father.*
• The students look at the words in brown flowers at the top of the page: *every, mother,* and *father.*
• Encourage the students to use the "say it as it sounds" technique when writing *mother* and *father.* They should say *mother* as though it rhymes with *bother,* and *father* as though it rhymes with *gather.*
• The students write inside the words *every, mother,* and *father* using a brown pencil.

Filling in the gaps
• The students trace inside the outline letters in the word *every,* saying the letter names as they do so.
• Then the students cover up all instances of the word *every* on their page and try to complete a column of this word, by tracing over the dotted letters, and filling in the missing letters.
• The students repeat these steps for the words *mother,* and *father.*

Complete the sentences
• Read the first sentence to the students, pausing at the two gaps:
  My ___ and ___ are my parents.
• Ask the students which of the three tricky words they have just learned might fit in the gaps in this sentence.
• They should write *mother* and *father* in the gaps.
• The students read the next sentence by themselves, and decide which tricky word completes the sentence.
• They write the correct tricky word on the line.

Dictation sentences
• Dictate the following sentences:
  He gets a comic every week.
  She painted a card for her mother.
  Father took us to the park.
• The students write these sentences on the lines in their *Phonics Student Books.*

Tricky word flowers
• The students look at the tricky words flowers at the bottom of their page.
• Read each tricky word with the students.
• The words are:
  also, of, eight, love, cover, after.
• The students color the flowers using a brown pencil.

Further blending practice
• Write the following list of words on the board, and blend them with the students:
  flair, everyone, care, parent, prepare.

Words and Sentences

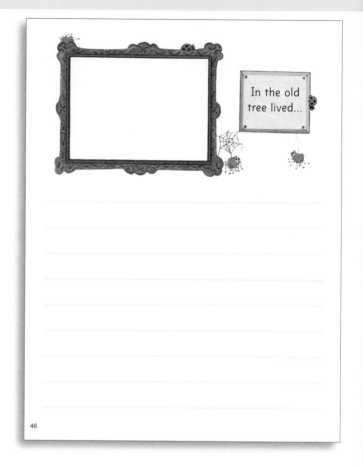

In the old tree lived...

46

Flash cards
- Practice some of the alternative letter-sound spellings taught so far, including ‹ph›, soft ‹c›, soft ‹g›, ‹igh›, and the three ways of writing the /air/ sound.

Words and sentences
- Write the title on the board, *In the old tree lived...*
- Read the title with the students.
- Ask the students what kind of creature, or creatures, might live in the old tree.
- Encourage the students discuss what they think the creature looks like, or the kinds of things the creature might like to do.
- Try to develop the students' ideas into a story.
- If the students struggle to come up with ideas, the class could read the Jolly Reader *The Tree That Blinked.*

Writing
- The students write the title, *In the old tree lived...* on the top line.
- They write a story about the old tree and its inhabitants on the remaining lines.
- The students could write their own story, or the write story discussed by the class.

Picture
- The students illustrate their story in the picture frame.

Note 1: spelling
- At this stage, the students' spelling will not always be accurate, but their work will be readable. Spelling gradually improves through reading many books, and learning the alternative letter-sound spellings.

Note 2: title
- Teachers should feel free to set their own writing subject. The title of the writing exercise does appear on the *Phonics Student Book* pages, but the picture frame is empty, and the lines are blank.

- It may be that the students would like to write about a recent holiday they have celebrated, or a story they have heard. If this is the case, teachers can set their own title, and guide the students' writing accordingly.

Further blending practice
- Write the following list of words on the board, and blend them with the students:
  repair, beaten, stare, glare, tearing.
- Write the following sentences on the board, pointing out the tricky words, and blending any unknown words with the students.
  1. My father will pay my train fare.
  2. You only say "snap" when you have a pair.
  3. Every day he sits in the same chair.
  4. My mother is wearing her new beads.
  5. In a square, every side is the same length.
  6. My mother and father are playing chess.

Comprehension

Flash cards
- Practice some of the alternative letter-sound spellings taught so far, including ‹ph›, soft ‹c›, soft ‹g›, ‹igh›, and the three ways of writing the /air/ sound.

Story: The Midnight Feast
- The students look at the story, *The Midnight Feast*, on their page.
- Read the story with the students.
- The story is as follows:

The Midnight Feast

Once upon a time, there was a king called Alfred. His wife was Queen Matilda. They lived in a castle, with a cat called Fluffy. One night, King Alfred was hungry. So he got up and made himself some cheese sandwiches to eat. Some crumbs from the sandwich fell onto the floor.

A mouse saw the crumbs from her mouse hole in the corner of the room. She could have a midnight feast, if she was quick and quiet. She crept out, and had just reached the crumbs, when Fluffy looked into the room. The mouse ran for her hole as quickly as she could. Fluffy ran for the mouse as quickly as he could.

The mouse reached her hole hungry, but safe!

Comprehension: The Midnight Feast
- Read the first question to the students:
  What is the king's name?
- The students might not be able to remember the king's name.
- If the students are struggling, encourage them to look for the answer in the story in their books.
- The students write their answer on the line next to the first question.
- The students read the remaining questions to themselves, writing their answers on the lines.

Read the story and answer the questions below.

Once upon a time, there was a king called Alfred. His wife was Queen Matilda. They lived in a castle, with a cat called Fluffy.

One night, King Alfred was hungry. So he got up and made himself some cheese sandwiches to eat. Some crumbs from the sandwich fell onto the floor.

A mouse saw the crumbs from her mouse hole in the corner of the room. She could have a midnight feast, if she was quick and quiet. She crept out, and had just reached the crumbs, when Fluffy looked into the room. The mouse ran for her hole as quickly as she could. Fluffy ran for the mouse as quickly as he could.

The mouse reached her hole hungry, but safe!

1. What is the king's name?
2. What is the queen's name?
3. What sort of animal is Fluffy?
4. What did King Alfred make to eat?
5. Who saw the crumbs on the floor?
6. Who saw the mouse?
7. Did the cat catch the mouse?

47

Further blending practice
- Write the following list of words on the board, and blend them with the students:
  royalty,
  throne,
  golden,
  crumbly,
  quickly.

Reading sentences
- Write the following sentences on the board, pointing out the tricky words, and blending any unknown words with the students.
1. Fluffy loves to chase mice.
2. Every mouse likes to eat cheese sandwiches.
3. Fluffy has ginger fur and a long tail.
4. Does the little mouse manage to escape?

Words and Sentences

Flash cards

- Practice some of the alternative letter-sound spellings taught so far, including ⟨ph⟩, soft ⟨c⟩, soft ⟨g⟩, ⟨igh⟩, and the three ways of writing the /air/ sound.

Words and sentences: celebrations

- Discuss a recent party, or celebration with the students. For example, the class might discuss a carnival, a festival, a family celebration, or a birthday party they have been to recently.
- Read the first incomplete sentence on the students' page:

    We had a party for ___.

- Ask a student to say one sentence about why he or she was celebrating. For example, "I got a new sister." "It was my birthday."
- You may need to stop the student at the end of their sentence, as most students will try to carry on.
- Read the next incomplete sentence on the students' page:

    We ate some ___.

- Ask a different student to say a sentence about the special celebration food he or she ate. For example, "We ate some cake." "We ate some carnival food."
- The students complete the sentences on their page and write some sentences of their own on the remaining lines.
- The students illustrate each of their sentences in the picture frames.

Note 1: spelling

- At this stage, the students' spelling will not always be accurate, but their work will be readable.
- Spelling gradually improves through reading many books, and learning the alternative letter-sound spellings.

Complete the sentences writing about a recent birthday, or a holiday celebration. Illustrate what you write in the frames.

We had a party for

We ate some

48

Further blending practice

- Write the following list of words on the board, and blend them with the students:

    festival,
    feast,
    celebrate,
    enjoyment,
    carnival.

Reading sentences

- Write the following sentences on the board, pointing out the tricky words, and blending any unknown words with the students.
    1. We all lit lanterns at midnight.
    2. We blew up one hundred yellow balloons.
    3. The children were wearing lovely costumes.
    4. There was drumming and singing at the carnival.